The Making of the Primary School

WITHDRAWN

Innovations in Education

Series Editor: Colin Fletcher (Lecturer in the School of Policy Studies, Cranfield Institute of Technology)

There have been periods of major innovation in public education. What do the achievements amount to and what are the prospects for progress now? There are issues in each slice of the education sector. How have the issues come about?

Each author analyses their own sphere, argues from experience and communicates clearly. Here are books that speak both with and for the teaching profession; books that can be shared with all those involved in the future of education.

Three quotations have helped to shape the series:

> The whole process – the false starts, frustrations, adaptions, the successive recasting of intentions, the detours and conflicts – needs to be comprehended. Only then can we understand what has been achieved and learn from experience.
>
> *Marris and Rein*

> In this time of considerable educational change and challenge the need for teachers to write has never been greater.
>
> *Hargreaves*

> A wise innovator should prepare packages of programmes and procedures which . . . could be put into effect quickly in periods of recovery and reorganisation following a disaster.
>
> *Hirsh*

Current titles in the series

Bernard Barker: *Rescuing the Comprehensive Experience*
Jan Stewart: *The Making of the Primary School*

The Making of the Primary School

Jan Stewart

Open University Press
Milton Keynes · Philadelphia

Open University Press
Open University Educational Enterprises Limited
12 Cofferidge Close
Stony Stratford
Milton Keynes MK11 1BY, England
and
242 Cherry Street
Philadelphia, PA 19106, USA

First Published 1986

British Library Cataloguing in Publication Data

Stewart, Jan
  The making of the primary school.—(Innovations in education)
  1. Elementary schools—Great Britain
  I. Title II. Series
  372.941   LA633

ISBN 0-335-15142-6
ISBN 0-335-15115-9 Pbk

Library of Congress in Cataloging No. 85-29684

Typeset by Rowland Phototypesetting Limited, Bury St Edmunds,
Suffolk
Printed in Great Britain by M & A Thomson Litho Limited, East
Kilbride, Scotland

Contents

Series editor's foreword: the making of this book   vii
Acknowledgements   ix

Section one Primary Schools: A Range of Provision   1
  1 First impressions   3
  2 Contrasting types of primary school   7
  3 Never the twain   17
  4 Contrasts in primary school organisation   19

Section two An Environment for Learning?   29
  5 Hall in a day's work   31
  6 Within these walls   33
  7 Can I go with paper, Miss?   45
  8 Design matters   47

Section three Is It the Way that You Do It?   63
  9 Joining the revolution   65
  10 Pressure from the progressives   68
  11 A style of her own   80
  12 Effective teaching   82

Section four Conflict in the Curriculum   101
  13 A question of standards   103
  14 Battles over basics   106
  15 The power of the project   115
  16 Problems with projects   118

Section five Differences or Needs?   129
17 Bomber   131
18 Special needs   133
19 Crossed by categorisation   135
20 Equal opportunity   153
21 No difference   155

Section six Conflicts and Resources   163
22 Eggsperiments   165
23 Even the kitchen sink: conflict over resources 167
24 When is a rabbit not a rabbit?   181
25 The micro: another white elephant?   183

Section seven Beyond the Teacher's Day   207
26 Food for thought   209
27 Deals on meals   211
28 Overpaid and underworked?   224
29 And what did you do at school today, Teacher? 225

Notes and references   235
Index   253

Series editor's foreword: the making of this book

Jan Stewart's reputation has been, principally, for developing the use of microcomputers in primary schools. This book extends her reputation in all directions; here she explains and evaluates virtually every aspect of the primary school. She writes as a teacher who wants to know what is happening and who needs to understand the causes of events. She is determined to weigh up the usefulness and truthfulness of competing ideas. Her affection and loyalty for teaching, teachers and pupils are compelling. In this way the book goes to the heart of a host of questions:

- Why do so many adults view primary school as 'the happiest time of their education'?
- What are the origins of the primary school?
- When did individual differences become 'learning difficulties' and with what result?
- How has the maxim 'a place for everything and everything in its place' influenced primary schools?
- Where did 'projects' come from?

This book is the richest available source of evidence from, analysis of, and experience within, primary schools.

The book's development was fascinating and the process accounts for its structure. The very first outline of chapter headings was a kaleidoscope of keenly heard phrases, a string of pearls brought up from the sea-bed of a teacher's daily life. When I asked about 'Can I go with paper, Miss?' and 'Eggsperiments', Jan Stewart developed her perspectives by beginning with a delightful story. What she had learned in different schools and classrooms sometimes stretched her imagination and at other times strained her credulity. Each story focused the mind upon how primary teachers look at themselves and their tasks. It became essential to open each section with its founding stories in the hope that the reader could see through the author's eyes. The purpose of this series is, after all, to show the fresh connections that need to be made between the personal and the professional, the practical and the political.

Having agreed that each section would open with a story, our discussions led straight to substance. The draft was coming to say three things. First, there were many dark corners that needed illuminating; primary teachers were too often in the dark over the origins of their commitments and their confusions. Secondly, the development of primary schools had produced many contrasts – in areas ranging from buildings to beliefs and from techniques to teachers. These contrasts needed to be evenly and equally compared. Thirdly, the fabric of primary school life is a tapestry of debates over principle and dilemmas upon practice. The conflicts, too, had to be brought out into the open. It became possible to understand primary schools if one understood the conflicts about them and within them.

The working title of the draft became 'Contrasts and Conflicts'. It was clear that this approach was challenging a review of almost every study that might have something to say to the practising teacher. The scale and scope altered dramatically. Chapters became as long as the relevance of their material. Opening with contrasts led to the continuing conflicts. Each section was reaching towards real and imaginary choices. The practical eye of the teacher, the ear of the story-teller and the clear head of the natural scientist worked together to harvest small grains of truth.

In this way, the book's present title emerged: it was brought forth by effort. The series' faith is that some teachers have got it right, some of the time. Jan Stewart had begun from that point and then portrayed innovation on a much broader canvas. The route was through reliving moments of learning with great generosity. The direction lay through a fearless integrity towards contrasts and conflicts. The result was a book that one can believe about the making of primary schools.

Colin Fletcher

Acknowledgements

I would like to thank the following people for their comments and help: Gaye Allen, Valerie Ashley, Roger Beard, Sandra Beer, David Benzie, Hugh Benzie, Heather Brown, Daniel Chandler, Wayne Connolly, Jon Coupland, Pamela Eden, Graham Field, Lynn Fletcher, Angeline Grace, Tony Hoile, Doreen Johns, Janet Lancaster, Pat Lowe, Sue Lowrie, Eric Lunzer, Betty Male, Pauline Ormerod, Mike Walters and, David Whalley. Also Colin Fletcher whose advice has been invaluable and the children and staff of Dartmouth and Stoke Fleming Primary Schools.

Copyright note
'When is a rabbit not a rabbit?' is reprinted from *ITMA Newsletter 9* with their kind permission.

Figures 1 and 10 are Crown Copyright and are used with the permission of the Controller of Her Majesty's Stationary Office.

Figures 2,3,5,8 and 9 first appeared in Fraser, R; Stewart, J. *et al.*(1983) *Micros in the Primary Classroom, Modules 4, 5 and 3* Harlow: Longman (for the ITMA Collaboration) and are re-printed with their permission.

Figures 4, 7a and 7b first appeared in Stewart, J. (1984) *Micros in Project Work: Course Reader* Winchester: MEP and are reproduced with both the permission of MEP and the respective authors Alistair Ross, Malcolm Hall and the ITMA Collaboration.

Photographs were taken by Richard Stewart.

Primary Schools: A Range of Provision

CHAPTER 1

First impressions

The inhabitants of the grim terraced streets surrounding High Rise School once gained brief fame through mention in Richard Hoggart's *The Uses of Literacy*.[1] Since then, as before, they have lived in the shadow of the towering school that represents one of their few hopes of escape. It has served their community for generations. It continues to serve.

It was 1965 when I first first visited High Rise. The message on the gate declared its authority in large letters, 'No Unauthorised Person Allowed on These Premises'. Hesitatingly I entered and, passing under the entrance clearly labelled 'Boys', mounted the well-worn stairs to the second floor. It was mid-morning, yet not one child's voice could be heard. Only the regular click of a typewriter pierced the silence, guiding me to the secretary and Mr Teague, the head-teacher. He eyed me carefully.

'So you're joining us in September?'

'Er . . . yes.'

Under the staffing arrangements at that time, new teachers were allocated to schools from a 'pool'. Neither of us had had any choice in the placement. It had been thrust upon us both like an arranged marriage.

'Well,' Mr Teague continued, 'we have books for every subject in this school and I expect you to use them.'

To emphasise the point a pile of textbooks was thrust towards me. They indeed covered the whole curriculum.

'You'll be taking 2A. Another new teacher will take 2B so that you can work together.'

At that moment a bell rang out. It was playtime. Doors opened and the plod of many footsteps echoed from the nearby stairs; but there was little noise. Declining a cup of strong tea, I joined Mr Teague on a tour of the school. We crossed a hall surrounded on three sides by classrooms. The walls were attractively decorated with children's work. Entering my own future home I noted paired desks fixed in rows, neat displays of work and a stuffed fox.

'Our main problem,' said Mr Teague 'is noise. You may teach in any way you wish but I suggest you keep the children in their desks – and quiet. You'll have no discipline problems if you heed my advice.'

We returned to the stairs. Boys with prefect badges were positioned like sentries. Pupils marched past them to their classrooms like the components of a well-oiled machine. To teach art, science and practical maths to these individuals seated in silent rows was going to be a challenge, but there were several months to plan tactics. In September I began a very happy probationary year.

The following Easter, that of 1966, I attended an evening interview at a new school in the Cheshire green belt. My husband was moving into the area and few jobs were available. I was grateful for the appointment and surprised to be offered a meal at the headteacher's house before beginning the long journey home. Eastlea was obviously an innovatory school. Children were unstreamed. There was no differentiation between the infant and junior departments. Classroom desks were arranged in groups. It was spacious and equipped like an Aladdin's cave. There were books galore but no compulsory sets.

The whole summer was spent planning, collecting equipment and marshalling ideas. By the first day of term the staff had met and spent several hours on joint preparation. We were all ready. At 8.30 a.m., having checked materials and equipment, I sat with my new colleagues for a welcome cup of tea. At 8.55 a.m. the deputy head picked up a bell from the table and headed for the playground. Few staff moved.

'Do we go and meet our classes?' I enquired, remembering the practice at High Rise. A young teacher, Tony, laughed.

'Heavens, no,' he said. 'Most of them will be in by now anyway. The bell's just to hurry late-comers.'

I felt myself pale. Children already inside! I had not considered that. As I hurried down the corridor towards my room, deafening noise confirmed my worst fears. There, seemingly leaping around on every desk and piece of furniture, were 2S – all forty-five of them. Standing by the door I conjured up my strongest playground voice.

'And what sort of behaviour do you call this! Sit down at once!' A pause. Bottoms slowly negotiated chairs.

'That's better.' Murmurs. I quickly pounced on the nearest unsuspecting child. 'Did I say that you could speak?'

'Nnn . . . oo, Miss.'

'No, Mrs Stewart,' I corrected. The training at High Rise had not been in vain, and desperate times called for desperate measures. After a long pause I continued dramatically.

'I will now leave the room. When the door is closed you will each lift your desk lid. Inside you will find a book. You will take out the book and read it.' A hand was raised. Thinking quickly I continued, 'If you cannot read the book you will look at the pictures. I do not wish to hear one desk lid open or close, one voice speak. When I think you are all reading, I will enter.' A pause. Incredulous looks were exchanged. I left. All was quiet. Desk lids gently creaked. Pages turned. Smiling as if nothing had happened I re-entered.

'Good morning, 2S.'

'Good—' At that moment the classroom door opened and in burst Tony. Children spilled noisily out of his neighbouring room and crowded round the door.

'Hi folks!' he yelled. 'Great to see you back.' There were odd tentative murmurs in response. He lowered his voice to a whisper. 'Just a word of warning. We don't do this sort of thing here.' I fixed him, his milling children and the general audience with a blistering stare.

'I'm afraid I do. Good morning, Mr Digby. Good morning, 2S.'

Surprisingly it was a good morning. The children were successfully rearranged into groups and embarked on a range of tasks. At break I consulted with the deputy head.

'That class,' she consoled me, 'have been fiends since they were infants. They saw off two teachers last year. You were right to start them off as you mean to continue.'

Before break was over I returned to the classroom and busied myself in the corner mixing paints. The children entered and settled immediately to their work. I stifled a smile. By the most formal means I had embarked on an era of innovation, experimentation and informality.

The bulk of my teaching career was spent at Eastlea. I would probably still be there but circumstances changed and I joined the staff of a local college of education. Within a year I was on the move again, this time to Devon. Over the phone a position was negotiated at Ford Farm Primary School. The headteacher painted a picture of an idyllic setting – a country school with small classes and squirrels scampering across the lawns. Reality was somewhat different. Although newly erected, half of the classrooms consisted of wooden huts grouped around the playground. Two huge housing estates sprawled around the school's perimeter, separated only by a strip of land earmarked for a motorway. The land had a derelict air but did, indeed, house several dreys.

I arrived the day before term started to prepare the room. The hut was to house twenty-five remedial children chosen because they had not yet transferred from reading in ITA (Initial Teaching Alphabet) to TO (Traditional Orthography). My whole summer had been spent mastering the intricacies of reading and writing in the medium of ITA.

On first appearance the new environment looked spartan and unpromising. However, the headteacher did not flinch at my list of requirements. Indeed, within half an hour she had produced all of them.

'Just ask if you need anything else,' she remarked cheerfully. 'I can usually find most things.'

The first morning arrived. Greeting my new charges at the hut door I helped them find pegs for their coats and seated them on the thin carpet. They were a motley crew of different shapes, sizes and handicaps. I began the register. Suddenly a figure clasped itself around my legs and began sobbing bitterly.

''E's Tom,' drawled a voice. ''E allus croys. 'E carn't tork proper.'

Kerry's lip also began to tremble. I rapidly produced a box of tissues.

'Don't cry,' I said gently. 'I've found your name on the register, Tom, and when we've finished we're going to have a lovely story.'

Kerry blew her nose hard. Tom applied a screwed-up tissue to each eye and left them there mumbling something that I assumed to be 'Glasshopper'. The joke was enjoyed by the Kung Fu fans of the class and our laughter relieved the tension. The story began. Thumbs slowly moved to mouths. Eyes glazed. *Charlie and the Chocolate Factory* was weaving its magic spell yet again.

The small class was easily organised into an integrated day. It seemed the best way of coping with such varying ages, abilities and problems. They also needed a relaxed working atmosphere. What delightful children they proved to be. By the afternoon we were able to wander informally down the nearby 'valley', the overgrown area destined for the motorway, on the first of many nature walks. By the end of the week they had covered the walls with their work. As we fastened coats to go home for the weekend Kerry clung to my skirt.

'I loves 'oo, Mrs Stooart,' she sighed. Tom commented and grinned.

'Pardon, Tom?'

Kerry translated. ''E says I'm daarft and 'oo torks funny.'

So much for first impressions!

CHAPTER 2

Contrasting types of primary school

Whilst generalised statements and assumptions are commonly made about primary schools, they do, in fact, vary enormously in type. High Rise, Eastlea and Ford Farm indicate only part of the breadth of provision. Availability of places or local education authority policy may vary the starting age of school from four to five-plus; while the upper limit may range from ten to thirteen years. Between these vastly disparate ages pupils may attend a variety of school types ranging from separate or combined infant and junior schools to first and middle schools. This variety has generally resulted from successive attempts to meet the changing needs of older pupils. Removing the small and playful enabled the bigger and more serious aspects of education – the 'real stuff schools should be made of'! – to continue uninterrupted. Nevertheless, British primary schools have evolved their own distinct ethos. They have influenced not only educational provision for young children across the world but also their secondary counterparts. This chapter describes the somewhat shaky foundations on which the solid edifice of primary teaching has remarkably been built.

Infant schools

Originally state schools were very much concerned with keeping children out of mines or factories and providing a more literate and numerate work-force. But few catered for the youngest age groups. Sunday schools did not provide infant places until the mid-nineteenth century; parochial and charity schools only admitted children after their seventh birthday, and early monitorial schools had no arrangements for children under six. The British and Foreign School Society even had rules preventing the admittance of children under that age.[1] Consequently infant provision tended to fall upon the dame schools, where the majority of pupils were aged between two and seven. At their best these

> discharged the function of public nurseries for very young children and served as places of security as well as of education, since they were the most obvious way of keeping the children of poor families out of the streets in towns, or out of the roads and fields in the country.[2]

However, the teachers were often elderly, infirm or ignorant, the classrooms merely crowded and dirty kitchens.[3] Their very existence probably did much to inhibit the development of state infant schools in the pre-1870 period. The fees, equivalent to 1p or 2p per day, provided a good income and encouraged the dames to oppose any superior competition.[4]

Nevertheless, infant schools have a long tradition. The first was established in 1769 by J. F. Oberlin at Waldbach in Alsace. It became the model for similar establishments in France, Switzerland and Germany. The first British infant school was founded by Robert Owen in 1816 at New Lanark in Scotland. Two years later James Buchanan, an Owen employee, moved to Brewers Green to open a second school. Others rapidly followed, including Wilderspin's famous school at Spitalfields and David Stow's at Drygate, Glasgow. One of the principal functions of these early schools was to provide a place where children could receive care whilst their mothers were at work. For example, Robert Owen's school allowed entry at three years, thus releasing mothers for employment in his cotton mills. Buchanan's school title, 'The Westminster Free and Day Infant Asylum',[5] also reflects its pastoral leanings. Its role was preventive and compensatory but in a social and moral rather than educational sense:

> Infant schools are designed to prevent evil, and to train young children in the practice of virtue and kin feeling, particularly in those cases in which parents from their vocation are unable . . . to take proper care of their offspring.[6]

Where places allowed, young children moved into the normal school system. By 1870 nearly half the elementary school population was under eight, and pressures arose for separation of the older from the younger pupils. Matthew Arnold, writing in 1852, clearly expressed future concerns:

> In the institutions I have visited during the past year, I have continually felt the want of infant schools. It seems that schools are clogged and

impeded in their operations by a mass of children under 8 years of age
. . . [more] than from any other cause.[7]

However, a lack of specialised infant teachers somewhat impeded
the move. Therefore, in 1854 a Committee of Council for Education directive was issued preventing training colleges obtaining
benefits unless they provided courses for the training of infant
teachers.[8]

In 1870, attendance at school became obligatory. A compulsory
lower age had to be decided and precipitated much Parliamentary
debate. Lord Shaftesbury proposed a starting age of four. Forster,
after whom the 1870 Act is named, preferred the age of six. Disraeli,
leader of the opposition at that time, was prepared to support the
proposition whether the age was five or six.[9] The final choice of five
seems to have been primarily a political compromise and was,
interestingly, much lower than that of other countries.[10]

When the Revised Code of 1872 made three-year-old children
eligible for a grant, greater pressure was placed on schools. Until
then, Standard 1 of the elementary school began at six years. This
was the age at which children began examinations so that teachers
could receive 'payment by results'. Infants, therefore, became
literally those children below Standard 1. The increase in infant
numbers following the 1870 and 1872 Acts soon caused further problems. The London School Board had, even in 1871, sought a
solution by increasing the starting age of Standard 1 to seven years.
Separate infant schools could then cater for children below seven,
junior schools for seven- to ten-year-olds and senior schools for
older children. It also recommended that infant schools or classes
should contain mixed sexes and be usually taught by women
teachers.[11] This form of organisation, the birth of the separate
infant school, was adopted by both London and the larger school
boards.

Infant schools and classes gradually became divided into younger
'babies', aged three to five years, and 'older infants'. The younger
age class eventually became known as the nursery and from 1905
separate nursery schools developed. Thus the infant school became
one that catered for five- to seven-year-olds as it does today. If
children remained in infant classes there was still a move for their
physical separation. This is highlighted in rules for planning and
equipping schools. Those for 1871 stated that infants should not be
taught in the same room with older children.[12] In 1904 access to
the infant room via a classroom for older pupils was prevented in
all-age schools.[13] Separation into a school or department was finally
ensured for the under-sevens, albeit for questionable motives.

Junior schools

Although, theoretically, separate junior schools developed simultaneously with separate infant schools, in practice they did not appear outside densely populated areas. Instead, junior children were housed in senior schools catering for seven- to twelve-year-olds. The evolution of separate schools for the juniors resulted mainly from changes in secondary rather than primary schooling. Education Acts of 1870, 1876 and 1880, for example, gradually extended the maximum age for compulsory education. By 1890 the larger school boards had been forced to organise separate junior departments containing Standards 1 to 3.

Payment by results was gradually abolished and in 1902 new forms of secondary school appeared. Until that time these had mainly provided places for privileged children whose parents could afford to pay the fees. The 1902 Act abolished the 2,559 school boards and 788 school attendance committees, replacing them with 330 local education authorities (LEAs). County and county borough councils, who had always controlled education 'other than elementary', became responsible for both types of school. Municipal boroughs with populations of over 10,000 and urban districts with over 20,000 had responsibility for elementary education only but could assist or take over the secondary schools. Board schools that came under the councils became 'provided schools' because their buildings were provided and maintained by the LEA. They were often called 'council schools'. Voluntary schools became 'non-provided schools'. Most higher grade schools became secondary schools and LEAs were able to build additional schools of this type where necessary.

The view now began to gain ground that children from elementary schools who could benefit from secondary education should be allowed to do so. In 1907 the Free Place System was formally established. This created a link between the elementary and secondary schools in that the latter had to recruit at least 25 per cent of their intake from able elementary school pupils. In return for this and other conditions the secondary schools received a grant from the LEA. The new system required some kind of test for those wishing to take advantage of it. This became known as the scholarship and was to have a restrictive influence on the primary curriculum, particularly for older pupils. As the secondary school course extended over four years, the scholarship had to be taken at around eleven or twelve years, from which the emotive name 'eleven-plus' was derived.

In certain areas selective 'central' schools were developed which operated a transfer system in much the same way. Their curricula, however, were given a more practical bias, but they did not gain official recognition until the 1918 Education Act.[14] This not only enforced compulsory education up to fourteen but required special provision to be made for the older or more intelligent children in elementary schools. No children were to be debarred, through inability to pay fees, from any form of education by which they were capable of profiting. All fees in elementary schools were therefore abolished. The number of pupils taking up scholarships rose continuously, trebling in the twenty years following its introduction. Pupils slightly, below the standard for secondary schools were offered places at the central school. Later non-selective central schools were developed for all non-scholarship pupils. In turn, these became the forerunners of the present secondary moderns – another emotive term which was to label the second-class citizens for several generations to come.

Such changes set the scene for the 1926 Hadow Report, *The Education of the Adolescent*.[15] This finally proposed the division of elementary schools into the two stages of junior and secondary. To differentiate them from their non-selective counterparts, the secondary schools became 'grammar' schools. Separate junior schools finally received official blessing and, such was the urge to rid the secondary phase of its younger burden, developed with startling rapidity. By 1938, 48 per cent of seven- to eleven-year-olds were housed in separate schools, a number that was to vary surprisingly little in succeeding years.

Combined primary schools

The term 'primary' has always described a range of educational provision for young children. It first appeared in *The Education of the Adolescent* to depict the period of schooling that ends at the age of eleven or twelve. However, the subsequent Hadow Report on *The Primary School*[16] used the term to cover both junior and all-age establishments to eleven years. At the time there was considerable conflict over whether junior and infant schools should be separated or combined. The Hadow Committee supported separation. Opponents reminded them that breaks in school life tend to retard progress. Furthermore, as development is continuous, there is no need to break a child's education abruptly at seven. They were also at pains to point out the unsatisfactory record of existing separate junior schools and the problems of uneconomic over-small infant schools.[17] In 1925 a Board of Education circular (No. 1,350) had drawn attention to the trauma experienced by children when transferring school. It was suddenly and mysteriously withdrawn.[18] The

Hadow Report Committee went ahead with the recommendation for separate infant and junior schools. Ironically, this was because of the needs of the youngest children:

> The training in the best infant schools is largely dependent upon atmosphere, and it is found in practice that this atmosphere is difficult to maintain when older children are present . . . a common playground for infants and children over seven . . . is serious, as even under the most careful arrangements the older children are apt to be rather self-assertive and inclined to bully the little children . . . the older children in a good infant school . . . often display a remarkable spirit of independence and initiative . . . In a primary school containing . . . older pupils they could hardly occupy such a position and the valuable ethical effects of this arrangements would be lost.[19]

Thus the juniors were given their own schools because both the oldest and youngest pupils needed to be separated from them. However, the Hadow Committee did suggest that teachers in separate institutions should ensure that the transition in teaching methods and general discipline should be made as smooth and easy as possible for the pupils.[20] They admitted that junior schools had once been merely places in which children passed one, two or three years on their way from the infant to the senior stage but hoped that the new four-year school with its longer course would have a more definite objective.[21]

The Hadow proposals remained largely conceptual for some years. All-age schools survived where numbers or buildings prevented separate reorganisation. These tended to be rural areas though older urban schools were also affected. In 1933, 59 per cent of elementary schools still contained primary children. The 1944 Education Act gave additional pressure to separation by fixing the lower and upper limits of primary education, and by 1955 only 12 per cent of primary children were being educated in schools with senior pupils. The all-age primary schools were a legacy from these small elementary schools. They, in turn, tended to have low pupil populations. Between 1947 and 1965 the numbers of small schools fell drastically, though, interestingly, it was to be the infant rather than combined schools that declined. According to Plowden, primary schools better matched the distribution and density of populations on new housing estates than separate schools.[22] This was true of Eastlea and Ford Farm.

Recent years have seen a further decline in the totals of separate infant and junior schools. Falling rolls have generally resulted in their amalgamation. Thus the all-age primary school is now becoming the commonest form of organisation in most areas. However, whilst in any age there will be an ideal, it will be defied where expedient. Thus one primary school was recently forced to reorganise on separate lines. Expanding rolls had necessitated a new school. Unable to afford a complete new primary, the authority erected a new building for the juniors on a separate site. The infants remained in their eighteenth-century two-room structure, gaining only a new headteacher.

First and middle schools

During the innovatory 1960s authorities gained permission to submit proposals for the establishment of schools with age limits below ten years six months and above twelve years. But such proposals could only be for new schools. The intention was to allow some experimental transfer patterns to be tried rather than a major change of structure.[23] There followed the establishment in some areas of 'middle schools' catering for children between the ages of nine to thirteen.

Such new ideas occurred within a pattern of changing attitudes towards selection and secondary education. The 1944 Education Act had suggested three types of school for the older pupils – 'grammar' for the most able, 'technical' for other bright children with practical skills and 'secondary modern' for the majority. In practice, few technical schools were built. It also proved difficult to test children's suitability for grammar and technical schools. The commonly used verbal reasoning tests had an error factor of around 20 per cent. Practical skills were even more difficult to assess. Such concerns plus the problems of an inflexible class-bound society helped stimulate the demand for comprehensivisation. It proved an issue that still causes conflict and debate. Even today a third of primary children are assessed for secondary education by a selection procedure. However, in areas where selection was rejected new types of organisation could be tried.

During the mid-1960s there was, again, the pull of secondary reorganisation (with the raising of the school-leaving age), combining with the push of primary reports. The age of transfer to the secondary sector was challenged. A break at eleven was claimed to cut across an important phase in learning and attitudes towards it. The rigidity of streaming and subject specialisation in some comprehensives was also criticised, as was the over-long time spent in such schools.[24] Certainly it is difficult to create an homogeneous community in schools catering for pupils with such disparate ages as eleven and eighteen-plus. Indeed, there is considerable pressure today for schooling to end at sixteen and for tertiary education thereafter. The Plowden Committee saw the solution in raising the transfer age to twelve.[25]

A further recommendation aimed at ending the strongly criticised practice of staggered entry into the infant school.[26] This results in varying lengths of schooling for children, which mitigates unfairly against the youngest. It also necessitates promoting children termly in order to cope with each new intake. The Plowden Report recommended entry into school during the September following the fifth birthday with optional nursery provision for all in the previous year. A three-year infant course was to follow with a transfer at eight years. Justifications, as in its 1931 counterpart, centred on the value for many children in remaining in an infant atmosphere with

> the opportunities they provide for play and the talk that accompanies it, the stress they put on individual learning and the skill with which teachers select from the various methods of teaching reading those that suit themselves and the individual children.[27]

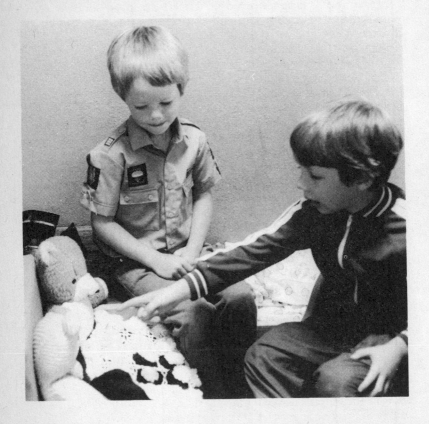

Infant schools provide varied opportunity for play and the talk that accompanies it.

Research from the National Foundation for Educational Research (NFER) and other bodies, showing that 40 per cent of children at eight needed an infant style of teaching,[28] was also quoted in support for the argument. Schools containing children from five to eight were to be called 'first' schools and those from eight to twelve 'middle' schools. In 1966, Circular 13 allowed local education authorities to change the age of transfer to twelve or thirteen but only if they could show some clear practical advantages in the context of reorganisation on comprehensive lines, or the raising of the school-leaving age, or both.[29] Despite Plowden rhetoric, the secondary tail was therefore continuing to wag the primary dog even in this type of reorganisation.

From the inception of first and middle schools there was conflict about the ideal ages for transfer. The Plowden Committee saw eight and twelve as the ideal years. This, they argued, gave adequate time for the first and middle schools to develop their own ethos. It also provided reasonably long secondary courses for the then early leavers. Others preferred splits at nine and thirteen and reorganised on this basis. In some areas combined schools for five- to twelve-year-olds developed. These were generally sparsely populated regions but exceptions include Milton Keynes. Thus authorities reorganised in these new ways according to their own beliefs and needs. There does, however, tend to be a distinction between middle schools catering for twelve- or thirteen-year-olds in the degree of specialisation they employ. Typically the 'eight-to-twelve' schools adopt a curriculum in the first three years similar to that of the higher primary school classes. Only in the final year does some specialis-ation occur, and this often less than in the early years of a conventional secondary school. In contrast the 'nine-to-thirteen' schools have, since their inception, always been seen as something other than simply an extended primary school. At their best they have tended to develop their own curriculum and ethos. Where staff have mainly been recruited from the secondary sector, however, the methods may be more didactic than those of primary schools and involve subject specialisation in all but the first year.

The first middle school arrangement has still not been widely adopted across the country but where it exists it seems to gain strong support from staff and parents alike. Indeed, plans for further reorganisation or reversion to transfer at eleven in some areas have recently been successfully resisted by parents.[30] Schemes involving a nine-to-thirteen organisation are, however, more expensive than conventional primary schools because of the extra staff and facilities required. As populations fall they become vulnerable to reorganisation and as a form of schooling they may well be short-lived.

The Leicestershire Plan

Finally a very small number of LEAs have adopted a system originating in Leicestershire whereby primary schools cater for children up until ten years. Pupils then transfer to a separate school for the next four years, transferring at fourteen to 'higher' schools for their sixteen-plus and A-level examinations.

Summary

The varying elements that make up the primary phase of education, therefore, have not necessarily developed at the right time in the right place for the right reasons. They also defy overall rationale. Infant schools originally arose to meet and compensate for the needs of working mothers. When such children became absorbed into the state system they were seen as interfering with the serious business of learning and became rapidly separated from the older pupils. Junior schools similarly evolved from the expansion of secondary education and, ironically, the need to preserve the by then established infant school approach. There was little support for combined primary schools even in the 1930s when the term was first coined. However, they persisted in rural areas and then met the fluctuating needs of many post-war housing estates.

In the 1960s abolition of the eleven-plus in some authorities led to further experiments in primary organisation. First and middle schools were developed in some areas and the Leicestershire Plan in others. The varying provision reflects conflict over suitable ages for transfer at the differing stages. Whatever the organisation, however, first/middle school reorganisation could go ahead only if it benefited a move to comprehensivisation. The needs of older pupils therefore continued to dominate policy up to the present day.

The result of all these changes is a confusion of provision. Parents may indeed have the choice of every available school type within a single authority. However, the problems that some forms of organisation were supposed to solve – for example, staggered entry into school – are still with us. Changes, such as the current move to combined primaries, still would seem to be as much a result of administrative and financial convenience as real educational need.

CHAPTER 3

Never the twain

During my year at High Rise I became a regular traveller on the number seven bus route. Starting on the residential side of the city, this meandered down into the centre and out into the depressed, industrial area beyond. Familiar faces joined and left the route at their prescribed points. Like homes and staff-rooms, a pattern of seating evolved into which newcomers were quickly initiated.

'Don't sit there, luv. Mrs Batty gets on at next stop and allus 'as that place . . . Mr Musgove's 'ad that seat for fifteen years, but 'e only gets on at City Square.'

Only two of us ever alighted at High Rise. My co-traveller went first and briskly vanished from sight. Struggling with bags, books and visual aids, I usually staggered off to a welcoming committee of pupils cast out from home and seeking illicit, early entry into school with offers of help. They at least carried the luggage and it was a welcome breath of informality in an otherwise formal and highly organised day.

January arrived and with it the snow. The bus was inevitably late. As I unloaded the usual selection of bags my co-traveller turned and offered a helping hand.

'I'm going your way,' she said, 'and we're both so late that a slow walk won't matter. How are you enjoying teaching?'

I was startled to find that Mrs Patterson was, in fact, a colleague, but in the girls' school occupying the ground floor. She confessed to little knowledge of staff or practice in the boys' sector despite teaching for ten years in the same building.

'We're like separate countries going about our own business under separate leaders,' she laughed. 'And there haven't ever been any road links built in my time.'

From that day Mrs Patterson and I sat together for our journey – we established our seats like other regulars and exchanged information and gossip about our relative institutions. They seemed more like worlds than continents apart. It was pleasing to be in the happy sociable staff-room of the upper storey rather than in its petty and mean-sounding counterpart below.

Like Mount Everest to the climber the girls' school demanded exploration simply because it was there. Did the hall floor really shine like a mirror through obsessive polishing and little educational use? Was there really little display because it might spoil the walls and look untidy? Like most teachers I always remained for some time after school but on Thursdays I stayed particularly late. It was an opportunity for mounting work and completing marking or organisational matters before the weekend. The caretaker generally threw me out when he was ready to go home. One such night I descended the stairs only to see the entrance to the girls' school open. Like a naughty child I stole inside. There was no light but the moon reflected in the infamously shiny floor to cast a ghostly glow on to the surrounding walls. I peered around trying to make out Mrs Patterson's name on one of the eight doors. Suddenly a voice boomed out:

'Do you know you're trespassing?'

The diminutive figure before me scarcely looked like the formidable headteacher I'd heard about, but I guessed she was. I flushed, caught in the act, and explained my position and interest in the school. The words fell on stony ground.

'Well, when you've finished snooping,' she exclaimed, 'kindly leave the way you came.' She looked down at my fashionable stilettos. 'I don't want those heels on my hall floor!'

CHAPTER 4

Contrasts in primary school organisation

As well as there being a range of types of primary school there are also widely differing forms of organisation. Marked contrasts result from the degree of separation or segregation of sexes, ages, abilities and teaching groups. High Rise, for example, was a single-sex streamed junior school. Eastlea and Ford Farm were combined primary schools with mixed-ability classes but separate remedial groups. Some classes in both these schools also contained mixed age groupings. Finally there is the pervasive element of the class itself which persists as the most common form of organisation in schools in spite of experiments for which the arrangement is not necessarily fundamental. This chapter examines these different forms of organisation, their rationale and implications for teaching and learning.

Single-sex and mixed schools

Whilst infant schools have always tended to be co-educational, junior schools have varied in their composition. For example, in 1925 approximately half the nine-year-olds in the country were attending single-sex schools. By 1965 only 3 per cent were being educated in this way (including those at High Rise). The tradition for separating the sexes probably originated in the private sector. Today private schools still demonstrate a certain prejudice against co-education even at the 'preparatory' level. In the nineteenth century such feelings were echoed in state schools and even the smallest contained separate departments for boys and girls. When mixed departments were first advocated it was because of an interest in educational efficiency rather than equality of opportunity.[1] By 1895 the arrangement was gaining popularity in smaller schools. But in urban areas separation of the sexes still remained the more common practice. Even by the 1930s co-education was still not fully accepted by society. The Hadow Report tentatively states that the authors could find

> no valid objection on general sociological and educational grounds to 'mixed' primary schools, provided that due regard be paid to the differing needs of the boys and girls in the matter of games and physical exercises.[2]

The Committee did not consider it desirable to lay down any firm rules on co-education. They simply noted that the arrangement worked well for junior children in urban areas, where mixed schools were administratively convenient. However, mixed schools spread with increasing rapidity after publication of the report. By 1947, 66 per cent of junior schools and departments were co-educational, rising to 92 per cent in the following eight years. The two High Rise schools were forced to amalgamate when they were reorganised into a middle school during the late 1960s. Today few single-sex junior schools remain.

Horizontal and vertical grouping

Age groupings, even more than sex groupings, often result from organisational rather than ideological factors. In larger schools, for example, classes have generally been organised so that they contain children born during one school year. Such horizontal grouping has been common practice since the Revised Code of 1862 instituted a system of six 'standards' corresponding to the then six years of school life. At that time children transferred from the infant school to Standard 1 of the elementary school as soon as they were six. This was financially advantageous to schools under the payment-by-results system. From that age the normal rate of progress for a child became one standard per year. Accelerated progress through the standards was generally discouraged as no extra grant was paid for pupils beyond Standard 6 even though schools with further standards did exist.

Whilst payment by results ended in 1898 the idea of promotion by standards survived. However, when the eleven-plus was introduced children were thought to have a better chance of a free place at secondary school if they were in the top standard by that age. Bright pupils were therefore accelerated through the system ahead of their age group. Similarly, less able children sometimes remained in the lower standards, repeating the same work year after year. From this practice come derogatory comments such as, 'He couldn't even get out of Standard 1.' Where age groups are mixed in this way there is vertical grouping. This has always been practised where a school's size prevents classes of a single age span. It became less common in junior classes during the post-Hadow period because of the recommendation of streaming for this age group. The Hadow Committee on Infant and Nursery Schools, however, welcomed what it termed the experimental use of vertical classification though they felt such an organisation would be effective only under a teacher with 'special gifts'.[3] However, necessity, rather than experimentation, has made verticle grouping a regular feature in infant school organisation.

Since 1870, regulations on the statutory age for commencing education have resulted in infant schools having termly intakes but annual outputs of pupils. This causes severe organisational problems. Sometimes reception classes are kept small enough in the autumn term to allow for additional intakes at Christmas and Easter. However, this means the youngest pupils not only having the least time in school but beginning in the largest classes. An alternative arrangement involves one teacher taking all reception children for one term. On the arrival of a new intake these have to be promoted into the next class with a consequent upward movement of the oldest children. Occasionally the top class are kept as one group and termly promotion is restricted to the two lowest classes. These and other practices have generally proved unsatisfactory. A whole class of reception children can be difficult to organise. Where pupils are promoted termly, they, teachers and parents have too little time to establish important relationships. The whole school can be affected, pupils and teachers having to adjust to continuous class changes. The Plowden recommendation of an annual September intake for children over five was never implemented. It would, of course, require the provision of nursery education for all pre-school children. A solution evolved by teachers themselves has been that of vertical or family grouping.

A vertically grouped infant class always has some children from each age group. A small number of reception children are added each term to spend the whole of their infant schooling with one teacher. The arrangement has many advantages. New children enter a stable regime into which they can be quickly initiated. The prolonged contact with one teacher provides security and also allows a child's progress to be measured over the whole infant period rather than a single year or term. Activities can therefore be more successfully matched to the child's ability. In a vertically grouped class, children tend to be more able to work at their own pace. A bright, younger child will have the activities and stimulation of the older age groups.

Less able, older children will similarly have apparatus and tasks within their abilities. The atmosphere tends to be one of co-operation rather than competition, children sharing and helping each other.

Criticisms of vertical grouping, like those of all-age elementary schools, centre on the disadvantages for certain pupils. Somerhill and Clark, for example, claim that the older ones might suffer most:

> Where classes are large and space restricted it is especially difficult to extend these children fully and to give the time and attention they need if they are to explore and experience widely. They themselves say that they like to be away from the youngest children because they often find them too demanding and distracting.[4]

Plowden commented that the younger pupils themselves may be overshadowed by the older ones, imitate them too closely, and have insufficient play.[5] For such reasons schools sometimes form a separate class of final-year children, thus restricting vertical grouping to the two younger age groups. Others create a separate reception class and vertically group the others. One compromise can be to allow occasional age groupings within the timetable for certain activities:

> Red butterflies [able final-year pupils] had one hour on each of two days plus one whole day, during which they pursued selected mathematical topics in detail, enjoyed more advanced singing and instrument work and stories, and adventured into some quite intricate handwork and art and cooking, as well as doing a lot of writing.[6]

When discussing vertical grouping the Plowden Committee recognised that it would not be acceptable in all schools[7] but claimed that where prevalent it resulted in the most lively infant work in the country.[8] They were more tentative about its use with older children, acknowledging that there is no available evidence to show whether a double age group is advantageous at the junior level. Plowden also recognised that such organisation demands great skill from the teacher.[9] Success in teaching such a class may particularly vary with its size. Nevertheless the arrangement has become popular in some junior schools.

The 1978 HMI survey[10] showed that 35 per cent of seven-year-olds were vertically grouped even though their actual numbers allowed for horizontal organisation. As children increase in age the practice similarly appears to decrease, only 19 per cent of eleven-year-olds being voluntarily vertically grouped.[11] Junior groupings also seem more popular over two rather than three age groups.[12] Generally, however, mixed-age classes at the junior level are an organisational convenience in schools too small for single-age school year groups. Both Eastlea and Ford Farm schools were forced to group some classes vertically. However, the implications of such practice can be far-reaching. Teaching classes of mixed age groups and abilities does require great skill. The professional strategies that must be adopted under such a system are complex and sophisticated. Vertical grouping therefore presents teachers with a demanding situation. If they do not necessarily support it and have it inflicted upon them the claimed advantages can be seriously reduced.

Streaming

Streaming involves classifying children into homogeneous groups by ability. At High Rise there were two streams, 'A' and 'B', for each age group. The main recommendation for this form of organisation came from the 1931 Hadow Report – widely acclaimed for its progressive, child-centred attitude. Such seemingly conflicting values and prescriptions from its writers reflect learning theories of the time.

The 1930s saw psychologists such as Cyril Burt and Percy Nunn asserting that intelligence was fixed by hereditary factors and unaffected by education or environment. Both were influential members of the Hadow drafting subcommittee for *The Primary School* report. Streaming was also seen as a way of recognising and helping teachers develop individual differences between pupils – the essence of a child-centred approach:

> One great advantage of the self-contained primary school is that teachers have special opportunities for making a suitable classification of the children according to their natural gifts and abilities. On the one hand, immediate treatment of an appropriate character can be provided for retarded children, and on the other hand, suitable arrangements can be made for specially bright children . . . Where classes are large, the task of the teacher will be lightened if the pupils are carefully classified according to their capacity . . . in the smaller schools steps might well be taken to organise at least one separate class for the abler children.[13]

Eminent educationalists such as Susan Isaacs, renowned for their activity methods, therefore gave this form of organisation their full support,[14] and the junior school was an ideal environment in which it could flourish. From its inception a proportion of top pupils were selected for secondary school places. After the development of the tripartite system following the 1944 Education Act the idea of streaming for the three types of secondary school gained increased importance. Competition between schools for grammar school places encouraged the practice, as did the large-sized classes of the time. By 1962, 96 per cent of junior classes were organised in this way. Eastlea escaped because of its small numbers and a changing mood in the times. The 1960s, for example, saw a move to comprehensivisation in the secondary sector.

With the abolition of the eleven-plus, junior schools became freed of their selective role and de-streaming gained popularity. Galton *et al.* see de-streaming as a teachers' movement rather than one promoted by authorities (though LEAs and the HMI did give their support and encouragement once de-streaming was under way).[15] Their reasons could have been educational, though de-streaming was also said to ease the teacher's and school's managerial problems:

> as was well understood at the time, it tended to obviate centres of disaffection with the C and D streams in large urban and suburban primary schools (by the same token it was also seen as tending to equalise disciplinary problems amongst the school staff as a whole).[16]

Today, where selection persists so, too, does streaming. There is also evidence that arrangement of classes into mixed abilities and/or ages does not completely eradicate the practice. Teachers normally arrange such classes physically into groups. There are many ways in which this can be done. As Ridgway points out:

> the basis for them, in differing situations, can be age, ability, teaching convenience, teacher specialisation, assigned or self-chosen tasks. Groups may form because of the magnetism of a dominant child, the preference of children for each other or a piece of equipment, or simply because of the physical location involved in carrying out a task.[17]

Friendship groups are probably the most informal of all arrangements. Sometimes, though, they may be unsatisfactory with young children because of the tenuous nature of relationships at this age. Rivalry, cliques or over-dependence on a partner can also result and some friends may simply distract each other.

The most formal division of children is into permanent groups. Research as to the form such groups take is somewhat ambivalent. The 1978 HMI report suggested that it frequently relates to some academic achievement such as reading ability or mathematical skill.[18] Galton and colleagues found similar arrangements for the curriculum – children being labelled by work card or textbook level. However, their physical seating within the classroom tended to be heterogeneous.[19] As groups in primary schools rarely work co-operatively the different findings may be insignificant. Whether physically grouped around a table or by work level, whether named by colours or Greek letters, children tend to know the group ratings. Once a teacher decides that these children are 'As' and these 'Cs' streaming results. The effects on the pupils are the same as in the streamed class.

Research into streaming has produced conflicting findings. Yates and Pidgeon declared in 1959 that, on the evidence available, it was impossible to establish a case for or against the practice.[20] Subsequent research by Daniels[21] and Jackson[22] supported this. Studies comparing streamed and unstreamed schools did, however, find differences in the attitudes and characteristics of their relative teachers. Those in streamed schools, for example, tended to be less permissive in their attitude towards children's behaviour and more in favour of corporal punishment and selection at eleven. Their methods were more formal and, on average, they were older.[23] Teachers in streamed schools also tended themselves to be streamed; those with most experience and who were concerned with hard work, examination results and obedient behaviour gaining allocation to the highest ability classes.[24]

As schools have moved towards mixed-ability teaching such findings have become less pervasive. However, as teachers continue to stream informally within mixed classes, the effects on children may well continue. One of the most worrying findings is that such labelling tends to depress the ability of less able children despite, in some circumstances, increasing performance amongst the most able.[25] Thus placement of a child on the 'bottom' or 'top' table may well become a self-fulfilling prophecy.

Such results cause more concern when one considers the methods used for allocation to ability streams or groups. The Hadow Committee was at pains to warn teachers about assessing children too early and advised them to group by potential rather than attainment:

> our psychological witnesses stressed the desirability of classifying by capacity rather than by attainments; the method of assessing ability at this age by a simple test in reading and calculation might yield misleading results, since, for example, retardation at the end of the infant stage is frequently due, not to any inherent defect in the individual child, but to prolonged absence through illness, or to unfavourable home conditions. Moreover, the freedom and variety of the methods of teaching now employed in many infant schools are apt to render mere attainments a rather untrustworthy criterion of general ability at this stage.[26]

Generally the advice was ignored. Seven-year-olds were frequently streamed and a common means of grouping young children today is still by reading attainment. Such assessments tend to favour girls, 'bottom' tables and remedial groups containing more than their share of boys. Older children who have entered school in autumn and spring also benefit, there being more 'Easter intakes' amongst remedial children than other groups.

Labelling in one aspect of learning tends to persist across others. There was little movement between streams in the past. Today the high level of literacy demanded for learning in most subjects tends to make assessment of the ability of slow readers a difficult task. Observers have, indeed, been surprised at the performance of remedial children when problem-solving within the new medium of a microcomputer.[27] Hopefully such findings will encourage educationalists to review both criteria of assessment and policies of labelling children in the future.

Summary

Primary schools may differ widely in the way sexes, ages, abilities and teaching groups are separated. The practice of segregating the sexes predominated in the private sector and became echoed in the state system, at first as an ideology and then as an administrative convenience. The Hadow Committee remained neutral to the practice though their Report was followed by a rapid decline in the number of single-sex primary schools. However, today a few still exist.

Contrasts in the age groupings within primary classes often result through organisational compromise. Horizontally grouped classes have their basis in the old elementary school 'standards' where each class corresponded to a particular age grouping. However, where entry numbers are small or fluctuating, schools have always been forced to mix children of different ages in one class. This is particularly true of infant schools where termly intakes are not matched by termly outputs of pupils. Infant teachers have experimented with a variety of arrangements to solve the problem, one of the most popular being vertical grouping. However, where children of varying ages are grouped together concern arises over the disadvantages for certain groups. There is inadequate research to support or refute such claims. Certainly it is an arrangement that demands considerable teaching skill. Success or failure of the organisation may also vary more than in horizontally grouping with class size. With its increasing occurrence in primary schools, the disadvantages of vertical grouping for teachers and children would seem to warrant further research.

In contrast to vertical grouping, a declining practice in primary schools is class streaming. Originally streaming was recommended as a means of helping teachers cope with individual differences. It was therefore advocated by many eminent child-centred educationalists. However, like horizontal grouping, it was most easily practised in schools with large annual intakes of pupils. The advent of the smaller school, systematic research and a move to comprehensivisation in the secondary sector all helped reduce streamed classes.

Nevertheless, teachers have continued to group children according to specific ability within mixed-ability classes. Such labels can prove a self-fulfilling prophecy for children. Indeed, labelling by sex, age and ability can all mitigate against the educative process, there tending to be as much variety within labels as between them. Like infamous medics handing out tranquillisers or aspirin for all ills, those who label too freely in school tend both to diagnose and to prescribe inadequately or even disastrously. Hopefully, as our understanding grows such practices will decrease.

An Environment for Learning?

CHAPTER 5

Hall in a day's work

The design of High Rise offered few advantages to its users. Classrooms surrounded a central hall. Fortunately this could accommodate the whole school for morning assembly. At other times, however, it trapped us in our classrooms providing a constant background of TV, PE and music to interrupt our train of thought. Only at Christmas did I realise some of the advantages central hall schools may have offered to their original users. Christmas is always a wonderful time in primary schools. It offers stimulus for a range of aesthetic experiences and a topic that is of natural interest to a young audience. Following on from Hallowe'en and Bonfire Night it forms the culmination of an exhausting but exciting term.

At High Rise, Christmas was approaching fast. The staff had already enjoyed a weekend social evening at a local restaurant and now it was time for the pupils' Christmas dinner and parties. They had been planned to occur on the same day, preceded by an end-of-term staff meeting in school time. The organisation for the latter was well up to standard. Each class was provided with at least an hour's work. My own had to complete party hats for the afternoon celebrations and progress to standard work in the basic skills. At 11 a.m. prompt doors were opened so that occupants of rooms could be viewed by the head boy placed centrally in the hall. Mr Teague gave clear instructions. No child was to move or speak. Any pupil disobeying the order was to be brought into the hall by the head boy to be dealt with later. With silence established we all descended to the staff-room below.

It was an enjoyable meeting made more informal than usual by the provision of sherry and orange juice. The agenda was frequently interrupted by jokes and asides as parts numbed by a long hard term became refreshed and rejuvenated. At 11.45 a.m. we ascended, some more unsteadily than others, to the school above. Few of us could suppress giggles at the sight that met our eyes. There, scarcely the height of the head boy's desk, stood the youngest child in the school. His sins were solemnly related to Mr Teague. Had he really had the audacity to move not once but twice from his place? Had he really made noises so that the rest of the class giggled. Had he? *Had he?* A large tear trickled down the tiny cheek. Mr Teague then boomed his most feared words.

'Follow me, young man!'

The whole school gasped. Few made the trip to the inner sanctum of the head's study. Even fewer wished to repeat the experience. I watched somewhat saddened as the miscreant dragged his feet towards certain doom. However, Gwyneth his teacher didn't seem too perturbed.

'Hark at the criminal of the century,' she giggled. 'Little devil!'

I protested, 'Oh, Gwyneth, it is Christmas.'

She smiled at my concern. 'Don't worry,' she said. 'Harry'll only tell him off and threaten him with missing the party this afternoon. At two o'clock he'll ask for an apology and then let him join the others.'

I still looked doubtful, so she continued, 'You know, Jan,' she said, 'old Harry's firm but he's fair and a real softy at heart. That's how he runs a good school in an unlikely area.'

Sure enough, the afternoon saw little Terry seated outside Mr Teague's study with a pile of work before him. Tears were still flowing fast. At two o'clock I was just gathering up the paper from 'pass-the-parcel' when a small figure caught my eye. It was Terry, hurrying across the hall.

'And don't run, boy,' a voice boomed behind him, 'or we can arrange an afternoon of walking practice!'

CHAPTER 6

Within these walls

High Rise was built at the turn of the century. When I taught there in 1965 over half the primary schools in England and Wales were either of this age or even older. In contrast both Eastlea and Ford Farm were erected during the early 1960s to cater for the school population of new housing estates on the outskirts of cities. Spacious plots of land had been put aside for this purpose. In both schools corridors and chains of classrooms spread out in long fingers from a central administrative palm. All three schools have, within the last twenty years, seen neighbouring establishments constructed with some element of open planning.

The first open–plan school in Britain was conceived during 1956.[1] Like all prototypes before, it reflected specialists' interpretations of teachers' and children's requirements for effective education. Such interpretation frequently occurs against a background of conflicting pressures. Since 1833, when Exchequer funds were first used for educational building, government approval of school plans has been mandatory. However, for some years controls were not strictly applied, allowing dubious practice in certain areas. The Schools Inspector for Devon, for example, boasted in 1876 of

> the relative cheapness of elementary schools in the South West . . . and recommended particularly the saving which was to be made when a school was built without the services of a professional architect.[2]

By 1902 architects were employed by all the school boards and their professional publications did much to inform and influence new trends in the field. Following the Second World War regular

Building Bulletins from the DES Architects and Buildings Branch have served a similar purpose. These specialists consult closely with LEAs who, together with the Exchequer, provide money required for all but independent and voluntary school buildings.

Before any new school is built today there are numerous consultations between architect, LEA administrative officers, area advisers or inspectors and (sometimes) practising teachers. Any draft plans, however, must meet cost-per-place limits set by the government and minimum standards set by official building regulations. The final design is often a compromise between conflicting architectural, financial, educational and health considerations. At different periods one aspect may be considerably more influential than another.

The problem presented to teachers by school architectural procedures lies in the transformation of any structurally adequate and cost-effective new type of building into a prototype copied within or across authorities. Evaluation of design in terms of learning and teaching is generally not practised. Indeed, the assumption is usually made that a successful building for one group of teachers and children will operate equally well for another. The effects of such a decision are, of course, long-standing, for schools last longer than people or educational theories. The result has been a legacy of school buildings that pose inherent problems for their contemporary users. This chapter describes some of the types of building modern teachers might find themselves in, their architectural features and background ideologies.

One-room schools

The earliest type of European school, widespread in the Middle Ages, consisted of a single room in which a large number of children were taught by one qualified teacher and several assistants. It was to such a school, in Madras, that Andrew Bell was appointed superintendent in the 1790s. When Bell met resistance from his assistants for using sand to teach early writing skills, he gave the task to an eight-year-old pupil, John Friskin. The latter was so successful in his task that he was appointed teacher to the lowest class. An account of the project, aptly called *An Experiment in Education*, was published in 1797, after Bell returned to England. It ran to five editions.

Later, and quite independently, Joseph Lancaster evolved a similar idea but for very different reasons. He had established a one-room school in Borough Road, London, in 1801. Lancaster's school attracted increasingly large numbers of pupils, for whom he could not afford to employ the necessary assistants. Facing severe financial difficulties, he began using the older children, whom he called 'monitors', to teach the younger. Believing his idea to be original, he described it in a pamphlet with the euphemistic title *Improvements in Education*, in 1803. Such was its fame that Lancaster secured the patronage of George III.

Both Bell and Lancaster contributed much to the widespread development of the 'monitorial system' and in turn continued the building of one-bedroom schools. The economy of the system was attractive on all counts. Lancaster boasted that it allowed one teacher to educate a thousand pupils; Bell, that ten schools of a thousand pupils could be supervised if the buildings were close enough.

Generally schools were somewhat smaller! A typical Lancastrian school room of 70 × 32 feet held 320 children, allowing seven square feet per child. This was reduced to six square feet in most monitorial schools. As well as being cheap, the schools were rigidly organised. Lancaster revelled in this. Down the centre of the room was a line of long desks for writing, and to the sides semi-circles of studs marking the pupils' and monitors' positions for reading. It was Lancaster who coined the phrase 'a place for everything, and everything in its place' – and he kept to it.[3] Each pupil had a number for nail, hat, desk and slate. Armies of monitors not only taught, but repaired pens, ruled paper and called registers. Pupils marched to places and desks.

Bell was more flexible in his system, having fewer monitors but larger classes. Writing desks were placed around the walls and central areas marked by squares for each class. This arrangement was adopted by the early 'national' schools, though the central area soon became fitted with movable benches that could accommodate approximately twelve children and a monitor for reading. A further development, particularly in infant schools, replaced desks with a stepped floor or gallery on which children could sit. Here they received 'simultaneous instruction'. This innovation was introduced by Samuel Wilderspin, founder of the Infant School Society in the 1820s. In tiers (physically and sometimes literally) facts could be learned and infants drilled mechanically through question-and-answer routines. Responses often satisfied diverse criteria:

> Two pints will make one quart,
> Four quarts one gallon strong.
> Some drink too little, some too much,
> To drink too much is wrong.[4]

Wilderspin's galleries became popular even for older children. An Education Department circular of 1872 argued that their proper use improved the general intelligence of children.[5] A memo in 1898 argued their retention in the hall of the Jonson Street School because they had 'great advantage over desks [for] games and object lessons . . . word building or mechanical arithmetic'.[6] Galleries could still be found in primary schools of the 1950s, the last in London being removed during 1952.

Wilderspin and David Stow also introduced the idea of having a separate classroom attached to the schoolroom in which smaller groups of children could be taught. This design was recommended by the Committee of Council on Education in 1851 and embodied in the *Rules to Be Observed in Planning and Fitting up Schools* issued from 1863 until the end of the century. It was the precursor of a system of separate teaching classes.

In 1962 over half the total of primary schools in England and Wales had originally been built in the nineteenth century to these designs. In the following eight years two thousand were closed and six thousand improved. This left a further six thousand to be improved or replaced. Many nineteenth-century school buildings, therefore, still exist. They tend to be voluntary or church schools in rural areas, and built originally to the two-room design. Where single-room schools still exist they tend to have been divided into several classrooms or extended, the original room generally becoming the school hall.

Central hall designs

Towards the end of the nineteenth century building was strongly influenced by trends in Prussia, whose schools were regarded as exemplars of their day. In the Prussian system classes of eighty children were allocated to their own rooms with a separate teacher. A general schoolroom or central hall was also available for use. In 1872 the newly formed London School Board built the Jonson Street School in Stepney to this design. By 1878 the Birmingham School Board had followed suit.

The system initially helped the boards cope with the rising school population resulting from the 1870 Act. The resulting large classes required large buildings and separate classrooms. However, such designs were less suited to the use of pupil teachers, who were easier to supervise in the single-room plan and its derivatives. In the early days, objections to the Prussian designs were mainly on this count. Indeed, in 1872 regulations clearly stated that each standard should be taught, as far as possible, in separate classrooms, but 'as each school is under the supervision of one master or mistress, this principle must in some degree be subordinate to the necessity for such supervision'.[7] Thus when the London board built the Jonson Street School, it ensured that building was under way before submitting the design to the Education Department! The architect was immediately summoned to Westminster where battles with officials ensued, particularly over the large size of the school hall. Although finally accepted at a Department meeting, the (anonymous) comment, 'I do not think you will beat the Germans',[8] was recorded in the minutes. This indicated more a resignation to rather than support for the design.

Early in the twentieth century pupil teachers were largely replaced by student teachers. These were recruited at sixteen and worked in school for two years before embarking on a training college course. Elementary school staff could therefore be given more responsibility to control their own classes in their own rooms. The central hall school spread rapidly throughout the country, 80 per cent being built to this plan by 1910.[9] Claims that classes of sixty children could easily be controlled in such schools were made. Headteachers, however, maintained overall authority for discipline by partially glazing the walls surrounding the hall. This provided an adequate view of all class activities for supervisor or visitor. The design was thought to engender a healthy community spirit as well as good discipline in the pupils.

Central hall schools tended to be built in heavily populated areas of inner cities. At the time the design saved land which was in short supply. Many are still in use, including High Rise. In 1965 organisation here was as originally conceived. A single-storey building contained the infants; the main building housed girls on the ground floor with boys above. Many designs occupy three storeys and there are examples even today of playgrounds in central hall schools being placed on the roof to save space. However, High Rise had and still has normal play facilities.

Veranda and quadrangle designs

Early in the twentieth century urban development patterns began to change. New schools were built on the outskirts of towns where more spacious sites were available. The birth-rate also declined so that there was less emphasis on building large schools. The inter-war period saw a general concern for the physical well-being of the poorer social groups. A new welfare policy was pursued by central and local government authorities affecting housing, medical provision, school meals and buildings.

In reaction to the overcrowded, smoky slum conditions of the many inner-city homes came the demand for cleaner, brighter, more airy schools. By 1905 'open-air schools' – buildings opening fully on at least two sides, with verandas – were being built for ailing children. Such schools were thought to be an investment in more than health:

> Far better that debilitated children should, through the open-air schools, be able to live, and grow, and develop, than that through inattention they should be allowed to drift into schools for the mentally defective, or otherwise become a burden on the rate payers.[10]

Doctors became increasingly involved in school design. George Reid, county medical officer for health in Staffordshire, for example, launched a vigorous campaign to improve ventilation in his local schools in 1902. At the time the central hall design, so resisted in 1872, had become virtually compulsory. Thus when Reid and Hutchings, Staffordshire's architect, submitted a design with classrooms separated from the hall along an open veranda, it contravened existing building regulations. Lengthy and animated discussions with the Board of Education ensued. The latter felt that the design would allow too much light and fresh air into the building. Reid argued that such 'cross-ventilation' was essential for a healthier working environment. Finally, after some modifications, two experimental schools in the design were allowed. A Board of Education architect assessed the completed buildings and was impressed: 'It was remarkable that when I walked into the classroom there was no smell.'[11]

Reid's ideas received much publicity. He was particularly supported by George Widdows, Derbyshire's county architect, who designed an extraordinary range of experimental veranda schools for his own area. These greatly inspired others. However, the idea was accepted by the Board of Education only in 1914 when the revised building rules stated:

> it is desirable to place the hall so that noise in it will not disturb the work in the classrooms. For this reason, as well as for ventilation and freedom from dust, the classrooms should not open directly from it. The hall may therefore be altogether or partly detached.[12]

'Cross-ventilation' became the important factor in school design. Indeed, by 1931 the Hadow Committee was claiming that the more closely the design of primary schools approached that of open-air schools the better.[13] By 1936 the Board of Education was advising that 'the ideal should be envisaged as a single storey building, opened out to the air and sunshine in every part'.[14] The pavilion or veranda designs were an obvious solution and there was now both the space and the support for building them. Teachers were enjoying the increased autonomy presented by the separate classrooms. The hall, once the centre of school discipline, could now be used, not only for assemblies, but for physical exercises and music – two increasingly popular activities at the time. The medical profession also supported the designs. The glazed folding doors, which replaced side walls, could be opened during the summer to provide a free flow of air. The verandas provided shelter when doors were opened in less clement weather. In winter, high level clerestory windows above the verandas could be opened for ventilation. The simple designs were also cheap though aesthetically unattractive. Indeed, Seaborne and Lowe claim that, although the most healthy of all English school buildings, they established

> the principle which was to govern much twentieth-century school design that, by comparison with hygienic and pedagogic consider-ations, architectural style was of slight importance.[15]

Opposition to veranda schools came mainly from traditionalists who feared they might lose their identity and cohesion by moving away from centralised plans. One compromise was to build class-rooms around a quadrangle with the infant department at one end, the hall opposite, and both linked by two rows of junior rooms. The design was thought to have many advantages, including:

> access from one part of the building to another . . . verandas on the inside . . . and good opportunities for architectural treatment in the enclosed courts and corridors, which can take the form of a kind of cloister.[16]

A number of veranda schools, of varying designs, are still in use.

Corridor designs

A common criticism of veranda schools even at the time of building was that they allowed too much fresh air into classrooms. An obvious solution was to close in the veranda section to form corri-dors. This became the practice in the inter-war years. Schools built from that time until just after the Second World War were the most spacious designs ever conceived. At their most extreme they were developed in 'finger plan'. Here the hall and administrative offices formed the schools' 'palm' with long 'fingers' of classrooms radiat-ing from it. The separation of teachers was often increased by the placement of store cupboards between adjoining rooms. Children were equally separated by arrangement into 'streams', the more able striving for places in the local grammar school. Separate cloak-rooms, playgrounds and playing fields added to the division. But the space required made the designs expensive and they were never developed on a wide scale.

During the post-war period a dramatic rise in the birth-rate was accompanied by a severe shortage in land and materials. Schools now had to be built more cheaply. This led to much bureaucratic scene-shifting in the background of continuous dramatic production. By 1950 detailed cost limits had been imposed on schools. By 1954 the building regulations had been revised twice. The result was a reduction in teaching area and in the cost per place in new buildings. By 1956 the Ministry could boast that the price of schools was 20 per cent less than in 1949 despite a 50-per-cent rise in building costs.[17] Savings were made by reducing the height and floor-space of schools. The first did bring schools more into proportion with the children using them. The second change was less popular. Dual use of space was introduced. Thus a hall served as a dining room, a classroom as a teaching area and corridor. Designs became more compact, some reverting closely but not completely to the central hall plan.

The era also brought other changes in the form of flat roofs and increased use of texture and colour. New building techniques were developed. Hertfordshire County Council, for example, built two hundred primary schools between 1945 and 1961 by using mass-produced standardised components that could be speedily erected into a light steel framework on site. One of these schools received a Royal Institute of British Architects medal for its design. Outside trees, shrubs and lawns gave a domestic character to the surrounding grounds. The school was becoming a smaller, friendlier and more homely environment:

> . . . we see a school no longer as a mere machine for giving lessons, but as a social unit concerned with the all round development of boys and girls.'[18]

This was also a period of rapid building, so many schools of this period are in common use. They include Eastlea. Here you enter into an attractive central area with dining room and administrative offices. Beyond lies a corridor leading to three closely grouped infant classes and, perpendicular to this, the junior department. Here, two lower classrooms are superimposed by two upper-storey rooms for the older pupils. Children, therefore, literally go up to the top classes at nine years of age. Between the two departments lies a staff-room with its own kitchen and cloakrooms. Outside are attractive gardens and generous play facilities.

Internally, Eastlea was difficult to maintain. Its walls were badly finished and the flat roof leaked. All staff helped regularly with decoration and school funds provided paint, pinboard, shelving and even new staff-room curtains. Conscientious ancilliary staff ensured that the school gleamed at least at beginning of term. We all formed part of the bucket brigade on wet days!

Open-plan designs

During the 1960s there was a move from traditional class teaching to group work; from separation to sharing. Different forms of organisation, for example vertical grouping, were tried, resulting in new methods such as the integrated day. Parents and ancillary staff became increasingly involved in school activities. It was a time for experimentation, educationally and architecturally. The most popular plea regarding school buildings was for 'flexibility'. More open designs developed and when the Amersham and Finmere schools were built[19] they began a trend which was to have greater effect on teachers and teaching than any other design. The Plowden Report describes the reasoning behind the two prototypes:

> The 'teaching area' was conceived as the whole school environment, rather than a series of individual rooms. The design . . . offered opportunities for changing ways of learning as the children grew older . . . 'School' includes the buildings, garden, play area and games space. Outside and inside provide an integrated learning environment. Inside, there are small working areas, each with its own degree of privacy and a character of its own, opening onto a larger space sufficiently uncluttered to allow children to climb and jump, dance and to engage in drama.[20]

The Amersham school (see Figure 1) was only semi-open plan. The eight individual classrooms were distinct from each other but grouped to allow easy access between rooms and the shared practical areas. In the Finmere school, folding partitions could be closed to create separate rooms if required. It was a small rural school but for many designers provided 'the solution for some of the most pressing problems'.[21]

The prototype for the large urban open-plan school was the Eveline Lowe School in Southwark. Here different areas were created for different activities. Carpeted quiet corners, tiled wet regions and carefully designed furniture and fittings created a resource-based rather than teacher-based environment. There was no hard and fast division between group spaces. The whole area was for learning.

The concept of open planning was extended and modified through the 1960s, reaching its peak in the 1970s. At its most extreme a school might bear a remarkable resemblance to the early two-room designs, e.g. the Eastergate primary school in East Sussex. More popularly, 'home bases' where classes of children could meet on occasions have been retained on the recommendation of Plowden, the DES[22] and the NUT.[23] In 1980, Bennett *et al.*[24] suggested that the wide variety of designs under the classification should be viewed in terms of

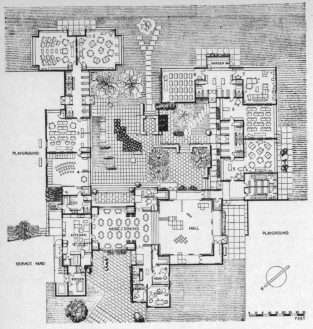

Figure 1   Amersham Junior School: a semi-open plan design, 1958

differences in size (i.e. the number of teachers the school was designed for) and the type of shared facility (whether practical or quiet areas and/or teaching space). In this way it was possible to identify eight basic types. These were by no means homogeneous, a fact frequently overlooked by early researchers.[25]

The open-plan movement has had more than its fair share of criticism. A commonly expressed view is that it is forced upon the teaching profession for purely economic reasons. In 1978 Peter Rattenbury, staff inspector for the DES Architects and Buildings Branch, denied this, stating:

> Any money saved by reducing the number of interior walls has been deliberately ploughed back into an increase in area and an improvement of fittings and finishes.[26]

DES figures on space standards, however, show that these have steadily fallen over the last decade, and many architects have claimed that they cannot design a conventional school within current cost limits.[27]

If the perpetuation of open designs has been for economic reasons the origins were not. The 'open society' dream of the 1960s expressed itself in many ways. In architectural terms it resulted in open-plan offices and homes as well as schools. Educationally, classrooms and schools became more open. Teachers emerged from their isolated classrooms to work together in teams; parents were given greater opportunity for decision-making and participation in school. The new designs attempted to support, and some would say encourage, this change in attitude and teaching. How successful they have been and whether teachers favour the designs continue to be the basis for much research. Whatever the findings all new primary schools will have at least an element of open planning in their design. 1982–83 saw the production of only twelve new schools, though a further twelve were replaced, two remodelled and twenty-two extended. There has also been a firm statement from the DES that it will not revert to 'cellular designs'.[28] Open designs have now existed for twenty-five years. At a recent conference celebrating the fact, there was at least one supporter who claimed: 'Open education has not been tried and found wanting. It has been found wanting but not tried.'[29]

Summary

Primary school buildings may therefore range from an original eighteenth-century single classroom to a modern open-plan complex. New schools, unlike some of their predecessors, are now architect designed. However, they must meet cost limits set by the government – an amount that can vary enormously depending on the financial state of the country. There are also pressures from the medical profession and teachers. Resultant designs generally show a compromise between architectural, financial, educational and health concerns. Innovatory ideas tend to become prototypes copied within and between authorities. A whole fashion in one design might literally sweep the country until new ideas or constraints produce another prototype. As with houses, however, schools outlive their original designers and occupants. Success of a building with one group of users is not necessarily repeated with another. Teachers therefore often inherit outmoded or inadequate designs of school providing subtle architectural constraints on their teaching.

The earliest one-room schools were necessary to ensure the successful supervision of large numbers of children by a limited number of qualified staff. The monitorial system perpetuated the use of the design, though, eventually, a second small room became attached to the main schoolroom to enable the tuition of small groups of pupils. These two room buildings tend to persist in rural voluntary or church schools.

Within these walls

The introduction of compulsory education greatly increased the school population. Larger buildings with separate classrooms were needed to house it, particularly in inner-city areas. The central hall design, emanating from Prussia, solved the problem. However, as it contravened existing building regulations the first to be built in Britain was partly erected before planning permission was sought. The central hall design still enabled supervision of a whole school by a single teacher. With the development of teacher training, however, staff could be given greater responsibility for their own pupils.

Recruitment in the First World War revealed a poor level of health amongst conscripts. In the inter-war period there was consequent pressure to improve the general physical condition of the nation. School was the ideal environment to begin preventive methods. Pressure for school meals and more airy buildings both affected design in the period. Using the example of open-air schools for the delicate, veranda and quadrangular designs were developed. These provided cross-ventilation in classrooms and increased the use of halls for physical education and music. Users complained that the designs allowed too much fresh air into classrooms, so verandas became enclosed to form corridors. At their extreme these corridor designs became long fingers of classrooms spreading from a central administrative palm. The design supported both the increased autonomy of teachers and the segregation of pupils into streams.

A dramatic rise in the birth-rate in the post-war period coincided with a shortage of land. School buildings therefore had to be cheaper. Regulations and cost limits were manipulated to effect the required results. Teaching area was reduced and ceilings were lowered. The concept of dual usage was introduced. Halls doubled as dining rooms and gymnasia; classrooms became corridors as well as areas for learning. Such changes, combined with less closed attitudes amongst teachers themselves, encouraged the development of open-plan designs. Early and generously equipped prototypes were followed by a rapid acceptance of the concept. Now most new schools tend to be either open or semi-open in design.

Generalisations in research about the advantages or disadvantages of open-plan schools tend to ignore the lack of homogeneity between them. Also, standards set in the spacious prototypes of such schools have declined considerably. Contemporary versions have less space and more children. How does this affect teaching and learning? Are the original ideals being realised under the new constraints? What are the implications of designs that impose methods upon teachers? Widespread implementation of open designs for financial convenience with little evaluation of effects represents the unacceptable face of current school building practice. It is one that has been continually masked but now needs reassessment.

CHAPTER 7

Can I go with paper, Miss?

It was my first day of teaching. The lesson was continuing smoothly and the children were working hard at their tasks. However, all did not seem well with Jonathan. Writing somewhat hesitantly with his right hand, his left gripped his stomach tensely as he shifted restlessly in his seat.

'Are you all right, Jonathan?'

'Can I go to the toilet, Miss?'

By now the trembling lip and clenched posture told all.

'Yes. Please be quick.'

The child stumbled towards me. Glancing cautiously back at the now rapt audience, he whispered, 'With paper, Miss.'

'Sorry?'

'Paper, Miss!'

The tone was urgent. Paper? Paper? I looked around puzzled. The appeal became desperate.

'In the cupboard, Miss!'

Fortunately there was only one cupboard. But it contained all the class resources and equipment. We flung the door open. Chalk, paper and books tumbled to the floor. Leaning across, the child's experienced eye located it . . . the toilet roll! Tearing off a good arm's length and ignoring cries that only two sheets were allowed, I thrust my unfortunate charge towards the door. He had a hall, two flights of stairs and a long playground to negotiate. Neither of us knew if he could make it.

A good five minutes passed.

'Kingsley,' I said, 'could you go and see if Jonathan is all right? You'd better put your coat on and take his too. It's started raining.'

At that moment the door opened. With relief I saw that, though wet, my charge was looking much better. As he returned to his seat, I finished tidying the cupboard. From then on the toilet roll was to occupy the foremost, most prominent position.

In 1966 indoor lavatories were installed at High Rise. They were placed in the existing cloakrooms so that coats had to be housed in the already cramped classrooms. Fitted cupboards were erected for this purpose. Each day now began with a coat-hanging routine to enable the forty pupils to reach their pegs. From the start, children complained that coats and shoes remained damp in inclement weather. Consequently heaters were installed in each cupboard's base. Classrooms were now not only smaller but damper as condensation gathered in the ill-ventilated space. The children, however, now had only two flights of stairs to negotiate to use the lavatory.

CHAPTER 8

Design matters

In all my years as pupil and student I never experienced outdoor lavatories. It was startling in the mid-1960s to find a school that did not reach the norms of sanitation existing within virtually all pupils' homes. But compared with the staff and pupils of Bishop Carpenter School, North Newington, we at High Rise were lucky. Even as late as 1985 the headteacher and forty-two boys of this school shared two washbasins and two toilets.[1] The five women teachers and fifty-five girls at the school similarly had four washbasins but only three toilets between them. Since 1975 the staff of Bishop Carpenter School have constantly had their request for staff cloakroom facilities vetoed by the DES despite having funds and plans available. For many years they used the toilet in the nearby headteacher's house. But when he moved from the area the new head lived too far away from the school for this practice to continue. The school also had no hall or PE facilities and the school office had been converted into a classroom.

Lack of such facilities typifies the architectural constraints that exist in schools. They can be unpredictable and unexpected yet their effects on teachers and pupils can be dramatic. Lavatories, cloakrooms, water supply, windows, lighting, heating, acoustics and the arrangement of space within a school are all potential sources of problems and conflict within the learning environment. The persistent use of temporary huts as teaching areas is also a bone of contention within the profession. Adequate programmes of replacement, adaption and maintenance of schools would, of course, reduce these issues but are generally not available. This chapter describes the architectural constraints teachers and pupils can face in school and discusses the background problems surrounding their adaption or removal.

The limitations of loos

It may seem trivial to place lavatories high on the list of important school design factors, yet it has been shown that their poor condition can generate a dislike for and inability to adjust to school in many pupils. The outdoor lavatories at High Rise were obviously a problem; yet 65 per cent of schools suffered such facilities in 1962.[2] In today's schools lavatorial problems remain high on the list of children's complaints about conditions. Indoor lavatories also can be as cold, dark and insanitary as those outside. Toilet doors with no locks or insufficient height and depth can reduce privacy, and hard rather than soft toilet paper causes discomfort. The lavatories themselves should also be of appropriate size for their users. The ease of locating boys' toilets in most primary schools through the simple sense of smell illustrates the problem. In temporary huts it is further exacerbated by absorbent wooden floor surrounds which are difficult to dry or clean.

In some schools it is the absence rather than the condition of toilets that causes problems. Many temporary huts accommodating over thirty pupils may house a single lavatory. Such a level of provision would be quite unacceptable in homes containing a fraction of these numbers. Staff toilets may be equally inadequate in school. High Rise had one shared lavatory accessed through a half-glazed door in the staff-room. It offered little privacy. The separate staff facilities at Eastlea were luxurious by comparison, although eight females had to share the same provision as two males. Only the generosity of the headteacher in relinquishing his own cloakroom reduced the inevitable break-time queues.

Conflicts over cloakrooms

In comparison with toilets, problems with cloakrooms tend to be few. Indeed, in the past their provision was often so generous that modern users can convert them to accommodate coats and learning activities simultaneously. Cloakrooms, however, need to be carefully sited. Access through practical or quiet areas in open-plan schools can produce severe limitations on teaching. The storage of coats on movable trolleys is an even greater source of irritation.[3] Such structures may occupy valuable teaching space and usually have to be replaced by standard hooks and lockers because of functional inadequacy.

Children line up for games outside their 18th century two-roomed school with its 20th century porta-cabin lavatory. Most of the classes are taught in temporary huts with no water supply.

Essential supplies

Water supply in schools is another factor that needs careful thought and consideration. Both hot and cold water supplies to cloakrooms are an obvious necessity. Where only cold water is present wall heaters are sometimes used but may issue water at such a temperature as to be a danger to young users.

Classrooms with no water supply present problems that can severely restrict the curricular activities. Obvious examples are in science, art and craft. At High Rise the only water supply was both cold and sited down a flight of steep stairs. I well remember devising a 'three bucket system' for survival! During painting the first was used for clean water, the second for washing or soaking used brushes and pots and the third for emptying our dirty water. Mops and cloths were situated nearby in case of accidents. Science required a similar arrangement though additional containers were required for the experiments themselves. Final cleaning of apparatus in both subjects took place in the cloakroom with water supplied from the staff kettle! It would have been easier to exclude such subjects from the curriculum altogether. It is to their credit that few staff at High Rise did so.

Lighting and learning

Teachers in the older designs of school frequently find the lack of natural light a problem. Windows may be too high to look out of or reach. Originally some were even stained in Gothic ecclesiastical style. This gave children an uplifting sight but not necessarily a working light! Lack of windows in older schools often results in poor ventilation and those classroom smells so frequently mentioned in past Inspectorate reports. However, new schools may equally suffer. The centralised working areas of open designs frequently lack windows. Solutions have had to be found because of strict regulations on both the amount and direction of light. A popular measure in single-storey buildings has been to place windows in the roof. But difficulties with cleaning and a tendency to leak have made them unpopular with staff. A second solution has involved amending the building regulations themselves. This was carried out in 1969, allowing 'the modification of minimum daylight factor' and thus the increased use of 'permanent supplementary artificial lighting of interiors'. Although Bennett and colleagues did find teachers in open-plan schools happier with their lighting than any other facilities,[4] concerns have been expressed over the amount of time teachers and children are spending in artificial conditions. But

Bennett's teachers did not face the problem presented in one school known to me. Here, the maximum height of the wedge-shaped hall (some 22 feet) required the erection of scaffolding for each replacement of a blown bulb. The staff are certainly not satisfied with their lighting!

If inadequate provision presents one end of the lighting spectrum, a surplus of window must represent the other. Veranda-style schools, designed for improved ventilation, are often too successful in their task. One I experienced as a student allowed such blasts of air through the opening door that carefully mounted wall displays required constant repair. In winter the extra windows caused low temperatures and draughts, the outside veranda being virtually a wind tunnel. Staff of veranda schools interviewed by Seaborne found similar problems.[5] Even the closing in of verandas simply replaced them with cold and draughty corridors. Many, too, mentioned the lack of privacy caused by the large numbers of windows in their rooms, resulting in a peepshow effect.

The lack of privacy through surplus windows occurs in many schools. Glazed walls surrounding the halls of central hall designs are consequently quickly covered by staff. At High Rise, pin-board was used. It provided valuable additional display space as well as reducing visibility from the hall. Windows in walls and doors to corridors in other types of school tend to become similarly covered.

Corridor windows on exterior walls may cause problems for pupils rather than staff. Positioning at the wrong height around playgrounds may, for example, lead to serious accidents to energetic children hurtling, arms outstretched in their direction. However, by far the greatest complaint about surplus windows concerns the 'hot-house effect' they generate. Whilst glass is recognised as a cheap building material it offers a most unsuitable south-facing wall. Excessive use of windows in such positions causes great discomfort to room occupants. The usual solution is to fit blinds. Their effectiveness, however, can be equally dependent on the windows they cover. In many cases it is impossible to have the blinds lowered and the windows open simultaneously. As one teacher explained: 'We have the dubious choice of having the windows open and frying, or the blinds down and roasting.' The opening of windows may be curtailed because the blinds rattle excessively in streams of fresh air. Close proximity to a road, airfield or playground may also restrict opening. My old hut at Ford Farm, for example, now borders on a motorway producing an intolerable level of fumes and noise.

If windows do not open, or when open do not close, there are additional problems. An essential item in older schools is the window pole. Literally a long pole, this terminates in a hook that engages with the opening mechanism of the highest windows.

Carefully placed by deviant pupils, it has provided an ideal booby-trap for generations of unsuspecting teachers. Those tempted to open windows without the pole – an occasional necessity with more difficult windows – need both a head for heights and an agility not renowned within the profession.

Freezing and boiling in school

With variable school temperatures the opening and closure of windows becomes essential. Many adults can recall freezing in the morning at school and boiling in the afternoons. Before central heating, both schools and children were often damp. Indeed, the Hadow Report urgently requested driers for clothes and boots. Lack of such facilities created not only discomfort but also widespread rheumatism at the time.[6] All today's schools have some heating. Even so, temperatures can be difficult to maintain in cold weather, though few schools actually close under such circumstances. Indeed, it is not unknown for teachers to supply supplementary heating from their own homes. Types of heating can also be crucial. 'Hot air systems' create cold regions in the spaces occupied by younger age groups while wasted warm air rises to the ceiling. Equally the system may perform with excessive zeal. Bennett visited one school where the temperature on occasions had exceeded 100°F!

Central heating renders schools, like other institutions, vulnerable to the vagaries of fuel shortages and suppliers' strikes. The number of days lost from both factors has become increasingly significant and remains a permanent threat throughout the winter months. But heating is an essential though expensive facility in schools. Experiments to reduce bills have included a transfer of holidays from the summer to the winter period. In milder areas of the country, savings were enormous. In others, costs from burst pipes and problem boilers counteracted any fuel savings achieved.

Space to learn

One of the major savings in school costs is, of course, connected with a reduction in space. Chapter 6 has already demonstrated how financial cuts since the 1950s have reduced the floor areas. Whether this has resulted in the 'better designed and more successful primary schools' claimed by Pearson is questionable.[7] In older schools the term 'teaching space' referred to classrooms, and 'non-teaching space' to corridors, cloakrooms, dining rooms and administrative offices. Single, two-roomed and central hall designs had the least

non-teaching space, corridor designs the most. Pearson claims that
they

> sprawled about their sites and lacked essential cohesion. They were
> difficult to organise and small children were even known to lose their
> way in the maze of corridors. It was not unusual to find sixty per cent
> of the floor area given to non-teaching space. What uneconomic
> instruments of education these schools were.[8]

These schools at least had space, though sometimes in the wrong
place. They were often easily adapted to meet changing needs in
teaching and learning. Joan Dean, for example, describes a range of
ways this has been done in *Room to Learn: Working Space.*[9] These
ways include changing cloakrooms to accommodate both coats and
working areas, developing corridors for practical tasks, adapting
furniture to new needs and increasing storage provision.

As floor area reduced, so did non-teaching space. Indeed, pure
circulation space was virtually eliminated as corridors merged with
classrooms. Doors were removed – 'as these stop the flow of ideas
from imaginative people who initiate them or from gifted children
who develop and extend them'.[10] Separate classrooms became
'shared teaching space'. The open-plan school evolved.

The practice of using every square metre of a school as teaching
space has tended to reduce floor areas even further. Architects work
to a calculated 'minimum teaching area' (MTA) which Bennett
claims has resulted more from historical accident than research.[11]
Certainly the amount of MTA has varied enormously over the years.
In 1968, when open-plan schools were gaining popularity, the
average space allowance was 3.81 sq m (41 sq ft) per pupil. By 1975
this had fallen to 3.0 sq m (36 sq ft), and a DES survey of 1977[12]
found a further reduction to 2.5 sq m (27 sq ft) in some schools.

In defining MTA, circulation space is often classed by architects as
teaching space, to cut costs and meet existing limits. The main
problem with MTA is that areas used for continuous circulation still
tend to count as 100 per cent teaching space. In open-plan schools
this includes practical areas, 66 per cent of which in Bennett's
study formed the main circulation space between home bays and
entrances, cloakrooms or lavatories. Pearson claims that this is
reasonable because, in the early open-plan schools, 'The interesting
discovery was made that people could circulate through . . . areas
without disturbing unduly the work of others.'[13]

Unfortunately, this has not been universally discovered. Where
circulation occurs it increases noise and distraction, causes organisational problems and tends to reduce the use of such areas for
teaching. In central hall designs, children are often imprisoned in
surrounding classrooms whilst the hall is in use. In open-plan

schools a small home bay may house more children than planned because work in practical areas causes insurmountable problems. Bennett therefore suggests that circulation space should not count as 100 per cent teaching space in planning statistics.[14]

The use of areas for teaching and circulation is part of the move towards dual or multiple use of space in schools. How this policy affects school feeding is discussed in greater detail in Chapter 27. However, it is probably true that wherever dual use is introduced it presents organisational constraints on teaching and learning that are not always easily overcome. Mrs Shrimpton at Ford Farm taught at one end of the school hall. Unlike classrooms at High Rise, however, she had no door or dividing wall to reduce the sound from lessons in the neighbouring area. The situation was further exacerbated by the use of the hall for dining. Her own children's desks accommodated the packed lunch group. Both factors necessitated her adopting an almost nomadic existence, her class following her to others' rooms or cloakrooms. No work or display could be left out without interference, and several minutes had to be spent cleaning up remains of crisps and chocolate cake in the post-lunch period. As long ago as 1967 the Pilkington Report was advocating a re-examination of policies allowing dual use of certain spaces in school and a reconsideration of circulation and supervision problems.[15] Unfortunately the support given in the same year to open-plan designs by the Plowden Report left the recommendation unheeded.

Problems with space can also occur through poor detail at the design stage. An inadequately sized hall, dining room or staff-room can present untold constraints on staff and pupils. In older schools classrooms were often spacious but lacked facilities for practical work. Modern schools may lack an area where a whole class can meet together except informally seated on the floor. They frequently have only enough chairs and desks for 70 per cent of pupils because of the assumption that not all children will need to be seated at any one time! Only 5 per cent of quiet rooms in Bennett *et al*'s study were used, because teachers found them too small. Such decisions may constrain teachers and dictate teaching approaches even more than those of the past. In overcrowded schools problems are further exacerbated as quiet and practical areas are utilised for basic teaching. Here lack of space and poor design can combine to create an unacceptable level of noise and stress for all concerned.

Bennett produced a minimum list of facilities for any new open-plan school.[16] This recommended:

1 A home base that will accommodate the whole class comfortably, a suggestion supported by Plowden,[17] the DES[18] and the NUT.[19]
2 A more general area, where children from different classes can

mix, make contact with teachers other than their own and utilise shared resources.

3 Smaller extensions of the general area suitable for small groups and away from the distractions of the larger general area, for specialised use, e.g. crafts and home economics.

4 An enclosed room or rooms suitable for either quiet or noisy work.

5 An outside covered work area.

The appropriate balance of these spaces will depend on the age of the children and the preferred teaching style of the teachers. Many would agree with Bennett that this is a 'vexed question for both architect and educator'.[20]

Once agreed, facilities also need to be well arranged at the design stage. Rooms isolated from mainstream activity tend to be underused because of problems of supervision. Quiet and practical areas tend to suffer from poor siting in most open-plan schools.[21] Quiet rooms also cause problems in needing to be away from other work areas but close to the home base. Problems in siting tend not to improve as architects, having designed a school, do not have opportunity to see the results of their ideas in operation. As one said: 'Frequently a school is built and no one goes and tells the head and staff how the building is intended to be used in practice.'[22]

Noise that annoys

Connected with the use of space in school are problems with noise. Classrooms surrounding the old central halls are constantly invaded by noise from PE, music or assemblies. Pupils utilising the hall inevitably have their enthusiasm curtailed through fear of disturbing the rest of the school. Noise is obviously also a problem in open designs. A wealth of researchers such as Kruchten,[23] Bennett's team[24] and Strathclyde Regional Council[25] have found it to be the most undesirable aspect of such schools and one closely related to disruption, disturbance and teacher stress. One quarter of staff studied by Pritchard and Moodie had to compromise in their teaching to avoid disturbing others.[26] One in five pupils in the Canadian SEF (Study of Educational Facilities) survey made negative comments on the noise in their open-plan schools.[27] Noise was also given as the main reason for timetabling constraints and the use or non-use of space.

Brunetti's research has suggested that density of population rather than amount of space is a more crucial factor when considering noise and open planning.[28] Pupils in open environments would therefore suffer more noise in overcrowded conditions than their counterparts in closed designs. Differing levels of tolerance may be another factor. Sixty-five decibels has been suggested as a reasonable level of noise in school. This enables teachers and children to communicate intelligibly to a maximum distance of 2.1 m (7 ft). When this is exceeded, friction, distraction and increased stress will result. Modern designs of school, however, are often acoustically poor. Increased use of carpets, curtains, tiles and special wall surfaces has not always been successful. As there is a wealth of publications on the subject, Bennett wonders if the reasons for poor acoustics are mainly economic or 'whether there is a misunderstanding or ignorance of the general principles of acoustic design among architects'.[29]

Maintenance and adaption of buildings

Once erected, buildings have to be maintained. Programmes for maintenance within LEAs have, however, been singularly lacking. Many schools are therefore in a serious state of disrepair. A major onslaught on standards of existing buildings came in the 1960s. The NUT 1962 publication, *The State of our Primary Schools*,[30] and the 1963 pamphlet *School Buildings: A Survey of the Present Programme and its Limitations*[31] both attacked the government for the poor condition of many schools. The DES carried out its own survey in 1962,[32] and the 1967 Plowden Report[33] made a plea for an annual grant of 7–10 million to be made available for ridding primary schools of their worst deficiencies. In the 1970 General Election campaign all major political parties promised to give the matter urgent attention. By October of the same year 38 million had been allocated for the purpose. The 'deficiencies' causing most concern related to essential services such as water supply and central heating. Money for adapting designs or maintenance was less forthcoming.

Problems surrounding the maintenance of school buildings have reached crisis point in the 1980s. One indication is the number of accident claims from staff injured by collapsing furniture, broken slates, unfilled potholes and similar defects. These doubled in 1984, causing alarm to the teachers' unions.[34] For many schools the maintenance of unused rooms (usually caused by falling rolls) has to be met from school funds. Consequently a room that could incorporate a library or resource area may remain locked and unused if money for cleaning and heating cannot be found. Often basic maintenance of a building, as at Eastlea, has to be carried out by staff or parents. A 1985 report by the National Economic Development Council found that some schools had not been painted for twenty-five years, and in most of the fourteen LEAs visited the maintenance cycle had slipped from five years to at least eight.[35] May 1985 finally saw an outcry from the Inspectorate on the condition of schools, which were said to be in such a poor state that they were affecting children's work.[36]

School buildings too sometimes need to be extended or adapted. Building features praised by some will be hindrances to others. Changes in methods of approaches to teaching may require adaption of facilities. This is true of many buildings. Shop-fitters dedicate their services to redesigning and refurbishing the interiors of shops, offices and factories to meet new demands. Builders spend as much time maintaining, extending and altering the exteriors of premises, including homes, as erecting new structures. Educational establishments cannot generally expect such constant re-evaluation of their facilities. Indeed, major extensions of a school's facilities are again frequently having to be funded by parent/teacher associations rather than LEAs. Such a situation can obviously lead to greater differences between school standards in rich and poor areas.

Temporary buildings

Conflicts over maintenance and adaption can be avoided by LEAs through the erection of temporary buildings – wooden or pre-fabricated huts. Their use is one of the most common yet unpopular measures in school planning. Generally they result from problems in predicting a school's final population size. If numbers are likely to fall after the time of building, pupils in excess of the estimate are immediately housed in temporary huts. Unexpected rises in pupils are catered for in a similar way. Consequently, whilst educational advisers and administrators house themselves in palatial County Halls, children and teachers trek across frequently wet and muddy pathways to these inadequate structures, totally isolated from the rest of the school. The outdoor lavatories of the older schools have been replaced by outdoor classrooms in their modern counterparts.

Temporary or semi-permanent structures have, in fact, been used since the nineteenth century. In 1899 over 8,000 children under the London School Board were being educated in prefabricated iron buildings.[37] In large cities such accommodation was required to house the rising school population temporarily. It also provided one solution to buildings in mining areas where subsidence rendered normal structures impracticable. In line with current practice temporary buildings then became increasingly justified on the grounds that the school population might fall. Newcastle-upon-Tyne Authority, for example, claimed in 1905 that temporary schools were necessary because of the exceedingly precarious nature of the two major local industries, mining and fishing.[38] Such policies, claims Seaborne,[39] induced a 'schizoid condition . . . in the minds of many twentieth century architects'. He quotes as evidence the boast of Cecil Sharp, designer of the North Surrey District School, Averley, who in 1909 stated that 'after due consideration . . . I have been able to produce a building of temporary character and yet quite permanent'![40]

Of course, temporary buildings were, and are, cheaper than permanent ones. When the Board of Education appointed a departmental committee in 1910 to consider the cost of school buildings one of its first recommendations was that 'novel building methods and materials' should be encouraged.[41] It was one of several factors that persuaded architects to experiment with lighter and less durable school buildings. Arguments supporting such structures emphasised the need to allow more rapid change in teaching styles: 'it is not good practice, either from an educational or economic point of view, to make school buildings as solid or durable as churches'.[42] The argument was to be repeated in the Hadow Report of 1933 alongside an acknowledgement that, though initial costs of temporary buildings might be low, long-term maintenance might be high.

The increasing popularity of semi-permanent structures in the First World War did not result simply from financial considerations. In 1914 such buildings became exempt from local building by-laws and so could be quickly erected without normal planning consent.[43] In the inter-war period they were to provide an easy solution to the backlog of neglected building. Several authorities, including the West Riding, bought old army huts for use as elementary school classrooms. The Board of Education even offered a range of incentives to widen the practice, including a one third discount for purchasing LEAs. Army hut hospitals, regimental institute rooms and officers' and nurses' mess huts were considered particularly suitable.[44] Not until the early 1980s was the last Nissen hut in the South West demolished.

In the immediate post-war period other problems arose. The raising of the school-leaving age from fourteen to fifteen resulted in HORSA – the Hutted Operation for the Raising of the School-leaving Age. Many HORSA huts are still in use. The shortage of materials in this period also encouraged experimentations which were not always successful. Aluminium, timber cladding and concrete replaced steel. But the 1970s saw very high costs in repairing high-aluminia cement structures.

Complaints about temporary buildings concern both their facilities and siting. Generally they are noisy. The hollow space beneath their floors magnifies the sound from moving feet and furniture. Temperatures are over-variable. Internally facilities are poor –

storage space and water supply may be totally absent; where lavatories and sinks exist they are often inadequate. By their very presence huts can also reduce the facilities of a school. Playing areas or gardens are frequently lost. Playground supervision can also be made more difficult, huts acting as a magnet for children wishing to hide or indulge in dubious acts.

However, the major complaints about huts surround their physical isolation from the rest of the school. In wet and cold weather children must be dressed in outdoor clothing for all visits to the main building. Problems of supervision may prevent teachers from taking breaks. Trapped in isolation they are removed, not only from a hot drink, but also from the companionship and exchange of ideas the staff-room provides. Psychological isolation is a further problem. It is difficult for any head to generate a feeling of belonging amongst physically separated staff and children. Such groups may even cause wide divisions in a school by creating their own sub-group culture. The separation is ironical in schools built originally for shared and co-operative teaching. Yet open-plan schools constantly open with a provision of huts. There are even examples of more children being housed in temporary buildings than in the main fabric of a school. Clearly the practice should be re-examined.

Summary

It is commonly argued that good teachers can teach anywhere. This is possibly true but evades important issues. All schools contain architectural features that frustrate and constrain their users. Badly designed lavatories are a main source of irritation for children and can frustrate adjustment to school. Cloakrooms accessed through teaching areas can induce considerable organisational problems and limit teaching; and lack of taps and sinks in classrooms can reduce the curriculum. Schools also tend to be designed with either too few or too many windows. Excessive use of glass can result in high temperatures and a lack of privacy. Lack of windows can reduce ventilation and necessitate the use of artificial lights. Windows also need both to open and to close.

Schools dramatically vary in their heating and ventilation. Those built to the veranda and quadrangular designs often offered too much ventilation such that draughts or even gales might rush through to chill pupils and teachers. Central hall schools and some modern open-plan buildings often lack fresh air and can be both stuffy and smelly. School temperatures are equally variable.

Many design problems result from attempts to cut costs. A south-facing wall of glass can be cheaper than bricks but will roast the classroom occupants. A flat asphalt roof may seem financially and visually attractive when compared with its tiled counterpart but many leak constantly and require more frequent replacement. A more controversial means of saving money, however, is through reducing space, but not a corresponding number of children, in schools. Whilst a concept of minimum teaching area (MTA) does exist, the amount has varied enormously over the years. There is also conflict over what should count as teaching, non-teaching and circulation space in schools. Veiling the use of classrooms as corridors with claims of enhanced learning and teaching opportunities does not prevent the untold problems such a ploy can cause. Indeed, the Pilkington Report recommendation, that the whole question of dual use of space should be re-examined, needs immediate implementation.

Children and teachers need basic facilities in school. These include areas where a class can gather and work as a whole; also a desk and chair. The practice of providing furniture for only 70 per cent of pupils in new schools (on the basis that not all will be seated at one time) ignores the psychological need we all have for a place or base of our own. It also forces a method and form of organisation on teachers that they may not support or practise. They should also be protected from excessive noise, which can damage health as well as concentration. Noise is the most undesirable aspect of open-plan schools and the one most closely related to disruption, disturbance and teacher stress. Temporary buildings also are poor acoustically. Whether a general ignorance of the wealth of publications on acoustic design amongst architects is the cause of such problems or whether it is another side effect of financial limits has not been resolved.

Once erected, buildings have to be maintained. Such a programme, however, is costly and LEAs have always neglected it. Both trade unions and the DES have pointed to the serious condition of schools. This has reached crisis point in the 1980s and teachers and parents are simply funding and supplementing such work in their own time with their own money in desperation.

The considerable duration of school buildings also necessitates a programme for adaption to new ideas and methods. But financial parsimony prevents this occurring. Thus, whilst office and business premises undergo frequent major adaption, teachers and pupils must suffer outmoded designs and facilities. Again, many schools are simply subsidising such improvements from their parent/teacher association funds.

Temporary structures avoid maintenance and adaption problems. They are generally used in schools because of problems in predicting a school's final population. They are also cheaper than permanent

structures. Huts tend to be inadequate and unpopular. Their isolation from the rest of the school can cause organisational and
psychological problems for staff and children. The use of huts in a
school designed for co-operative teaching and learning is particularly
unfortunate. Predictions on population are notoriously difficult to
make. Schools therefore cannot be seen as finite units waiting ten or
twenty years to reduce to some expected norm. Generally they
should house all pupils. 'Empty' space caused by fluctuating birth-
rates can always be used by the surrounding adult population if not
by the pupils themselves – a 'mothers and toddlers' group, for
example, or leisure courses. The practice may even be profitable,
many groups being willing to pay for the use of space for such
activities.

The illustrated problems would seem to indicate that architects
and teachers should unite and work towards a new understanding
of environmental learning needs unconstrained by traditional
pressures. Administrators should also realise that investment
in the physical plant of education, like that in education itself, is
necessary for the future of the country. Only then might an ideal
school evolve that will stand the test of time and become a real
environment for learning.

Is It the Way that You Do It?

CHAPTER 9

Joining the revolution

There has been a suggestion that the revolution in primary schools never happened. However, when I moved to Cheshire, there certainly seemed to be a major uprising in many schools and I was determined to be a part of it. A post became available in the most innovatory school in the area. It operated an extreme form of integrated day under a liberal, if not permissive, regime. I applied for the position. Moving from a city in those halcyon days when teachers were in short supply, I presumed the job was mine and judged it a mere formality when invited to attend for interview.

After travelling some hundred miles across country, the day was spent looking for a house and visiting the school. It was overwhelming to see a type of organisation I'd previously only heard or read about at college. Fears about discipline problems were easily quenched. Children seemed to be working in every corner of the school without any supervision. One teacher was glimpsed aiding the application of papier mâché to the higher reaches of a life-size model horse. Otherwise the school seemed to be in the hands of the children rather than the staff. It was a throbbing hive of industry. I examined the displays, noting useful ideas and the very high standard of work. I was going to enjoy teaching at Courtfields!

The formal interview was held in the evening at County Hall. Arriving at 6.30 p.m. I was amazed to see other candidates there. In fact there were six of them. Thinking there was some mistake, I asked if all were interested in the Courtfields position. The nodding heads confirmed my worst fears. Somewhat shaken, I viewed the opposition. My neighbour, a rather meek, dowdy looking person, was dismissed immediately. The two older applicants also looked non-contenders. The other three, all bright, smart and lively, could well have the edge as locals. My pondering was interrupted by a door opening. One of the Young Hopefuls disappeared for interview in the next room. Twenty minutes later he emerged flushed and anxious.

'I think I've blown it,' he said. 'They asked if I could play the recorder and I can't even play a comb and paper. What about you lot?'

No one else seemed to be able to play either. I stayed quiet. One to me!

The applicants were slowly whittled down and with the passing hours we relaxed and chatted. So far I seemed well up on being able to offer science and needlework which had now been added to the interviewers' list. Thank goodness for an O-level in dress design! Throughout the conversations Meek and Dowdy buried her head in a book, not even looking up when the next candidate was called. There were only the two of us left. I felt sorry for her. Thinking she was probably overwhelmed with nerves, I attempted to make conversation.

'I wonder which of us will be next?'

'Oh, you will.'

I smiled. 'How do you know that?'

Meek and Dowdy fixed me with a not-so-meek smirk. 'The person who is going to get the job always goes last,' she said.

It was as if a bomb had dropped. Young Hopeful stared aghast. 'But you don't play the recorder or teach science or needlework.' Meek and Dowdy grinned.

'Yes, but my father is a friend of the headteacher and I'm getting the job.' It was game, set and match. Meek and Dowdy was appointed.

They say that education is a continuing process and, that night, I had learned a lot. The lesson had also been expensive. Travelling and overnight accommodation had not been cheap, and only two more jobs were available in the area. I was to make further trips to Cheshire. On the third I was the final candidate to be called and I joined the staff at Eastlea.

Several months later I saw Meek and Dowdy pushing a pram outside the local shops. 'Are you on maternity leave?' I asked.

'Oh no,' she replied. 'A few weeks at Courtfields was enough for me. I was pregnant anyway when I took the post and thought I could always get out of it if things didn't work out.'

'Was it really that bad?' I was curious. Several people had told me that Eastlea, with its more moderate headteacher, had been a far better appointment than Courtfields, but I had still liked the school.

'Bad!' she exclaimed. 'The children asked questions and wanted to do things all the time. And the staff were so keen, staying after school, running clubs, having parents' meetings. It wore me out. Eastlea seems a lot easier.'

I smiled at the insult. Meek and Dowdy was no revolutionary.

Several happy years passed and one day I found myself visiting Courtfields again, but this time on teaching practice supervision. The school had changed little in the interim period and my student was coping very well with its informality. I chatted to the head-teacher about promoting science in the school, explaining my work at Eastlea.

'How long were you there?' she asked.

I told her. 'Oh, if only I'd known you were moving into the area then,' she said. 'I had a post going here. You could have had it for science.'

'I probably could,' I replied, 'but you turned me down at the interview.'

CHAPTER 10

Pressure from the progressives

Teaching is a complex and sophisticated task. At its simplest it involves inducing learning in others. But through the years arguments have raged over the content to be taught and the methods to be employed. Inevitably conflict arose between the innovators, many of whom were removed from the 'coal face', and the traditionalists who had inherited a Victorian legacy of well-tried formal techniques which had stood them in good stead in a lifetime of teaching. This chapter examines the nature of the progressive movement in teaching, and the history of its adoption by British primary teachers.

Class teaching

Early elementary schools aimed simply at achieving basic literacy and numeracy plus virtues such as punctuality, obedience and acceptance of authority. Payment by results raised the problem of teaching large numbers of children a set amount of information in a fixed time. Exposition and demonstration, generally called class teaching, became the popular approach. The method was formal and the teacher's role that of instructor, a giver of facts to be learned by rote. Lawrence describes the classroom atmosphere in his novel *Women in Love*:

> This day had gone by like so many more in an activity that was like a trance. At the end there was a little haste, to finish what was in hand. She was pressing the children with questions, so they should know all they were to know, by the time the gong went . . . and she leaned towards the children absorbed in the passion of instruction.[1]

The success of this approach depended on maintaining strict control over all pupil actions and activities. Rigid seating in rows or galleries and the strict question–and–answer technique described by Lawrence helped focus the attention of the whole class on the teacher during instruction. Routines and drills with Lancastrian overtones (see p. 35) ensured maintenance of discipline at other times, particularly during periods of potential unrest such as when giving out books or leaving the room. Salmon's 1898 book, *The Art of Teaching*, describes the philosophy of formal, traditional teaching: 'The whole routine of the school should be regulated literally by clockwork . . . nothing should be haphazard, nothing left to the caprices of children.'[2]

Early reaction against traditional methods

Didactic methods, with their strict instrumental approach to achievement in the basic skills and social discipline, seem to have always had their critics. However, the conflict faced by these early alternative educators was whether to develop individual autonomy or to encourage the children to learn in groups with the social and educational advantages of discussion and the creative exchange of ideas this can bring.

Rousseau (1712–78), one of the first exponents of activity methods, favoured a highly individualised form of education. Émile, his mythical lone pupil, learned alongside his solitary tutor away from the rest of society in the grounds of a large country estate. *Émile* caused a storm when published because of its inherent criticism of existing teaching methods.

Years earlier Rousseau had condemned education as an absurd system that served only 'to adorn our wit and corrupt our judgement'.[3] In *Émile* his stance strengthened. 'Everything is good as it comes from the hand of God,' he cries. 'Men meddle with it and it becomes evil.'[4] He suggested the abolition of formal teaching for the first twelve years of a child's life, substituting instead an education based on real experience through personal investigation and exploration of the environment. The recommended method of learning was discovery. His instructions to tutors were firm:

> Teach your scholar to observe the phenomena of nature; you will soon rouse his curiosity, but if you would have it grow, do not be in too great a hurry to satisfy this curiosity. Put the problems before him and let him solve them himself . . . Let him not be taught . . . let him discover.[5]

Émile, in its denial of original sin, was a condemnation of the strict and harsh discipline that permeated schools of the time. Its emphasis on children following their own interests, playing and running across the countryside criticised a curriculum emphasising Greek, Latin and the basic skills at the expense of science, art, craft and physical exercise. The emphasis on a broad curriculum and learning through interest was to become one of the main characteristics of the progressive movement.

An emphasis on active learning is fundamental to the work of Froebel (1782–1852). This German teacher was to have a very direct impact on the education of young children in British primary schools. Froebel's ideas reflected the psychology of the time. Humans were thought to have innate capacities and characteristics which could be either fostered or stunted by experience. Froebel considered that the best growth occurred through varied and contrasting activities which it was the job of educationalists to provide. He also recognised the conflict that might exist between individual and group interests in learning:

> The human organism needs experiences as an individual and also experiences as part of a human group, therefore education should provide opportunities for both individual activities and group undertakings. The child needs to learn how to keep these two aspects of his life in harmony.[6]

Although he is generally seen as a pioneer of the kindergarten movement, Froebel regarded education as a continuous process. He saw the well-educated person as being a balanced, well-adjusted individual who had a zest for tackling new problems, facing new situations and mastering new knowledge – someone, as Curtis and Boultwood point out, looking to the future instead of to the past.[7] For many years Froebel hoped to set up an education centre with schools, a technical college and a training institution for mothers. His belief in activity, expressive work and the use of constructional equipment for learning was intended to penetrate all these stages of education. Instead they became an essential part of the education of nursery and infant children, to which Froebel initially turned his attention. The use of constructional equipment and sense training with this age group was given further impact through the work of Maria Montessori (1870–1952).

At the turn of the century the ideas of John Dewey (1859–1952) began to influence the education of older children in the United States. Dewey acknowledged the influence of Froebel on his views. He believed that all schools should be like the good kindergarten and preferred to employ teachers with Froebel training even though his school accepted pupils up to thirteen years of age. Dewey considered that the school should educate children in co-operative and mutually helpful living; the learning activities were to arise from the impulsive attitudes of the pupils; the teacher was to notice how these individual tendencies became engaged in the process of living together, so that he (the teacher) could learn how to introduce into the school, at the child's level, the occupations and pursuits of the outside world.[8]

Dewey's significant contribution to education was to define stages of problem-solving and suggest it as the main vehicle for learning in school. In his own establishment pupils were allowed to pursue activities they themselves thought worthwhile. First they had to formulate a purpose for the task which Dewey saw as being dependent on observation, previous knowledge and judgement. A plan of action was then drawn up and consequences of the action considered. The idea was then either rejected, re-evaluated or put into action. His approach led him to conclude that the whole of education could be implemented through cookery, textile making and workshop activities. Furthermore, whilst pupils must mature socially, they can learn only by constantly developing their own ideas and hypotheses in the pursuit of individual aims and purposes.[9]

Change in the inter-war years

Dewey's influence on British education is debatable. Findlay, writing on *Principles of Class Teaching* in 1902, made thirteen references to his ideas. In contrast, A. S. Neill, writing in 1945, did not include Dewey on his list of contributors to the Summerhill philosophy. However, the work of Dewey's disciples had considerable impact. Kilpatrick modified Dewey's Problem Method into the Project Method. This was widely practised in Britain during the inter-war period and still influences the primary curriculum today. Experiments by Parkhurst at Dalton also incorporated many of Dewey's ideas but explored the effectiveness of individualised study. Routine class lessons were abolished and children were given opportunity to progress at their own rate through individual assignments, and opportunity to follow interests. The Dalton Plan was adopted quite widely in British schools during the 1920s and was still being practised during the 1960s.[10] Generally British versions of the plan reduced the pupil's amount of free choice and introduced individual assignments whilst retaining the class (rather than laboratory) structure.

The inter-war period was an ideal time for reconsidering educational practice and exploring new ideas. Payment by results, with its necessarily restricted curriculum, had ended in 1898. Although the Elementary Code laid down broad requirements, teachers now had greater freedom in choosing the content and methods of their work. A 1911 publication, *What Is and What Might Be*, was also gaining interest. This was written by Edmond Holms, an ex-inspector for elementary schools. It not only condemned the drill-and-skill approach of existing schools but described the alternative all-round, humanistic style of Egaria, a teacher who is thought to have actually existed. At the time, recommendations for practice in school mainly lay in the *Handbook of Suggestions for the Consideration of Teachers*. The preface of the 1918 edition stated:

> each teacher shall think for himself, and work out for himself such methods of teaching as may use his powers to the best advantage and be best suited to the particular needs and conditions of the school.[11]

In the 1920s many did exactly that.

The influence of the Hadow Reports

The 1931 Hadow Report on *The Primary School* claimed that a more general change in primary teaching was possible because of the new break in schooling at eleven years. The Committee made the much quoted though somewhat confused statement that the curriculum 'should be seen in terms of activity and experience rather than knowledge to be acquired and facts to be stored'.[12] Teachers were also asked to reconsider the teaching of separate subjects in distinct lessons.[13] However, there remained a concern for the maintenance of standards. Teachers were encouraged to continue providing 'an adequate amount of "drill" in reading, writing and arithmetic'. The Committee were also concerned about the methods and forms of organisation to be adopted for the new approach. They recognised that 'the diversity in age or attainment makes flexible and individual methods essential if good work is to be done'.[14] They recommended grouping children where such differences occur, for example in small rural schools. However, age groupings within a class were generally condemned as retarding pupils' progress. Mixed-ability classes were also said to function effectively only because of the 'genius' of their teachers.[15] They therefore recommended that, where possible, children should be streamed.

The 1933 Hadow Report on *Infant and Nursery Schools* was less guarded. The views expressed more closely matched the ideas of the progressive pioneers. Learning was to be individualised. The infant child was to be 'put in the position to teach himself'. The knowledge to be acquired was to derive, 'not so much from an instructor, as from an instructive environment'.[16] Like Émile, children were to spend a large part of their school day out of doors:

The field, the park, the garden, the woodland copse, the waste patch, all are full of interesting things which will hold the child's eye, arouse his wonder, stimulate his inquiries, give opportunities for discovery.[17]

Learning was to be through play.[18] Freedom was said to be essential.[19] The child was to learn the 'three Rs' only when he wanted to, 'whether he be three or six years of age'.[20] A range of apparatus was to be provided. This would help the child 'to acquire the habit of discovering things for himself' and prevent 'the damage to character which too often ensues when instruction is forced upon the child by an external and personal authority'.[21]

The 1930s to the 1960s

By the late 1930s progressive ideas had become official, being promoted by the Inspectorate, the Board of Education and training college lecturers.[22] However, such ideas became absorbed mainly into infant school practice. Streaming and an increasing emphasis on preparation for secondary selection ensured a general norm of class teaching at the junior level. In the late 1940s Daniel's influential *Activity in the Primary School* was published.[23] Such methods began to spread and certainly penetrated the lower junior classes of some schools. By the time the Plowden Report was published many changes had taken place which made the idea of informal methods more generally acceptable. Of major importance was the movement of leading authorities such as the West Riding of Yorkshire, Leicestershire, Oxford and London towards comprehensivisation. De-streaming in the primary schools followed and along with it came a general movement towards more experimental approaches. The Plowden Report was all the more infential for such changes.

The Plowden influence

In both its title and opening words the Plowden Report declared its child-centred philosophy. As far as the Committee were concerned children were at the heart of the primary school and occupied the bulk of the Report.[24] The emphasis was to be on their learning, not on teachers teaching. Class teaching in particular was rejected: 'There has always been much class instruction and we believe that there is still too much.'[25] Teachers who relied only on instruction were said to 'disincline children to learn'.[26] Instead children were to be the agents in their own learning. They would learn to read, write and draw when the need for such skills was evident to them.

Meanwhile they would follow their natural urge to 'explore and discover'.[27]

Discovery methods were proposed for reasons of motivation, providing the child with a pleasure in learning that is self-perpetuating.[28] They were also claimed to be more effective:

> The sense of personal discovery influences the intensity of a child's experience, the vividness of his memory and the probability of effective transfer of learning.[29]

Here the Committee were probably reflecting the views and research of Bruner,[29] Hendrix,[31] Kersh[32] and Keisler[33] who indicated that learning through discovery methods would be more pleasurable and purposeful, involve greater effort and result in firmer learning than presented tasks. Ausubel in 1963 had further suggested that transfer of knowledge in discovery learning would be more likely than in other situations.[34] The Plowden Committee expressed the view that the approach would also teach children to 'learn how to learn'.[35] This was a popular claim for discovery methods.

Other arguments tended to concentrate on the changing nature of knowledge – emphasising that in our world we are continuously receiving new information and developing new hypotheses. Therefore, they argue, it is hard to predict what knowledge children living in widely differing environments might find relevant and what ideas, in a rapidly changing society, may be important to them in the future.

In the classroom the Report supported an emphasis on individual learning:

> Individual differences between children of the same age are so great that any class, however homogeneous it seems, must always be treated as a body of children needing individual and different attention.[36]

It suggested that the school environment should be adapted so that corridors and foyers could become quiet places for personal investigation.[37] However, the Committee also recognised the problems individualised teaching would present in a class of over thirty pupils. For economy's sake they therefore suggested that 'a small group of children who are roughly at the same stage' might be taught together. Although they thought that ideally such children 'might be better taught individually' they considered that they would 'gain more from a longer period of their teacher's attention, even if it is shared with others, than they would from a few minutes of individual help'.[38]

Groups were also recommended for their social function: 'children learn to get along together, help one another and realise their own strengths and weaknesses as well as those of others'.[39] The educational value of co-operative group work was also recognised. Pupils were said to develop their own understanding from having to give explanations to others. Small groups, they claimed, offered timid children support and motivated the apathetic. Able children would benefit 'from being caught up in the thrust and counter thrust of conversation in a small group of children similar to themselves'.[40] Value was also seen in the use of small groups for planning and following up enquiries in maths and science and participating in school visits.[41] But in these arrangements the Committee were firm to warn that there must be 'opportunity for each child's individuality to show itself'.[42]

Beyond Plowden

Concluding their chapter on learning, the Plowden Committee endorsed the trend towards individual and active learning and expressed a desire to see more schools influenced by it.[43] The view gained support from influential members of the Inspectorate such as Blackie.[44] LEA advisers added subtle pressure. Those visiting Eastlea certainly began to ask, 'Why has everyone got a chair?'; 'Why is everyone doing maths at the same time?' 'Why are all the children working in the classroom?' Teachers not experimenting with new approaches began to experience a certain discomfort; those supporting the new ideas gained promotion. Arguments in favour of the approaches became even more persuasive. The value of children gaining autonomy and a degree of self-direction now became expressed in terms of the reduced teacher demand this would achieve. The approach was also said to lessen academic pressures on teachers. Bainbridge, for example, discussing the use of the approach in science, claimed that if only teachers could see their role as providing the setting in which a child could learn, then the task would not seem so daunting for them.[45] Visiting academics from abroad began to talk of the 'revolution' in English primary schools. Lectures on the 'English system' were frequent. Two forms of organisation, the integrated day and team teaching, particularly gained attention.

The integrated day

The integrated day and team teaching became means of implementing the new ideas. The idea of an integrated day was relatively new at the time of the Plowden Report. The Committee made no reference to it though they did mention the integrated curriculum and the idea of a free day.[46] The most influential book on the subject was published in 1968 and described the work at Church Hill junior and infant schools in Leicestershire. The authors, Brown and Precious, described an integrated day as one in which the full day 'is combined into a whole and has the minimum of timetabling'.[46] They elaborated on the term through a description of work in their own schools. These provided 'time and opportunity in a planned educative environment . . . for all types of development'.[48]

The lack of a fixed timetable was an important feature. Children were allowed to follow an interest in depth 'even though it may take several days'.[49] No limit was set to such explorations. They might 'go off at a tangent into any sphere of learning'.[50] The conflict between individualised or group learning was resolved by leaving the decision to the children themselves: 'the freedom to choose an activity, to be alone or with a group, is an essential feature of this environment'.[51] No fixed class structure was applied. Children were 'free to use the whole of the school' and were 'not strictly confined to one teacher in one room'.[52]

The book devoted a complete section to the importance of the learning environment in the integrated day. It provided suggestions on rearranging facilities in old buildings as well as advice on organisation of materials and resources. It particularly offered support for schools or teachers newly embarking on the approach. There was advice on discipline, teaching strategies, organisation and contact with parents and neighbouring schools. In other words, it not only reiterated the Plowden philosophy, it proved that it could be put into practice.

Team or co-operative teaching

Integrated day and discovery methods can place a strain on the abilities of individual teachers. In order to share expertise, various kinds of team or co-operative teaching were introduced into schools. Of course teachers in a school must always co-operate to a certain extent. They need to share resources and expertise; lead, follow and discuss common problems. Yet the separate class as a unit with its one teacher has remained a powerful entity at primary level. Team teaching originated in the United States and, in its extreme form, does away with the single class unit, organising staff into a team sharing responsibility for up to two hundred children. For teaching purposes, use is made of individual talents amongst the team. Children are organised into variously sized groups according to work being covered. A group learning to play the recorder might be small whilst one watching a film very large. However, the class structure continues to exist with groups of children being allocated a 'home room' and a 'home teacher' to register their attendance and look after their individual welfare.

Efforts at co-operative teaching have been variable in Britain. Specialists have for some years exchanged lessons with non-specialists for certain subjects. At Eastlea teachers co-operated and shared specialisms according to their own needs and friendship groups. Experimentation was also made with a 'free choice' afternoon where children were offered a range of activities to choose from. When the deputy headteacher planned to embark on an expedition to the base camp of Everest the whole school united for a project on the subject. Key sessions were given by individual staff followed by a free choice of follow-up activities. By integrating all team-work, full continuity was maintained in normal class activities.

Some open-plan schools have been deliberately designed for team teaching and the integrated day, having shared work areas and resources. Indeed, writers such as Rintoul and Thorne saw such designs as intentional efforts, to persuade teachers to 'experiment and innovate' with such practices.[53] Several researchers suggested that the intentions were justified. Teachers in open-plan schools were shown to interact more than their closed-plan counterparts,[54] and to talk more about curriculum planning, teaching and evaluation.[55] However, in their survey Bennett *et al.* found that this teaching could very enormously:

> Wide variety in grouping was . . . apparent in team teaching organisations, from specific age to four year spans. Team size varied from two to six teachers and length of teacher specialization for a given curriculum varied from half a term to a full year.[56]

Generally teachers enjoy working in teams when they perceive clear advantages and when they are allowed to plan the composition of the group and its size. Satisfaction with the approach seems high when this occurs. The quality of interpersonal relationships in teams is a vital factor, incompatibility and frequent team changes being a common cause of low morale.[57] Staff working closely together need to have complementary areas of expertise and levels of expectation regarding behaviour amongst the children. Leadership of a team is clearly important. Several researchers[58] mentioned the importance of the head, who must be a good organiser, able to delegate, committed to the type of building and dynamic and democratic in their leadership.[59] The head also needs to support team teaching attempts with extra staff or help, without which variety in group size is difficult to achieve. The approach also requires co-operation, careful planning and record keeping. Team teaching can therefore be a fruitful approach, but is dependent on many factors for its success.

Summary

Traditional teaching methods helped teachers present a set amount of information to large numbers of children in a fixed time. They involved exposition and demonstration in a limited number of curriculum areas. Strict routines and drills helped maintain the enforced discipline essential to the approach.

Didactic methods seem to have always had their critics. As early as 1762 Rousseau was suggesting that children learn better when they follow their own interests, explore the environment and discover information for themselves. His book described the ultimate individualised situation with its portrayal of one child with a solitary tutor. Froebel also emphasised active learning but disagreed about the form it should take. Like most psychologists at the time Froebel saw human capabilities as innate traits which teachers could develop or stunt according to the experiences provided. His ideal teacher would offer children a variety of contrasting individual and social experiences for their all-round development. Although interested in continuous education, Froebel first paid attention to the education of the youngest pupils. His emphasis on activity, the use of constructional equipment and expression greatly influenced infant and nursery practice in Britain, as did the similar ideas of Montessori.

Froebel also influenced John Dewey, who defined the stages of problem-solving and suggested it as the basis for all learning in schools. He also supported education in groups, but emphasised that learning was ultimately an individual activity. Dewey undoubtedly had some influence on British schools if only through his disciples Kilpatrick and Parkhurst. Kilpatrick developed the Project Method which is still practised in today's primary schools. Parkhurst explored a plan for individualised learning at Dalton in the United States. Both approaches enjoyed a certain vogue in Britain during the inter-war period. It was an ideal time for experimentation. Inspectors were indicating a need for a more all-round, humanistic approach in schools, and teachers were given greater autonomy to choose their own methods and syllabuses.

The Hadow Reports gave further weight to the progressive views. The Committee claimed that the curriculum must be seen in terms of activity and experience though they were concerned that standards for older children should be maintained and that mixed-ability classes might require teachers of some genius to be effective. They therefore suggested streaming of junior classes where possible. Their report on *Infant and Nursery Schools* was less guarded. Children of this age were to explore and discover out of doors and be free to learn as their needs arose. These views became official in the late 1930s, being promoted by the Inspectorate, training colleges and similar bodies.

Activity methods began to spread in the 1940s and, as some areas moved towards de-streaming and comprehensivisation in the late 1950s and early 1960s, gained popularity.

Such changes increased the influence of the Plowden Report. This not only endorsed the move to active teaching and learning but encouraged such practices to become widespread. The Report stressed the importance of individualised learning through discovery. This supported views expressed by many eminent researchers and educationalists who had indicated that learning through discovery was more purposeful, involved greater effort and resulted in more positive learning than presented tasks. Transfer of knowledge was also said to be more likely with discovery methods. Furthermore, such approaches would teach children to 'learn how to learn'. Despite this stress on the ideal of individualised teaching, the Plowden Committee suggested group teaching as an organisational and educational compromise.

Active and individual learning gained support of the Inspectorate and LEA advisers, who placed pressure on schools, causing some conflict with traditionalists. Arguments were proffered that discovery methods helped teachers by reducing the demands that other approaches placed upon them. Visitors from abroad showed great interest in what became called the 'primary revolution'. The integrated day, in particular, caught their attention. This form of organisation was given little mention by the Plowden Committee. The most influential book, describing the organisation in its ideal form, was published after their Report in 1968. It not only supported the Plowden recommendations; it proved that they could be successfully extended into practice.

The new approaches placed a certain strain on the abilities of individual teachers. In order to share expertise and problems, experiments in team teaching were tried. The idea originated in the United States where, in some cases, the class unit was abolished and teams of teachers coped with groups of children sometimes numbering up to two hundred. In Britain practice varied, ranging from simple exchange of classes to more innovative co-operative project work. Open-plan schools were seen by some as deliberate attempts to produce an environment conducive to team teaching and an integrated day. Some writers would claim that such interventions have been justified, but it would seem that team teaching, like other aspects of education, is dependent on many factors for its success.

CHAPTER 11

A style of her own

Like most teachers Miss Chiswick had a style of performance that was recognisable, yet was really her own. The whole educational year revolved upon the acquisition of facts ranging from multiplication tables to the names of oceans and continents. Like a well-practised choir we would periodically strike up on the agreed signal to begin our wearisome chants:

> Two pints make a quart;
> Four quarts make a gallon.
> Twelve inches make a foot;
> Three feet make one yard.

The system obviously worked for some pupils because I myself can remember the words even now. Others, unfortunately, merely mastered the tunes and were forced to 'la, la, la-de-da' in the background, dreading inevitable exposure. It was as if Miss Chiswick could lip-read at fifty paces and her pale, pinched face scanned her throng continuously ready to pounce.

Light relief involved a flannelgraph map of the world. It seemed a wonderful activity, competing in teams to stick names or pictures in the proper place. Afterwards, however, the chalk appeared and with it the inevitable test of facts and memory. 'Products of the world' always generated inward groans. Rationing had limited our experience of so many items. Some we had not seen at all. Others such as fruits had familiar names but their illustrations appeared different from the dried chopped versions we obtained in packets. Pupils with good memories battled to recall the mysterious words. Others looked around, puzzled for help.

'Johnson! What's wrong with you?'

Andrew Johnson's amazing memory for dubious jokes and rhymes was less effective in academic matters. He gulped. 'I can't remember what comes from Cyprus, Miss.'

The response came sharp and fast like machine-gun fire:

> Citrus fruits from Cyprus.
> Citrus fruits from Cyprus.
> All together . . .

We began our chant and with every 'Again!' increased the crescendo until our throats ached and Miss Chiswick was satisfied. Settling down to work, Andrew still looked puzzled. We all knew why, but no one dared ask. What on earth was citrus fruit?

CHAPTER 12

Effective teaching

Conflict within the progressive movement over aims and methods is relatively minor when compared with that between progressive and traditionalist. Like the length of women's skirts progressive trends in education act as a societal barometer, rising at times of liberal thought and permissiveness, falling under a barrage of criticism during periods of austerity and reaction. Objections to progressive education tend to take four forms. The first concentrates on the rhetoric that surrounds the movement – claiming that, at least, it is confused and, at worst, unsound. The second reaction is to link the progressive with the permissive, and freedom with licence. A third claims falling academic standards and neglect of the 'three Rs' under the approach. Finally there is the response of the middle-of-the-road doubter who claims that, even if desirable, such approaches need teachers of some genius to implement them.

These criticisms may be based in varying degrees on syntactic, intuitive or factual evidence. All gain authority when supported by empirical research. However, investigations of the effectiveness of different teaching methods have been fraught with problems (a fact not always appreciated by those who call for teacher assessment in the 1980s). This chapter reviews the criticisms generally levelled at informal teaching methods and explores the conflict that permeates researchers' quests for the most effective teaching style.

A question of syntax

Probably the most persistent, thorough and critical analysis of progressive rhetoric has come from philosophers such as Robert

Dearden. They have wrestled with phrases such as 'working from needs and interests', 'the integrated day' and 'learning to learn', clarifying them and sometimes setting out minimal conditions for their adoption.[1] They have also questioned some of the assumptions made in the progressive literature – for example, those of writers such as Brown and Precious who saw an integrated curriculum and team teaching as essential elements of the integrated day.[2]

It would also not be totally unfair to say that some analytical philosophers had a veritable field-day dissecting the Plowden Report. The Committee was accused of crimes ranging from 'appeals to authorities' who were not actually authorities on the theories under discussion[3] through to asking teachers for clear statements of educational aims whilst writing a muddled and confused chapter on the issue themselves.[4] Their belief that the inborn nature of the child is essentially enquiring, the basis for recommending discovery learning, was also challenged.[5] Consequently *Perspectives on Plowden*, a collection of critical articles on the Report, was produced.[6] It reflected a trend in 'report bashing' that gained impetus in the 1960s and has threatened report writers ever since. The movement was typified by Naish and his colleagues' catalogue of entertaining but disturbing characteristics that identify ideological documents.[7]

Such work has been less of a criticism than a revelation of the confusion within progressive rhetoric which has resulted in conflicting advice or comments in the literature. Whether this has resulted in a confusion of practice is unknown. However, a survey on the integrated day in 1971 revealed almost as many ways of effecting this form of organisation as respondents – some 181 teachers in all.[8] As Dearden says, in practice the integrated day would seem to 'represent anything from an embryonic university . . . to a wet playtime all day'![9]

Intuition and progressivism

Arguments against progressive claims, like those supporting them, may be based more on intuition than on analytical analysis of the movement's vocabulary. Such arguments may come from specialists operating on authoritative common sense, or lay persons operating on prejudice or fable. Aspects of the progressive movement that have been intuitively challenged by specialists have centred on their product claims. Perhaps the most powerful progressive claim is that discovery methods are more motivating for children. Gagne, however, has counter-claimed that one could equally argue that children like learning when they are able to achieve new ideas by combining familiar ones; also that in choosing tasks for themselves, there is a danger of entering a completely new learning arena or a problem with too many variables for satisfactory exploration. Thus self-chosen tasks might actually reduce motivation. [10]

Specialist critics have claimed that traditional approaches could lead to a more effective development of enquiry skills than progressive methods. They quote Bruner, who stated that discovery, like surprise, favours the well-prepared mind, [11] and Gagne, who claimed that how enquiries take off and where they come to rest could equally depend on a basis of knowledge of principles as on discovery. [12] Ausubel's criticism was that discovery methods were probably too time-consuming and inefficient, and that they could lead children to consider only one aspect of a problem at a time so that they over-generalised and jumped to conclusions. [13] Others have criticised the apparently confused and inefficiently haphazard nature of progressive teaching. Bainbridge, for example, quotes a headteacher who felt that the discovery emphasis of the Nuffield Junior Science Project could lead to 'mucking about, often to little purpose . . . the open-endedness and open-handedness . . . out and about in the woods attitude'. [14]

Intuition often forms the basis of arguments that modern methods lead to a decline in both academic standards and discipline in schools. Such claims frequently come from the general public. 'Today's children can't read and spell like they used to,' they cry. 'Their manners are also appalling and they are getting out of hand.' 'Why did the Plowden Committee boast of children lying around at the heart of primary schools? Why aren't they working there!' The criticisms seem to be passed from generation to generation. Certainly complaints of major employers such as Vickers Engineering and Boots the Chemists that young recruits could not read, speak or write English properly were as strong in 1921 as they are today. [15]

It is interesting that, of all the 'three Rs' only one begins with the letter 'R'. As the term derives from this mythological period of perfect literacy, one wonders whether that generation would have coped, as its modern counterpart has to, with phrases such as 'inter-galatic missile'! Unfortunately reflections on one's own schooling frequently engender pictures of the good old days against which the present, particularly if it is radically different and therefore difficult to understand, cannot easily compete.

Adding up the facts

Intuitive reactions such as those from the general public can be influential but can also be easily dismissed. Those from specialists or figures of authority cannot. The post-Plowden era saw a backlash against informal methods that is still being felt in the 1980s. It was partly influenced by a series of 'Black Papers' on education. Many prominent figures contributed, including astronomer and television personality Patrick Moore, and headteacher-turned-politician Rhodes Boyson. The first paper linked the progressive with the permissive and what the writers saw as 'evil' trends within society. The unrest in some universities and colleges was used as evidence, and the writers appealed to the public's common sense: 'The results of permissive education can be seen all around us in the growth of anarchy.'[16] Supporters of the progressive trends began to get cold feet. Conservative Member of Parliament Timothy Raison, who as editor of *New Society* had been one of the signatories of the Plowden Report, wondered whether unrest amongst students at Hornsey College did not owe 'at least something to the revolution in our primary schools'.[17]

A further claim of the Black Papers was that standards were being eroded through use of informal methods. Did they not after all, they said, 'absolve anyone from teaching and anyone from having to learn'?[18] As support, clever use was made of letters in the press. Quotes from teachers stating that 'the quest for perfect spelling [is] an absurd rigmarole' seemed all the more damning when viewed out of context, and served their purpose. Scepticism and doubt amongst the public increased. The criticisms gained support from two controversial studies of reading standards published in the same era.[19]

Eminent educationalists added fuel to the fire. Gardner claimed that an increasing number of first-year primary pupils were not starting to learn to read.[20] Betty Root also considered that 'children, through no fault of their own, are not learning to read . . . as they used to'.[21] As in 1921 there were endless letters to the press pointing out that school-leavers could not perform the most basic tasks. Not only were the claims gaining acceptance; but so were the conclusions that the fault lay with progressive trends in schools.[22] Then came the 'William Tyndale affair' exposing, as it did, some extreme results of permissiveness to the public at large.

The William Tyndale affair
When events at William Tyndale Primary School hit the headlines in 1974 they seemed to confirm many people's worst fears about progressive education. Here was firm evidence at last. The scandal centred on a parental revolt, led by Mrs Dolly Walker (a part-time remedial teacher at the school) against the staff and their teaching methods. She levelled criticisms at standards of work, behaviour of pupils and the attitudes of teachers. Yet a description of practices at

the school, published some two and a half years later in the Auld Report, could well have been written by the Plowden Committee:

> There would be no timetable, the children would be largely free to choose for themselves from a wide range of activities, including the basic skills, what they wanted to do, and the team teachers would move freely among the group giving attention and encouragement to small numbers of children and individual children as the need arose. It would also be the aim that each child would receive some tuition in the basic skills on a fairly regular basis, but the regularity and method of approach would depend on the team teacher's assessment of the child's willingness and ability to cope with the learning activity.[23]

The Auld Committee condemned Mrs Walker's behaviour in bringing 'untold harm' to the school. Nevertheless some of her claims were upheld. There was found to be 'a general malaise of aimlessness and boredom in the school [which] . . . led to bad behaviour on the part of the children'.[24] The findings seemed all the more damning when testimonials were brought to the enquiry showing the head and his principal assistant to be exceptionally competent teachers.

The Bennett Report

During the course of the Auld enquiry the Bullock Report was published. Its reassuring claims that standards of literacy were not falling received little attention from the press. A year later Neville Bennett's research at Lancaster University on *Teaching Styles and Pupil Progress* was published.[25] It purported to show that formal teaching produces better overall academic achievement without adversely affecting pupils' social and emotional development. The poorer outcomes in academic performance of children taught informally were not even balanced by any convincing superiority in affective development.

The foreword to Bennett's book contained a firm statement from Noel Entwistle that 'Perhaps the worst mistake that could be made would be for the opponents of the progressive classroom idea to use Bennett's report as a basis for arguing against the value of progressive classrooms all across the board' (pp. ix–x). Bennett also made a plea that political or educational capital should not be made out of the findings. But both politicians and the media used them 'to knock down their own particular bogeymen'.[26] The *Economist* saw it as a 'badly needed' piece of research, and Rhodes Boyson as 'momentous'. Lady Plowden astutely advised that it 'should be considered in depth'; and the *New Statesman*'s prophecy that 'it will be impossible, in future, for anyone to write about teaching methods without some reference to this work' has certainly come true.[27]

Here at last seemed 'proof' that progressive education was undermining standards in primary schools. The fact that the most effective teacher in Bennett's study was 'informal' was either ignored by journalists or dismissed as proof that these methods sometimes gain success with isolated, talented teachers. The research, however, became carefully scrutinised by contingents of researchers. Criticisms, as with many previous investigations in the field, were raised about both the research methodology and the statistical analysis. These once more highlighted the problems of investigating this contentious aspect of teaching.

Early attempts at identifying good teachers

Attempts at identifying good teachers have a long, though unedifying history. Most early research concentrated on isolating the characteristics of able teachers. Pupil and specialist opinions were sought using rating scales on such factors as management ability, instructional performance and professional attitude. Such efforts met with almost universal failure, and Morrison and McIntyre claimed:

> nor is there much hope for progress in this direction until a more analytic view of the activities of teachers is taken, until criteria are defined in such analyses, and until much more reliable methods of observation and assessment are used.[28]

Early attempts to identify the most successful style of teaching were equally fraught with problems. Of thirty-two studies examined by Anderson in 1959, eleven reported superior achievements in learner-centred classes, eight in teacher-centred ones and thirteen showed no differences at all.[29] A year later, Gage, in his *Handbook of Research on Teaching*, was forced to conclude that change in pupils seemed largely unaffected by teaching style.[30] But research continued unabated to produce further conflicting results. One important reason for this has been associated with the methodologies employed.

Conflicting dichotomies

Most research in this field has been based on the hypothetical existence of conflicting highly polarised teaching styles. The terms 'progressive' and 'traditional' are typical, but there have been many others. Flanders's corresponding labels were 'indirect' and 'direct' teaching.[31] The 1978 DES survey identified 'exploratory' and 'didactic' teachers. When researchers use such terms they have to break them down into identifiable characteristics. These are then translated into an observable form or questionnaire items. Flanders, for example described indirect teachers as those who accept feelings, give praise and both encourage and use children's ideas in lessons. In contrast, direct teachers were said to lecture, give directions and criticise. His observation schedule helped researchers record the frequency of such behaviours from which a dimension of 'directness' could be measured.[32] Bennett translated the terms 'progressive' and 'traditional' into eleven basic differentiating elements which he used as a basis for questionnaires.[33]

Conflict has surrounded the use of questionnaires as opposed to observation schedules in this field of research. Observation schedules were originally introduced to improve the categorisation procedures used to assess teaching style. They greatly aided research by removing the subjective assessment of rating techniques from the process of observation, offering instead a direct recording of classroom incidents and their sequence. They also enabled a straightforward analysis of the interaction between pupil and teacher and focussed on aspects of teaching that tend to affect pupil performance. Up to the time of the Lancaster research, however, many tended to be used for concentrating on 'a narrow range of the behaviour of a small and unrepresentative sample of teachers drawn from a population of unknown parameters'.[34] Bennett therefore rejected the procedure in favour of questionnaires to gather information on teaching style. In this he followed the tradition set by many researchers, including Barker Lunn who used the procedure when comparing the effects of streaming on junior school children.

However, questionnaires present problems when used for identifying teaching style. They offer only descriptions of practice based generally on management aspects of teaching – the organisational and curricular strategies, directed towards maintaining control and a balanced curriculum content in the classroom. They cannot measure what Taba and Elzey call instructional strategies (those used by teachers to develop pupils' thinking)[35] or the tactical exchanges that teachers use to gain control or encourage social and cognitive development. Taba argues that the instructional strategies of a teacher are the most important, the main function of teaching being, in her opinion, to develop pupils' capacity for thinking.[36]

Questionnaires can also be unreliable, with the frequent existence of a 'perception gap' between teachers' descriptions of what they do and actual practice. This was particularly noticeable in the Ford Teaching Project.[37] To overcome this problem Bennett was careful to check his teachers' responses against other factors, e.g. observations of a local adviser, and descriptions by the pupils of a day in their classroom.

Questionnaires must also be carefully designed. Often they ask teachers to answer by choosing one response from a limited number of mutually exclusive categories. These must not be ambiguous or misleading. Galton, for example, has criticised items on Bennett's questionnaire, pointing out that the one asking 'Do you give your children an arithmetic (mental or written) test at least once a week?' could truthfully receive a negative response from a teacher testing once a fortnight but she or he would consequently be grouped with teachers who never gave tests at all.[38] Galton also queried the item asking teachers to estimate how much of twenty-five hours' contact time they devoted to academic subjects taught separately, to integrated subjects and to aesthetic subjects. He pointed out that here two questions of content were included with two related to organisation with which they would be inextricably linked.[39]

During the 1970s there was increased interest in developing improved observation schedules for studying teaching. When the ORACLE (Observational Research and Classroom Learning Evaluation) project, led by Galton and Simon, received funding in 1975 for a study into the relative effectiveness of different teaching approaches, the researchers severely criticised 'the quality and usefulness of much evidence on teaching methods when it is obtained mainly through the use of questionnaires'.[40] Instead the ORACLE team used a highly structured, systematised observation schedule. This enabled them to record key strategies and tactics that teachers use in the classroom as the basis of their teaching style definitions. The project was planned for five years. Length of time, however, is not always a sign of research reliability. Gardner, who studied differences between experimental and traditional primary schools over twelve years, was criticised for the length of time her research took since different observers had to be used at different times in the period.[41]

A question of assessment
Analysis of the results from observations or questionnaires is used to produce a list of styles. Bennett, for example, isolated twelve different styles which he then further grouped into 'formal', 'informal' and 'mixed' teachers. Galton and colleagues in the ORACLE investigation identified four main types of teacher: 'individual monitors', 'class enquirers', 'group instructors' and 'style changers'. In all cases a number of teachers with the required styles have to be selected and 'outcomes' of their teaching measured by a pre-test/post-test procedure. Confusion exists, however, over what should be tested as educational outcomes. Most researchers, for example, settle for a narrow range of abilities within the basic skills. The Inspectorate, whilst surveying a wide range of activities across the curriculum in 1978, chose to test only progress in reading and mathematics. Bennett also restricted testing to progress in the 'three Rs'. These 'outcomes' are, of course, the easiest areas to measure. But such selection can be biased against informal teachers whose key claim is

that their approach provides for the all-round development of the child.

The first researcher to attempt a broad assessment of pupil performance under different classroom regimes was Gardner.[42] She developed means of testing such characteristics as initiative, imagination, concentration, neatness and confidence. Such a thorough attempt to truly assess differences between outcomes of progressive and traditional teaching was itself not beyond criticism. Wright points out that many of the tests, being constructed specifically for the study, were not standardised and many were dependent on the subjective interpretation of results.[43] However, it was a significant attempt to fully evaluate the results of differing teaching styles and was used as an exemplar for the ORACLE tests.[44]

Time on task and academic learning time

As well as formal assessments of progress, children's behaviour under different styles is often observed. A fundamental element of this is 'time on task', one of the claims against informal teaching being that it allows children to waste time. Bennett's survey on teacher opinions, for example, showed that

> the majority of teachers are prepared to accept that formal methods do not encourage time wasting or day dreaming . . . The majority of informal methods do not agree that their methods are guilty of this whilst the majority of formal and mixed teachers point an accusing finger.[45]

United States researchers have seen time on task as the most important determinant of pupils' learning, and Bennett emphasised this aspect in his report. Pupils in formal classrooms, for example, were said to engage more frequently in work activity than in informal classrooms, whilst high achievers in informal classrooms displayed a very low level of actual work activity, 'preferring to talk about it or simply gossip socially'. In Bennett's first report this was seen as one cause of the inferior results amongst pupils of informal teachers.

Galton *et al.*'s much wider and more detailed study of primary classrooms (in the ORACLE research) found that time on task never accounted for more than 3 per cent of variation in pupil achievement since working did not necessarily mean learning.[46] This was because of various time management strategies adopted by the pupils. Some, finding work repetitive or monotonous, worked slowly – a process referred to as 'easy riding'. Others were 'intermittent workers', only concentrating on tasks when the teacher's eye was upon them. Both of these types also refused to do more than the minimum of set work. Nevertheless, most of Galton *et al.*'s classes had their share of 'hard grinders' who worked consistently on any set task.

A more accurate predictor of achievement than time on task is thought to be 'academic learning time'. This is generally defined as

> time spent by a student engaged on a task in which few errors are produced and where the task is directly relevant to an academic outcome . . . only tasks measured by achievement tests [being] considered relevant.[47]

However, when Galton's team compared the progress of children who were continuous workers (i.e. 'easy riders' and 'hard grinders') with intermittent workers, no significant difference in progress was found.

Time on task does not embrace aspects of the range and quality of activities being undertaken. Wragg pointed out, for example, how his own daughter completed the same workcard three times rather than bother the teacher or waste time in a queue.[48] Working slowly or without motivation is also understandable in atmospheres where the reward for finishing one workcard is to be given another, or the work is boring and unchallenging. Grouws[49] has noted that United States evidence on academic learning time has mainly been concerned with low level outcomes and this seems to have been a general problem when measuring effects of teaching style in the Bennett research. Here the presence of higher order skills within the classroom as a measure of the demands being made on children was not possible as it would have required the type of sophisticated observation schedule used by Galton and colleagues.

A question of analysis

Researchers into teaching style generally have two statistical tasks. First they have to see whether analysis of observations or questionnaires does in fact produced evidence of distinguishable teaching styles and, if so, their number and characteristics. Dependent upon this, the second task involves seeing whether the determined styles have any effect on pupil progress. For the first task a method called 'clustering' is commonly used. This technique was developed originally by biologists for classification since it looks for similarities and differences between the items being studied. Bennett's cluster analysis revealed twelve styles of teaching. These ranged from teachers who favoured an integrated curriculum, pupil choice in seating, individual or group work and intrinsic motivation, to those preferring class or individual work, in separate subjects, assessed by tests, in silence and without movement.

Bennett's twelve categories of teacher reveal some of the problems faced when using clustering techniques. First, the usefulness of the final groups depends on the precision and relevance of the variables selected for analysis. It has already been shown that Bennett's

questionnaire presented problems on this count. Secondly, if information is scored as dichotomies then they must be true ones.
Some of Bennett's were not. Galton has pointed that certain of the
final groups seem, consequently, illogical. Some teachers appear to
favour both separate subject teaching and integrated work.[50] More
than half the time in informal classes was also spent on basic skills and
there was little emphasis on integration in science or social studies.[51]

Galton has also indicated a further problem with clustering, which
is the extent at which it is allowed to proceed. He pointed out that if
taken too far, the distinguishing features of groups are too general.
Thus, if one group asked more questions than another, 'the details of
the types of questions which different teachers ask, possibly an
important variable in the definition of teaching style', would be
lost.[52] If the process is stopped too early, then so many groups can
emerge that subsequent analysis of relationships can leave too small a
number of items (in Bennett's case, pupils) on which inferences can
be based. Galton criticised Bennett's twelve clusters and their subsequent merging into the three broad categories of formal, informal
and mixed styles on this count, since it left Bennett 'basing important
conclusions on tiny samples' (in one case of only four pupils). He also
pointed out that if the clusters defining informal teaching had not
been merged then these four pupils would have had to be further
subdivided.[53]

The unsatisfactory nature of the clustering technique led to doubts
over Bennett's claims on outcomes – the progress of pupils under the
supposed teaching styles. In 1981 two groups – Aitken, Bennett and
Hesketh; and Gray and Satterly – both re-analysed the original
statistics. Aitken and colleagues found that whilst results in English
remained better in formal classrooms, both formal and informal
teachers achieved similar results in mathematics, and informal
approaches had the best reading achievements.[54] It was a reversal of
the original results, the trend now indicating an overall superiority of
informal teaching. Gray and Satterly's re-analysis of the same results
interestingly confirmed Bennett's original findings in favour of
formal teaching. Comparing a range of post-Bennett research with
the original, they concluded: 'On balance . . . there would appear to
be some evidence that more formal approaches are more effective in
maths as well as English.'[55]

A question of significance
Within the confusion of evidence and methodology in research on
teaching methods there lurks the factor of significance – significance
of the assumptions of conflicting highly polarised teaching styles and
the statistical significance of their effects on pupil achievement. This
seems to be the Achilles' heel of most efforts in this field. Indeed,

Bennett's original findings were unusual in their statistical significance. Rosenshine noted that the relationships in Flanders's research were variable and not always significant.[56] Barker Lunn's results rarely found differences exceeding two standardised points.[57] Cane and Smithers, researching reading standards in different schools, had their statistics affected heavily by the results from one particular school.[58]

The results in the 1978 HMI survey should be treated with equal caution. Claims are made that

> In classes where a didactic approach was mainly used, better NFER scores were achieved for reading and mathematics than in those classes using mainly exploratory approaches.[59]

But, as Gray and Satterly indicate, there is no evidence of the size of these differences nor of whether the classes exposed to the two teaching styles were matched in other respects.[60] Bennett's re-analysed results were also not significant even at the 5-per-cent level.[61]

A number of researchers have commented that standards of significance place too much burden of proof on the researcher and might mask potentially interesting findings.[62] Others, such as Aitken and colleagues, comment that differences can be educationally significant without statistical significance.[63] Nevertheless, tests of significance provide important conventions for assessing reliability of results.

Do global teaching styles exist?

The question remains as to whether teachers can be classed into such global groupings as formal and informal, progressive and traditional. Assessing Aitken, Bennett and Hesketh's re-analysed categories, Gray and Satterly state:

> First, the differences between teachers within styles were far greater than differences between styles. Thus one found 'effective' and 'ineffective' teachers, no matter which teaching style they adopted.[64]

One problem seems to be that 'progressive' teachers, as defined by Plowden, might be rare. The Plowden Committee itself found only 10 per cent of schools were either outstanding or good 'with some outstanding features'.[65] Both Bennett and Bassey (in his survey of 900 primary schools in Nottinghamshire) have also indicated a shortage of progressive teachers.[66]

Perhaps this is a result of the 'Miss T. syndrome'. Miss T. is the subject of a Walter de la Mere poem that describes how 'Whatever Miss T. eats turns into Miss T'.[67] Some would claim that many teachers are Miss T.s, converting new ideas into preferred practice.

The phenomenon may well exist. When Froebel's ideas first reached infant schools the use of his 'gifts' and 'occupations' (structural apparatus and craft tasks) and even opportunities for play tended to be reduced to mundane drills.[68] Teachers in the 1980s seem to have similarly paid managerial attention to the Plowden recommendations of seating children in groups without absorbing any of the essential spirit of the co-operative group work that should result.[69]

A further explanation, however, might be that descriptions of teaching as formal or informal, traditional or progressive, are simply 'emotionally labelled catch-all terms'[70] that give little help to teachers wishing to improve their own approaches. Galton *et al.* not only attempted to describe practice in primary schools but offered an analysis of the aspects of teaching that seemed to produce the greatest effectiveness plus suggestions for future in-service and initial training.

Effective teaching: the ORACLE contribution

The typology of teaching styles adopted by Galton and colleagues was more sophisticated than any other previously used. Of the four types identified[71] the 'individual monitors' (22.4 per cent) organised the curriculum so that pupils worked on mainly individual tasks. This put the teacher under extreme pressure so that much of the time had to be spent telling children what to do or monitoring (marking silently or recording completion of tasks and achievement). Little use was made of high level questioning by this group. 'Class enquirers' (15.5 per cent), in contrast, managed most of the learning themselves, spending approximately a third of the school day on class teaching. During this time, new topics were introduced to the whole class and there were question/answer exchanges concerning ideas and problems. Once the children began work, class enquirers moved amongst them questioning and giving oral feedback. Much of the conversation related to the higher cognitive levels.

The third style identified was that of the 'group instructors' (12.1 per cent). Such teachers organised work in groups but structured it carefully, first giving out information, then joining group discussions to give verbal feedback on the pupils' ideas and solutions to problems. Their low level of cognitive questioning was balanced by a high use of open questions. Thus children were expected to explore a range of possible answers rather than one single solution.

Finally there were the 'style changers' (50 per cent), who used a mixture of the three styles. The infrequent changers occasionally made a deliberate change of style in response to pupil behaviour. A teacher moving progressively from class teaching to more individualised work during the year would fall into this category. Habitual changers, on the other hand, moved between class and individualised instruction in a more unplanned, almost spontaneous way, generally as a means of coping with undesired pupil behaviour. The third sub-category of style changers is the rotating changers. This is probably the least satisfactory of all ORACLE definitions as the teacher's style seems quite consistent; it is the children and the curriculum that rotate! Typically a series of curriculum tasks is set (and generally written on the blackboard). Children work through them in sequence either rotating physically around activity areas or changing to a new task on completion of an old one. Moran called this a 'rotating or circulatory environment', and it was adopted by 54 per cent of teachers responding to his questionnaire on the integrated day in 1971.[72]

Galton and Simon analysed the results of progress under the different styles and then attempted to isolate the strategies and tactics a teacher might employ to improve teaching. The least successful teachers, for example, had below average levels of interaction with pupils and even then spent a lot of time telling children what to do and paraphrasing instructions already given (i.e. making task statements). Intellectual demands were minimal so that there were few reasons for questioning and feedback.[73] Successful teachers, on the other hand, engaged in above average interaction with pupils. Galton and Simon described the nature of these interactions:

> They appear to devote considerable effort to ensure that the routine activities proceed smoothly; they engage in high levels of task statements and questions, and provide regular feedback. At the same time, they also encourage the children to work by themselves towards solutions to problems. The majority make above-average use of high-order interactions, including statements of ideas and more open-ended types of questioning. They also manage to avoid the need to provide children continually with instructions on how to carry out the set tasks. This comes about either because they prefer pupils to find out for themselves or because their initial instructions are so clear that there is little need to follow up by further exchanges.[74]

The ORACLE team concluded that increased levels in such types of teacher/pupil contact would help improve teaching. Their studies revealed three ways of doing this: through class teaching, frenzied individual teaching or group teaching.

The reinstatement of class teaching as a valuable strategy was based on the success shown by the class enquirers. They could involve a class of children thinking alongside them using probing, querying techniques, making 'a whole-class teaching lesson a stimulating experience, actively involving a high proportion of the children'.[75] Even at the lowest level teacher/pupil interaction was increased with the approach although many pupils were involved only in a passive way. Class teaching of mixed-ability groups is common in Scandinavia, Poland and the Soviet Union, though the average size of Scandinavian classes is much less than in this country. For teachers to develop good class teaching skills they would, according to Galton and Simon, need deliberately to include 'together' sessions for the basic skills, develop class management skills that would maximise the involvement of pupils and learn ways of encouraging pupils to be involved at their own level.

Certain factors unfortunately mitigate against the use of class teaching in many schools. Open-plan schools, for example, are often designed with home bays that deliberately prevent such teaching taking place. Vertical grouping would also mean a teacher devoting attention to one group of children whilst leaving others on their own for long periods of time. Total individualisation, seen as a superior strategy by the Plowden Report, is rejected as a solution by the ORACLE group because of average class size. They claim that the Report's stress on discovery learning and the probing, questioning character of the teacher's role in this arrangement are both 'misconceived' and impossible to achieve.[76] The attempt to teach individually placed Galton's teachers under continuous pressure. They principally coped by setting relatively undemanding tasks, merely occupying pupils until they had time to help them. When interacting with children, responses were didactic and managerial. There was little feedback on work. Children with incorrect responses were simply told to 'do it again'; those employing inappropriate methods to gain correct responses were given no opportunity to discuss other potential tactics. Thus the match between task set and pupil's developmental level was poor. (The same lack of match was reported in the 1978 HMI survey.)[77] Lack of feedback also encouraged a fear of failure in some pupils which prevented them responding positively to demanding work. Thus, whilst they would work quietly on routine tasks they became disruptive when more difficult or stimulating ones were introduced. Success under the method was achieved only by frenzied activity on the part of some teachers which increased the number of interactions.

Interestingly this relationship between feedback and efficient time management might require a re-examination of some other traditional practices in school. Southgate, for example, found that teachers who most listened to reading achieved least. The picture emerging from the research was of a hard-working teacher trying to listen to each child read aloud whilst dealing with a queue for spelling and other demands. Each reader on average gained thirty seconds of attention, too little time for any effective help. Some were taking as long as a year to finish one book. The team suggested a change of technique to perhaps hearing eight or nine children read each week, but for fifteen or twenty minutes each. In addition there should be 'set aside regular and increasingly lengthy periods when every child in the class reads in a quiet atmosphere without interruption'.[78]

The final ORACLE team suggestion was for an increased amount of collaborative group work in school. This they found was unfortunately 'a totally neglected art' at primary level.[79] Although recommended by Plowden as a means of overcoming the managerial problem of dealing with over thirty individuals, teachers found it difficult in practice. Thus, whilst children were seated together they tended to work individually rather than co-operatively on common tasks. The findings related to a range of classroom settings such as those in open-plan schools or those vertically grouped. They also paralleled those of Bennett in his study of open-plan environments.[80]

Galton and Simon consider that prerequisites for successful group work would include the children's ability to challenge each other, raise questions and reason. They would need to be tolerant,

Taking opportunity to discuss individual work with a small group from a typical primary class of over thirty pupils.

responsible and willing to listen to others. Such skills would need to be either taught or encouraged by teachers, who would also have to add structure to the work and ensure the provision of relevant resources.[81]

Classroom strategies would initially involve class teaching to inspire interest in a topic. The children would then work co-operatively in groups on carefully structured, relevant tasks. Periodically they would be brought together for class work to sustain interest and finally to draw the investigations to a conclusion.[82] Galton and Simon insist that such recommendations are not the basis for another revolution in teaching but suggestions for overcoming problems faced by current practice in school. They are 'suggestions for appraisal rather than preaching a new orthodoxy'.[83]

Summary

Criticisms of what has been called progressive teaching have therefore been syntactical, intuitive and factual. Analytical philosophers have revealed confusion and conflict within the progressive rhetoric which has led to a certain confusion in practice. Intuitive arguments against informal teaching methods centre on a lowering of standards and behaviour both in school and in society in general. The post-Plowden era saw eminent public papers supporting such intuitions in a series of Black Papers. Proof of the validity of such claims seemed to be shown in the William Tyndale affair when the extreme results of progressive approaches were brought into the public eye. Despite reassurances of the Bullock Report that standards were not falling, public concern persisted. A significant though controversial piece of research by Bennett at Lancaster was then published. It purported to show that formal teaching achieved better all-round results in the basic skills than informal teaching, without detriment to pupils' affective development.

Criticisms of Bennett's research procedure highlighted the problems faced when investigating this complex field. First there are the arguments as to whether questionnaires or observation schedules should be used in such research. Questionnaires are an inadequate tool for measuring teaching style since they have to be limited to assessing the organisational and curricular strategies of the task, ignoring the vital instructional strategies and the wide range of tactics employed by teachers for effective learning. The development of sophisticated observation schedules in the 1970s provided a more efficient tool for researches, such as Galton and Simon's ORACLE project.

Having identified teaching styles, many researchers measure educational outcomes in terms of only the crudest performance in the basic skills. This tends to mitigate against the progressive teacher whose key interest is in all-round development. Attempts at broader assessment are now more common but have not been without their critics in the past. Pupil behaviour tends also to be noted, including time on task or the frequency with which children are involved in working. Some United States researchers have seen this as the most important determinant of pupils' learning but later research has indicated that it accounts for less than 3 per cent of pupil achievement.

Statistical analysis is a further problem for researchers into teaching style. Clustering techniques may be unsatisfactory for analysing results from questionnaires if the validity of items is questionable. In addition, if analysis is complete too early a large number of groups may result, which if clustered further can mean inferences being made on the performance of a very small number of pupils. Statistical techniques also develop and improve, though this may not ease the researcher's task. When Bennett and colleagues and Gray and Satterly re-analysed the original *Teaching Styles and Pupil Progress* results in the light of new techniques, Bennett's re-analysis reversed his former findings, and Gray and Satterly's confirmed them. None of the new set of statistics, however, was significant. Achieving statistical significance has proved a problem to many researchers in the field.

All the research mentioned assumed the existence of contrasting and conflicting teaching styles in schools that could be measured for comparison. A more realistic assumption could be that such stereotypes of teaching style do not exist, although effective teachers do. Galton and colleagues therefore launched the ORACLE project to investigate teacher effectiveness. Using detailed, systematised observation schedules they monitored the teaching in a wide range of classrooms. Four basic styles were identified which did not correspond to any ideological stereotypes. In comparing a wide range of outcomes of the styles some indications of effectiveness were produced. The most successful teachers, for example, interacted with their classes the most. The ORACLE team suggested that increases in frequency range and quality of interactions could improve teaching. They suggested three possible ways that this could be effected. Class teaching was reinstated as a desirable activity but was assumed to be too difficult to implement in some buildings and organisational groupings. Further interaction through total individual work, however, was thought to be almost impossible, having been achieved in the study only by excessive and frenzied work by a few super-teachers. In consequence group work seemed the solution. This would take the form of initial class lessons followed by collaborative work in groups. Class teaching would be further used to sustain interest and draw work to a conclusion.

It would appear that the continued comparison of teachers as formal/informal and progressive/traditional is not only fraught with problems but also assumes a dichotomy of styles that may not actually exist. Nevertheless, such work has revealed the difficulties that might have to be faced if measures are introduced to enhance the promotion and pay of teachers according to effective performance. Not only will the assessment be difficult; teachers might not retain levels of effectiveness over different curricular areas or different academic years. The highest correlation achieved on 'teacher stability' is 0.5, and most results were lower, showing considerable variability in year-to-year effectiveness.[84] Measuring teacher effectiveness in the future, as in the past, is therefore not going to be easy.

Conflict in the Curriculum

CHAPTER 13

A question of standards

Carlton's campaign of untidy, over-concise work and carefully planned impertinence was proving something of a thorn in the student teacher's flesh. Her question, 'How would you make a cup of tea?' received the written response, 'With great displeasure. I prefer coffee.' He had made noises all through the story. Then he had spoiled her sociometric survey by saying, probably truthfully, that he could not choose two people to work with though he would least enjoy being with Miss Grant (the student) and Miss Grant. Carlton was, in fact, bored. Normally quiet and self-sufficient, he would, indeed, work with any of his peers. I quelled Miss Grant's anxiety that no one had chosen him as a friend by pointing out that no one had rejected him either. However, I had to agree that he was different.

Carlton's parents rated culture higher than care. With a classic BBC accent he stood out amongst our northern brogues. In normal attire of holey sweater and Wellington boots, he was whisked to museums, theatres and exhibitions across the country. Whilst other pupils had beans on toast, he had curried beans. Whilst they read Enid Blyton, he burnt the midnight oil with Tolkien. Carlton generally arrived at school late and bleary-eyed but welcome. His wit and talent, so wasted on Miss Grant, were a delight to the rest of us. However, this time I felt a few firm words and threats in his ear were necessary to ensure the student's survival. He'd won a few battles but he was not going to win the war.

When teaching practice was over we had three weeks until end of term. Thinking it would at least be different, we launched a project on the number sixteen. Here was an opportunity for the children to put their mathematics into practice. I could also informally assess their learning and understanding. The children were remarkably full of ideas that could be explored. Sums with sixteen as the answer were an obvious choice. Could they use any of the operations? Could they involve fractions and decimals as well as whole numbers? Should we have a prize for the most difficult sum? What about geometry? Could John try to make a sixteen-sided shape? Could Theresa make a set of triangles that all had one angle of sixteen degrees? Could Joseph and Sarah make a dictionary of 'teen' words and 'six' words. And so they continued. As one mini-investigation closed, so another began. Meanwhile a 'sixteen' frieze began to spread around the room.

Carlton was determined to make a set of magic squares adding up to sixteen. For hours he sat puzzling over the problem. A pile of discarded failed attempts mounted in the waste basket. We looked up other magic squares for adaptation and inspiration. I duplicated some blank squares to reduce the tedium of ruling lines. Yet the problem seemed to defy solution. Then one day two miracles happened. Carlton arrived early for school and he was clutching a sixteen magic square.

'I've done it,' he beamed, 'and I think I've got a formula!'

He proceeded to explain a complex process of calculation which could provide any magic square. Like many teachers of able children I simply listened, understanding more about his potential than the described process. By lunchtime an A1 sheet of sugar paper lay neatly covered with sixteen magic squares. It joined the other work displayed around the room.

Carlton's class stayed with me for a further year. At the end of that time he gained a free place at the local public school. He was surprisingly anxious.

'Will I be all right at public school, Mrs Stewart?'

'That depends, Carlton.'

A wistful smile appeared. 'I suppose I can be lazy and untidy,' he said, 'and Mummy says I won't have you to bully me!' We both laughed.

At Christmas, Carlton appeared on a visit bearing a box of chocolates and his homework book. He had been placed bottom of his class.

'Mummy says that they can't read what I write and I'd better turn over a new leaf,' he said.

I scanned the characteristically untidy but accurate contents of his work, then produced some clean paper. In a few minutes we revised the basics of italic script and points on presentation. As I had spent two years imposing such standards on him it did not take long for the skills to reappear. He painstakingly completed his homework. It looked impressive. At Easter, Carlton came top of his class, a position he was to hold until he moved on to higher education.

CHAPTER 14

Battles over basics

The constant claims that standards have fallen because of the progressive movement in primary schools have caused continuous conflict between the DES, the Inspectorate and teachers. This has been reflected in attempts at direct intervention by secretaries of state to make teachers more accountable. This chapter plots the rise in conflict and its impact on the primary school curriculum.

A gathering storm

When the first Black Paper[1] made claims of falling standards in school during the late 1960s, fingers were pointed at young teachers:

> the cult of carefree creativity has had a large following, particularly among younger teachers, who have welcomed the notion that rigorous marking of spelling, punctuation and other errors, as well as 'punitive' corrections, has a discouraging effect on juvenile writers and stifles their creative talent.[2]

Generally the accusations received a bad press. The government were also quick to attack the authors. Ted Short, Secretary of State for Education, called them 'thugs' intent on halting if not destroying many of the important post-war developments in education. Nevertheless the accusations caused friction between the teachers, the Inspectorate and the colleges of education. The Inspectorate blamed the colleges for the quality of teachers being trained. They stated, for example, that many did not understand the basic concepts they were to teach in mathematics.[3] In turn teachers also claimed that inspectors had advised that the learning of tables or the correction of spellings was unnecessary.[4]

There then came a period of severe economic crisis. The Labour government, having received the Plowden recommendations for development and expansion, had to cut educational as well as other expenditure. A certain disillusionment also began to set in amongst the British public. Education, once thought to be the answer to a wide range of social ills, was shown by some research to have little real influence.[5] The Black Papers were relentless. The changes in education – free play in primary schools, comprehensivisation, expansion in higher education and 'experimental courses in new universities' – were castigated as untried and 'revolutionary'.[6] In a time of economic crisis the government was also finding them expensive.

When the William Tyndale affair hit the press in 1974, the government panicked. Certain accusations caused embarrassment to them. Mrs Walker, for example, not only levelled criticisms at standards of work and the behaviour of pupils within the school; she also claimed the problem resulted from left-wing attitudes in the teachers. Their educational thinking, she said, was entirely germane to their political thinking. It was not that they could not teach but that they would not teach.[7]

A bidden curriculum?

The Auld Committee dismissed Mrs Walker's arguments of political bias amongst staff, but the affair opened old sores. A general feeling emerged that teachers were getting out of hand. Commenting on the William Tyndale scandal, a leader in *The Times* talked of 'the wild men in the classroom'. It equated progressive teachers (and indirectly all primary teachers) with trade union disrupters and demanded they be brought to heel. Neville Bennett's research fanned the flames. A 'Yellow Paper' was swiftly drawn up by the Inspectorate to brief the Prime Minister. In contrast to previous publications from the same body it seemed to challenge informal methods, and resulted in Jim Callaghan's Ruskin College speech.[8] This specifically criticised the use of such approaches by teachers.

The resultant Green Paper, *Education in Schools*, claimed, quite inaccurately, that progressive teaching was widespread. It had become 'a trap for less able or less experienced teachers [which] in some cases . . . has deteriorated into lack of order and application'.[9] The paper called for 'a core of learning', a 'protected area of the curriculum' to be established of which literacy and numeracy should form the most important part. This was a direct challenge to teachers' autonomy whereby, under the 1944 Education Act, only religious education was compulsory. The secretaries of state, however, seemed determined to achieve such a core – a bidden curriculum, as it were. Their 1979 report on *Local Authority Arrangements for the School Curriculum* criticised LEAs for not having 'a clear view of the school curriculum, especially its core elements'.[10] They considered that the authorities

> should give a lead in the process of reaching national consensus on a desirable framework for the curriculum . . . [which] could offer a significant step forward in the quest for improvement in the consistency and quality of school education across the country.[11]

In January 1980, under a now Conservative government, the DES itself produced such a framework.[12] The core primary curriculum was now defined with science, RE and physical education being added to the 'three Rs'. Proportions of the timetable were even suggested, not less than 10 per cent of time to be spent on each area, and more time on English than mathematics. The only method of teaching prescribed was for science where a process approach was recommended. On publication the document received immediate criticism and was said to be badly written and simplistic in its advocacy of a means–end curriculum model.[13] The sequel in March the following year demonstrated a much broader view of the common core.[14] This was now to consist of all the usual curricular elements, from music to geography, and craft to science, and even included simple technology. It was more a description of subject areas than a narrow core of basics.

Reaction from the Inspectorate

Pressure to aim for a broader curriculum could well have come from the Inspectorate. Their surveys had shown that, rather than standards falling, there was, certainly in reading, a steady improvement. Not only was the progressive teacher a threatened species, but the observed curriculum was boring and unimaginative, scarcely more, according to Richards, 'than a revamped elementary school curriculum with the same major utilitarian emphases'.[15] The over-dominance of the basic skills not only restricted the breadth of subjects offered but reduced children's performance:

> The basic skills are more successfully learnt when applied to other subjects and children in the classes which covered a full range of the widely taught items did better on NFER tests at 9 and 11 years of age . . . there is no evidence in the survey to suggest that a narrower curriculum enabled children to do better in the basic skills or led to work being more aptly chosen to suit the capacities of the children.[16]

Research has shown in fact a persistent emphasis on the basic skills. Bassey found that 52.1 per cent of the timetable was given to English and mathematics in nine hundred classes studied.[17] The ORACLE study[18] found these subjects forming an even greater 65.7 per cent of the observed curriculum. However, when adjustments were made for non-observed subjects the findings were remarkably similar to those of Bassey, Bennett *et al.* and the Bullock Committee. Indeed, the pattern seems remarkably consistent and predictable.

In contrast to the Black Paper authors and the secretaries of state, the Inspectorate have regularly pressed for a broadening of the curriculum. They responded to the DES framework for the school curriculum with their own publication, *A View of the Curriculum*.[19] They argued that as well as language, literacy and mathematics, science, aesthetics, PE and social studies (including religious education in a multicultural perspective) were all important. Examples of the skills, concepts and general areas of content to which children should be introduced were outlined. It was argued that a common policy for the curriculum

> cannot be a prescription for uniformity. Enabling all children to achieve a comparable quality of education and potentially a comparable quality of adult life is a more subtle and skilled task than taking them through identical syllabuses or teaching them all by the same method.[20]

The division between the DES and the Inspectorate has conspicuously widened. Whilst both have recently commented on the five-to-sixteen curriculum, the former has argued in terms of subject divisions,[21] and the latter have stressed the importance of skills, attitudes and areas of learning.[22] In *The Curriculum from 5 to 16*[23] the Inspectorate specifically warn of the 'limitations of a curriculum which is no more than a list of subjects'. They comment that it is difficult to define content without reference to the learning processes that will be involved and activities in other areas of the curriculum. Thus instead of supporting the secretaries of state they outline broad curriculum areas, and detail how they might fit into and across the curriculum and how they might be introduced at different stages. Concepts, skills and attitudes are defined and schools are asked to pay attention to the type and range of classroom activities that will promote them.

The quest for accountability

Much of this conflict stems from differing views of how a unified curriculum might be achieved. The Inspectorate favour discussions of policy at a local or even individual school level to broaden teachers' understanding of what the learning processes are and how they might best be promoted in school. The government favour a common core and regular assessment of progress and standards as a means of enforcing teacher accountability. Their curriculum must therefore be assessable, and relevant procedures, combined with LEA record keeping, be developed to monitor results. Whilst the Inspectorate's views allow them to place responsibility for curriculum policies and standards with the schools themselves, the DES places it firmly with the LEAs. Thus in *A Framework for the School Curriculum* it states clearly that 'authorities should collect information annually from their schools about the curriculum offered, together with school assessments of the extent to which the curriculum matches the schools' aims and objectives'.[24] As Kelly pointed out in 1977, the DES view has been 'not so much that teachers cannot be left to choose the right sorts of activity for their pupils as that they cannot be trusted to ensure that sufficient high standards are attained unless there is some kind of outside supervision'.[25] For example, to ensure public accountability, national research projects have been funded including an investigation into record keeping in the primary school and the provision of tests in mathematics and language for LEAs so that they can assess the performance of their pupils against established norms.

Such actions have increased the pressure on LEAs to demand more record keeping in their schools. Teachers have, in fact, always kept a variety of records. Some, such as the record book of work covered, have tended to be completed to meet the needs of the headteacher and adviser. Personal results of standardised tests and comments on personality and attitude have generally been necessary when a child is transferred to a new teacher or a different school. Teachers have also kept their own records of progress as a means of mapping a child's development and of improving their own teaching. Government persistence has resulted in formal LEA records being added to the list. This had placed increasing pressure on teachers and on advisers, who have had to adopt a more active role in ensuring such requirements are satisfactorily fulfilled. The Assessment of Performance Unit (APU) has been established since 1975. This unit aims at providing information concerning the general levels of performance of pupils in most areas of the curriculum. Its role is intended to be neutral, involving the gathering of information that will provide a picture of performance over the differing areas which can be compared in future surveys.

Thus whilst the Inspectorate press for teacher development, the secretaries of state seek public accountability. There is a certain amount of evidence, however, that the latter tends to effect a narrowing of the curriculum. The ultimate in public accountability is, of course, 'payment by results'. To raise standards the Revised Code of 1862 restricted the curriculum to the areas that were thought capable of accurate assessment. Teachers could then be paid according to the achievements of their pupils. Unfortunately it resulted in a very restricted curriculum with many important subjects excluded. It was therefore with some surprise that an inspector, James Bryce, found a school in the mid-1860s implementing a most detailed and effective curriculum for primary science. The 'school', a decrepit thatched cottage, was not under the state system. Nevertheless Bryce was moved to comment that, had it been, the teacher would not have been allowed to devote the four afternoons a week he did to that most difficult of all primary subjects.[26] By 1875 the Board of Education was forced to broaden the curriculum, and six hours of science per week were recommended for all pupils. Payment by results had to be abandoned.

Even today, where tests or assessments are introduced, teachers tend to concentrate on the aspects tested or to elevate them above those that are not. In regions operating the eleven-plus, books of exemplar tests are popular in home and school. The curriculum of the top two primary years can become one of regular tests and exercises in logic and verbal reasoning. Already a textbook exists that purports to help children achieve the science processes tested by the APU. Brown also claims that, as a direct result of the APU's work, advisers are recommending the teaching of aspects of learning that will be tested by the unit.[27]

The findings are all the more worrying when one considers that many important aspects of education are not easily assessed. The APU, for example, has made most headway in devising tests of performance in maths and science. Its slowness elsewhere is possibly because it has been at pains to find ways of measuring broad processes rather than narrow concepts and skills. Nevertheless, as Brown indicates, even in science, one of its more successful areas,

> the . . . skills which are definable and the outcomes which are precisely measurable will . . . be tested well in national monitoring. Only a limited attempt is being made to test the less easily definable skills like creative thinking and imaginative reasoning and their less reliably measured outcomes.[28]

In many other areas the quest to develop tests of performance has produced untold difficulties. The group exploring aesthetic development were quick to note that 'many people experienced in this field are convinced that no comprehensive or adequate conceptual model for aesthetic experience yet exists. Nor has any real insight been gained into aesthetic development during childhood and adolescence.'[29] In the area of personal, social and moral development, the APU decided not to proceed with national monitoring but rather to map dimensions of development in this area that teachers might observe and monitor for themselves.

Record keeping produces similar problems. Blenkin and Kelly argue that those produced by LEAs in response to government recommendations tended to be

> simplistic and gave teachers little scope to indicate the broader aspects of the work that children undertook. The elements that were considered worth recording were narrow and easily assessed and the teacher's attention was directed to the child's achievements rather than emerging processes.[30]

Objectionable objectives

The idea of expressing educational objectives narrowly in operational rather than broad humanistic terms has permeated many national publications, projects and attempts at records of performance for some years. Typical is the Schools Council project Aims in Primary Education, which states that 'if the teacher's aims are to help guide his practice, then they should be expressed in behavioural terms. That is to say that they should state what the child will actually be able to do when the aim is achieved.'[31] The NFER research project on record keeping in the primary school also advises the 'analysis of aims into more specific objectives which can be used as a basis for record keeping'.[32] Such a view can turn teaching and assessment into a narrow, deterministic, self-fulfilling activity rather than an open, creative and dynamic process. Nurturing the higher processes (and affective aspects) of education becomes more difficult and unlikely with this approach. Records become check-lists of narrow skills and concepts to teach towards. As Blenkin and Kelly say, in adopting them we 'are losing the strengths of the informal approach to education, and instead adopting an approach which restricts the freedom of both child and teacher'.[33]

An alternative view of assessment and the curriculum

Assessment is probably at its best when carried out by teachers as a means of helping them in their complex task. Of interest here is the Schools Council Progress in Learning Science Project,[34] where the emphasis is on helping teachers develop skills to encourage children's learning. It is supported by *A Guide to Diagnosis and Develop-*

ment which helps teachers devise appropriate experiences for children at different developmental stages and record progress. Assessment and recording are to monitor individual development and learning. Goodman's 'Informal Reading Inventory' takes a similar developmental approach. Here children's 'miscues', or reading errors, are recorded and used by teachers to develop an overall picture of individual strengths and weaknesses in reading on which they might build.[35] Both techniques are optimistic in learning terms. Children are not viewed as sick patients waiting for their daily dose of educational medicine that will remedy their deficiencies (what Chandler[36] calls the 'hospital approach' to teaching). They are seen to be bringing their own unique qualities, on which a teacher can build, to the learning process.

Many LEAs are reviewing their own assessment procedures. Several have already moved from a public-accountability approach to one of self-evaluation by schools. The ILEA, for example, issues, in addition to individual record cards, a list of questions on children, parental involvement, curriculum, organisation, staffing and staff roles to schools. Entitled 'Keeping the School under Review', this aims 'to assist a school to examine its organisation, its resources, its standards of achievement and its relationships'.[37]

Summary

Conflicting pressures have been placed on the primary school curriculum. The Black Papers coincided with a period of disillusionment with many aspects of society. Education was not proving to be the panacea of all social ills. It was also an expensive commodity. The William Tyndale affair appeared to confirm that progressive trends in primary schools might be getting out of hand. Initial government reaction was almost one of panic. Bennett's research exacerbated the problem. Measures to make teachers more accountable were demanded. However, there was conflict about how this should be achieved. The secretaries of state favoured isolating a core curriculum and monitoring national standards. The Inspectorate favoured a broad curriculum and the development of teachers' understanding of the educational processes are a local or school-based level.

The monitoring of standards has proved easier to order than to implement. Aspects of education that can be readily assessed tend to be the least worthwhile. However, once tested or recorded these aspects become elevated in teachers' minds above those that are not. There are also other unwanted side effects, namely the viewing of curriculum objectives in narrow behavioural rather than broadly developmental terms. Thus education has become viewed as a 'banging-in' rather than a 'drawing-out' process. This can restrict both teacher and child.

Pressures for accountability persist into the 1980s and form the basis of considerable conflict between teachers and employers. Where assessment is viewed as an externally enforced burden, resistance will persist. Forms of assessment that encourage self-evaluation and development of teaching skills may prove more acceptable to the profession. Some already exist and perhaps should be developed further. Inspectorate concerns that the curriculum in primary schools is too narrow are well founded. In her research published in 1984 by the NFER,[38] Barker Lunn showed that fairly mundane basic tasks occupy a major part of the pupil's day. Mathematical computation and silent reading occur daily. English comprehension exercises, spelling lists and tests, formal grammar and creative and descriptive writing each occur at least once a week in most classes. Alternatively the higher skills of problem-solving are conspicuous in their absence in school. The campaign for a return to basics would appear to have been successfully completed.

CHAPTER 15

The power of the project

The pupils were feeding back from their discussion groups. Carlton's group wanted to know if Persil really did wash whiter than other powders; Deidre's, the best materials for swimwear; Stephen's, why birds had feathers. Then it was Paul and Jonathan's turn. As they sat with arms folded and grim looks, things didn't look too good.

'Well,' I said, 'have you decided?'

'We're only interested in football,' came the response. 'We don't wanna do nuffin' on clothes!'

The response was honest rather than defiant. With very little reading and writing skill the two had at least found success in sport. Both were staunch members of the football team. Jonathan's other more dubious talent of fighting had also gained him the wary respect of both staff and pupils. Some, from either group, even bore the marks of his not infrequent outbursts. I had to tread carefully.

'This is difficult. Our project is about clothes and everyone is choosing an aspect that interests them. Now, I don't think you should give up so easily. Go to the library, find some books – on football if you like – and try again. You obviously need a bit of help.'

There was a pause; looks exchanged. I smiled encouragingly. Reluctantly the two got up from their seats and left.

With the other groups settled and planning their work for the next few weeks, I went to check on the 'footballers'. The 'school library' was a euphemism for a collection of reference books and encyclopaedias in a converted cloakroom between ours and the neighbouring classroom. Children passed through to go to the lavatory or collect their coats. It was, unfortunately, an area to mess around or pick pockets in as well as to do research. Paul and Jonathan were more inclined to the former, and my suspicions were therefore roused by the silence that greeted me.

As I rounded the corner of the bookcase an unbelievable sight met my eyes. The two were engrossed in a book, whispering:

'Cor, look at that!'

'Eh, let's 'ave a look!'

'What does it say?'

I was still suspicious, Jonathan's 'research' in the library tended to be a dubious activity. Being the slowest reader in the class he was nevertheless first to find the word 'bum' in Roald Dahl's *Charlie and the Chocolate Factory*. Now what was he up to? I could see it was a Ladybird book. 'Not *The Human Body*, again!' I thought. But no. Here they were genuinely browsing *The History of Football*.

The following Sunday a colour supplement compared today's footballers with those of the past. Features ranged from differences in clothes to costs of treating injuries. On Monday morning three class members produced copies. My own could stay hidden in its bag. The final group was now under way.

At the end of term Deidre's group produced a fashion show for the school. The whole class was involved, dressed in a range of holiday clothes from party dresses to beachwear. Behind the scenes a range of helpers organised the 'changes' whilst the commentary progressed:

'And now for the evenings. Here comes David in fashionable corduroy trousers in the new aubergine colour. This co-ordinates with his pink shirt and flowered tie. Very nice, David.'

The 'birds' group gave a lesson to another class on the structure of feathers. Hand-lenses and sets of feathers were provided and Stephen talked them through various observations with great expertise. The rest of the class watched with interest, noting 'good' aspects of his teaching.

There was a certain amount of hilarity in dressing Jonathan up in the footballer's knickerbockers of the past. Paul, resplendent as Georgie Best, was easily kitted out in normal school team 'strip'. The two marched down to the infant department with the rest of us following, to explain the differences between footballers past and present. It was a dramatic affair – particularly when acting out the nature of past football games. The group chosen for the scene enjoyed the tussle. We had spent a lot of time learning to mime a fight, and Jonathan's restraint was commendable. He even allowed himself to be 'knocked out' in the game – and grinned widely when the infants cheered. Apart from the socialisation within the project, both pupils learned to research, draw up and present statistics, to act, paint and sew. Their interest had been sustained over many weeks and they had both written and presented an acceptable report. Only a project could have stimulated such response.

On the morning of the final project presentation I awoke with symptoms of flu. With a temperature running high I staggered to school to experience the performance. It was a play: *The Emperor's New Clothes*. I remember little about it and accepted the headmaster's offer of a lift home at lunchtime. The class would be divided amongst the other classes during the afternoon. Christmas was approaching and I hoped to recover for the final week's parties and celebrations.

I awoke with a start and glanced at the clock. It was 6 p.m. and the front door bell was ringing. Dragging on my dressing gown I descended the stairs and was surprised to see Mr Snell, the head-teacher, on the doorstep looking grave. He had bad news. That afternoon Jonathan had made a violent and unprovoked attack on a senior member of staff. A strongly built, athletic woman, she had coped well with the situation but was badly bruised. I was shattered. I had worked so hard on that child! Feelings of guilt and despair descended. Mr Snell felt that the situation was very serious. Because of the child's home background outside agencies had already been brought in. An emergency meeting had decided Jonathan was to be sent to the local secondary school prematurely. Meanwhile he was to be excluded from school for seven days – up until end of term.

The parties and Christmas fun cheered us all during that week but a cloud still hung overhead. On the final day Jonathan arrived to collect his paltry belongings. The rest of the class were watching a film and I was arranging their Christmas decorations on desks to take home. He offered to help. As we stood together on the ladder unpinning and passing work to each other our eyes scarcely met. Finally I spoke.

'I'm sorry about what happened, Jonathan.'

Grunt.

'I'd like you to know we've enjoyed having you in the class and we're going to miss you.'

Grunt. Silence. I reflected on the power of the project approach.

'We were disappointed, though, at what you did to Miss G. You've never behaved like that with me.'

He grinned. 'I'd 'av looked a right cissy hittin' you, wouldn't I?' he said. 'You're not the size of tuppence!'

CHAPTER 16

Problems with projects

Concentration on the 'basics' narrows the curriculum. The 'three Rs' are seen as essential skills and everything else, including project work, as non-essential frills. The extent to which today's teachers adopt the approach is difficult to determine. However, it would seem that, on average, only 17 per cent of the curriculum is devoted to projects; also that the range and quality of such work are extremely varied. This chapter examines the origins of, and reasons for, the project approach and the conflict surrounding its implementation.

Background to the project approach

The idea of learning through projects rather than separate subject teaching is not new. In 1830 William Cobbett refused to allow his children to attend a state school, arguing that. 'Schools could only give a devitalised kind of instruction, an organised book drill that would do nobody any good.'[1] Instead, he taught them at home on lines similar to the project approach. When the Inspectorate recommended in 1897 that object lessons should be grouped into a connected theme they were also recommending a move towards curriculum integration that typifies project work. The method gained popularity in the United States, being advocated by both Dewey and Kilpatrick. Helen Parkhurst's organisation at Dalton, Massachusetts, where individual assignments replaced a rigid time-table, contained elements of a project approach.

It was to the United States that the Hadow Committee turned for information on projects, and a memorandum from R. B. Roup of

Columbia University stimulated them to devote four pages to the approach. By the 1960s enthusiasm was running high, although the Plowden Committee expressed some reservations. They wrote only three paragraphs on the subject. The first warned that research skills would not necessarily be developed through the project work. The second noted that linking the work of a class to one centre of interest might be artificial. The final paragraph described work that might develop from spontaneous interests (although their examples of children wanting to build an aviary and measure the area of an irregularly shaped field seem rather unlikely).[2] Ten years after Plowden the Inspectorate's interest had waned even further. The HMI survey[3] gave only brief reference to the integrated curriculum. The comments were at best descriptive, at worst unfavourable.

What is project work?

Projects were originally introduced as a means of involving children in purposeful activity as a learning experience. They were developed as a more easily organisable adaption of Dewey's problem method. The emphasis in a project is on research, enquiry and discovery. Kilpatrick formulated four phases for the successful project.[4] The first he called 'purposing' – the determining of a purpose for the activity:

> the teaching . . . takes the form of raising a succession of problems interesting to the pupils and leading them to reach, in the solution of these problems, their knowledge of principles which the teacher wishes them to learn. It is the method which an inquisitive boy is driven to follow, when he wants to find out how a steam engine or an electric bell works . . . In all instances the enquirer sets out ignorant of the scientific or mathematical principles, but keen to solve a problem that appeals to him: and the satisfaction of his desire is made to depend upon his discovering and learning the principles involved.[5]

Thus at Eastlea it was not enough for children simply to enquire about washing powders or birds' feathers. They had to specify what they really wanted to know, raising questions to which they would seek solutions.

Stage two involves 'planning'. This is a time for consulting various resources – published materials, brochures, pictures, slides and people. Both the extent and order of the enquiry must be decided and a plan of action and division of labour drawn up. The main theme has to be broken down into smaller topics and allocated to individuals or groups. Each needs a definite course to follow, a problem to solve and a certain piece of information to discover. The final outcome of the project must also be decided: whether it will result in a talk, play or slide-show. To whom will it be presented? The audience is important: if an infant class, then information must be presented in terms appropriate to the young age group; if parents or senior citizens, the presentation can be more sophisticated and informative. The teacher's role at this stage is complex. Basically she or he acts as catalyst and must know when to retreat or step out from the shadows, discuss or listen, lead or follow. She or he must sometimes keep a balance in the work covered, looking at the learning potential that might come from an initial interest – science that might develop from a fashion topic, the geographical potential of a tree study. Pupils must also explore the realms into which the project might extend. Some teachers encourage groups to draw up flow charts of connecting ideas. These can initially help develop early ideas but later act as a check-list of progress.

Stages three and four involve executing and judging the project. The teacher must now sustain interest and momentum in the tasks. Further problems may need to be presented to the group. The children's performance must also be assessed. The project is an excellent diagnostic tool. It shows a child's interests, strengths and weaknesses which may need to be developed or compensated for. As

Junior pupils absorbed in group project work.

in stage two, discussion and observation will be the principal tools. The teacher also needs to give a good deal of her or his own time. Plays and talks need to be practised and refined, friezes and models atractively displayed, photographs planned, shot and developed. The final stages, like those of any creative activity, are intense. Once complete, judging is vital. The success of a project must be viewed in relation to the original purpose. New skills and learning must be appraised; content and organisation assessed. At Eastlea the children themselves were involved in assessing each other's results and learned to give both praise and criticism.

Why projects?

Teachers adopt the project approach for the same reasons that they adopt progressive methods – to develop all-round education and to encourage children to work harder and participate more actively in the learning process. Many teachers argue that in integrated work the child rather than the subject becomes important; hence the popular but somewhat ambiguous statement that primary teachers teach children not subjects.

Supporters of project work also have particular views about knowledge, arguing that traditional subject boundaries are artificial and that subject teaching leads to knowledge fragmentation. Barnes and Dow, for example, write:

> pupils should be introduced to knowledge in such a way that they . . .
> recognize its power to give meaning to their world. Its value should
> be shared: thus acquiring knowledge should be socially enriching not
> divisive.[6]

Projects do tend to combine a number of conventional subjects. The pupils investigating the best type of beachwear at Eastlea, for example, studied history through looking at changes in beach fashions over the years by interviewing a grandparent and parent. They were involved in geographical and mathematical investigations when evolving a survey of where the class members took their last holiday and mapping the results. Scientific work involved investigating the properties of different materials for wear and tear, speed of drying and response to sun and salt. Many elements of language were also incorporated into their written reports and the organisation of a fashion show. The curriculum in project work is therefore integrated, developing according to the interests of the children rather than because of a teacher-planned sequence.

A further argument used in favour of project work is that it aids both the pursuit of knowledge and the acquisition of learning processes. The Plowden Committee, for example, stated:

> Rigid division of the curriculum tends to interrupt children's train of thought and of interest and to hinder them from realising the common elements in problem solving.[7]

Projects are also said to help children to learn how to learn. The term is unfortunately surrounded with some confusion. Dearden found five different possible interpretations amongst writers.[8] Some meant learning how to obtain information or developing methods of enquiry. The Gittins Report,[9] for example, emphasised that a child should 'be able to seek out information as he needs it', whilst the Schools Council Science 5/13 (SC5/13) team felt children should develop 'an enquiring mind and a scientific approach to problems'.[10]

For others the term has meant the learning of general rules for application in new situations, or how to exploit one's capacities to greatest advantage when studying. Finally the Plowden Committee emphasised the importance of children discovering the joy of learning. Critics have also pointed out that all these skills could be developed as effectively, and perhaps more efficiently, through a knowledge-based curriculum.[11]

The extent of project work in schools

A confusion of terms surrounding project work, not dissimilar to that surrounding descriptions of teaching styles, has made it difficult to assess its extent in school. Words such as 'projects', 'topics', 'centres of interest' and 'themes' are used synonymously in some texts and with different meanings in others. The Plowden Report, for example, contains the fascinating statement that 'A variation on the project . . . is the "centre of interest". It begins with a topic.'[12] In the same paragraph 'topic' is given new meaning: 'It has become more common to have several interests – topic is now the usual word – going at once.' Similarly the 1978 HMI survey makes six references to 'topics', one to the 'thematic approach' and one to 'projects', although it fails to index the latter. Other writers are just as confused. Leith attributes equal meaning to 'topic' and 'project work',[13] and Blenkin and Kelly use all terms synonymously.[14]

In 1968 Rance attempted to clarify the language surrounding the approach. 'Projects', he claims, set no limit on the eventual scope of the subject, include elements of research and the exploration of many conventional subject areas. He sees 'centres of interest' deriving mainly from natural history and being planned in advance by the teacher in a graded, structured way. 'Topic work', in contrast, he feels falls between the two extremes, being a 'more limited technique' than the project approach. Choice, for example, he says is limited in topic work, a child being free only to study 'within the limits approved of by the teacher'. The time spent on a topic is shorter than on a project, and teacher intervention is higher: 'she must decide the central theme – the limits within which she intends children to work and the kind of end product she requires'. He considers that a carefully planned and prepared introduction to the subject matter is also the teacher's responsibility.[15]

Teachers have understandably remained confused. In a study of nine hundred primary teachers, Bassey found that junior teachers separated 'thematic studies' and 'integrated studies' whilst infant teachers linked integrated studies and topic work into one category.[16] The expected difference between the two junior categories is vague. Alexander's explanation that 'thematic studies' refer in this case to 'bounded topics or projects as conventionally conceived', and 'integrated studies' to 'a topic based approach to a substantial part of the curriculum', does little to clarify the issue.[17] However, it was found that, on average, teachers devoted four hours per week of 17.4 per cent of the timetable to this type of work.

The Inspectorate paid little attention to the extent of project work in their 1978 survey report. RE, history and geography were said to be generally taught through topics such as 'helping others' or 'homes', and social studies through a thematic approach. Such practice was also indicated to be popular though no statistical data is available to quantify the extent. The survey itself could well be at fault here. Although the Inspectorate were asked to note the relative emphasis of prescribed topics for children's writing and 'other curricular areas',[18] the teacher's questionnaire on the curriculum listed only traditional separate subjects with no mention of projects. As the original purpose of the survey was to present a representative picture of the range of work carried out by primary children,[19] such an omission is unfortunate.

In contrast to Bassey and the Inspectorate, Bennett *et al.* found thematic approaches rare in the open-plan schools they studied.[20] However, the team concentrated on areas of the curriculum 'in the same manner as the HMI 11–16 curriculum report'![21] Consequently, when classes were observed using a thematic approach it caused problems:

> in this unit the fact of a thematic form of curriculum organisation makes differentiation between curriculum contexts somewhat problematic and reference to the actual activities table gives the reader a more reliable guide to the curriculum activities experienced by the teacher.[22]

Bennett *et al.* describe the thematic approach as 'an organisation whereby the curriculum is derived from a series of topics or projects'.[23] They differentiate this from the 'split day', a form of organisation whereby basic skills are taught in the morning and 'other work', including topic or project work, occurs in the afternoon. As the split day is by far the most common form of organisation in open-plan schools (see Bennett[24] and the Strathclyde survey[25]), the differentiation is unhelpful in assessing the real extent of project work in such schools.

Probably the most reliable information on the approach is to be found in the ORACLE study[26] and a 1978 survey by Leith.[27] The former found that 15 per cent of pupils' curriculum time was spent on project or topic work. Of the 167 teachers responding to Leith's questionnaire nearly all stated that pupils did project work in their classes. Thus the practice might be more widespread than research has generally indicated. However, the type of work that can be placed in this category may need more careful analysis.

Problems with project work

If teachers have had problems in adopting an integrated approach to the curriculum it is hardly surprising. Alongside the confusion over what project work is and how it can be recognised lies the government's and the Inspectorate's remarkably consistent view of the curriculum as separate subjects. Their publications have been repeatedly organised in this way, and government-financed projects such as those of the Schools Council have been subject-centred. Pressure for increased specialised subject teaching in primary schools has further encouraged a move away from integration. The trend has not gone unnoticed. The NUT, for example, was moved to comment after the 1978 HMI survey:

> Where schools have chosen an integrated curriculum on educational grounds they should not feel constricted by the Inspectorate reference to particular subjects into a type of planning more suited to the needs of the secondary school.[28]

Teachers have also experienced criticism levelled at all aspects of the approach from process to outcomes. Arguments have raged about the teacher's role. Whilst Rance recommends that teachers may make decisions on content (at least in topic work),[29] Blenkin and Kelly see this as gross interference:

> For some teachers, in their anxiety either to demonstrate that the children have interests, or to make the work more interesting to their own satisfaction and not necessarily their children's, have engaged

pupils in topics which begin with the teacher's interests, develop along lines that the teacher has planned out carefully and come to a conclusion when the teacher has exhausted his own resources.[30]

Teachers may intervene in the planning of project or topic work for good reason. They are often criticised for neglecting subjects and not achieving an adequate breadth and balance on the curriculum. There have been cries for what is called 'curriculum consistency'. Such criticisms may not be without ground. Bassey, for example, found some teachers spending considerably less than one hour per day on mathematics whilst others devoted nearly two hours to the subject.[31] Opportunities for language work showed even greater discrepancies, though linking the data from infant and junior teachers may have accounted for this. Bennett found similar variations with teachers devoting between two and a half and seven hours per week to mathematics and between four and twelve hours to language teaching. The amount of environmental studies offered also varied from seven hours to none.

The number of subjects offered varied similarly from school to school. Some covered five areas of the curriculum and others eight.[32] The Inspectorate also found that 'coverage of items varied from class to class and showed no overall consistency'. In 1978, 25 per cent of teachers taught no history or geography. No observational or experimental science existed in 80 per cent of primary classes.[33] This had improved by 1982 although there was still a neglect of three-dimensional and observational work in art, and no music was taught in 20 per cent of schools.[34] Richards, carrying out a detailed analysis of the variations, found most inconsistency in areas that tend to be given 'integrated' status.[35]

In response to such findings and the implicit criticism they entail, teachers intervene. They draw up flow charts showing how history, music, drama and all other curricular areas can be developed from a project. Connections are sometimes tenuous. 'The project is "Flight", so let's do angels in RE' syndrome can prevail. As the Hadow Committee pointed out:

> though subjects may at times be brought in naturally and usefully in the working out of a project, it is too likely that they will merely be 'dragged in' obediently to the supposed claims of a principle.[36]

Blenkin and Kelly also note that there is a great difference between a teacher planning a project on ships and planning what might develop from a child's interest in making a model boat.[37]

Too much teacher guidance can also be counter-productive. Under complete control, the moods and interests of the children may be ignored while the theme is played out insensitively to the bitter end. I well remember Jack. After returning to school in

September he excitedly announced that his class was to carry out a project on whales. That week a whale was drawn to full dimensions in the playground. Subsequent tasks involved gathering information on different types of whale and their lifestyles. Films, stories, slides and a zoo visit added to the enjoyment. By half-term, however, Jack's interest began to wane. 'What did you do at school today?' received a disconsolate, 'Oh, whales again'; and finally, 'Can't you guess?' The children returned to school after their half-term break on Hallowe'en. Waiting for him to emerge at 3.30 p.m. Jack's mother watched the other children carrying their witches' hats, turnip lanterns and ghost puppets. Jack dragged his feet towards her, his hands quite empty. 'Are you all right?' she asked. 'No,' he replied. 'It's still bloody whales!'

As well as content, the quality of project work has come under criticism. The Bullock Report commented on children copying verbatim from their reference books. The Report writers assumed that the children had not been shown how to make well-structured notes, how to integrate notes from a range of sources or how to use flow charts and other techniques to indicate their findings and further lines of enquiry.[38] Certainly there are some beautifully presented project reports in school from which children have learned nothing. Project work may also be badly matched against pupils' abilities. The Inspectorate noted this when history and geography were taught as topics,[39] and that the approach tended to lead to repetition rather than an extension of children's knowledge and skills.[40] They recommended more assessment by teachers of all areas of the curriculum. Perhaps thinking of project work, they advised:

> Careful assessment of the children's progress has implications for the teacher's approach . . . it is not sensible for teachers to attempt to use a teaching technique that is clearly beyond their operational skill and is therefore inefficient.[41]

A more positive approach would be to help teachers with the assessment of effectiveness of their approach. Leith, interestingly, suggests that the Inspectorate themselves have not found the task easy.[42] Their brief in the 1978 survey included evaluating the extent to which work in school was matched to ability. She points out that whilst they probably saw much project work in evidence they were probably unable to comment in length upon it because of the difficulties of assessing such 'match' in the approach. Indeed, very little has been written about project work assessment. In 1975 an Open University course commented that it could be particularly difficult because of the diversity of project titles and content.[43]

In the same year Ashton worked with a group of teachers on the nature and objectives of project work as part of the ORACLE project.[44] As a result forty-seven criteria were listed under eight headings. These related to the personal choice of topic, the planning of the project, the selection of resources, the extraction and presentation of information and the level of motivation in its planning and execution. From these an assessment sheet was developed which was evaluated by Leith in 1978–9. Thirty teachers agreed to be involved. After two terms none had used the procedure. A further term found the same negative result. Leith was puzzled. She wondered if teachers simply carry out projects because they have an aura about them and meet demands for an individualised curriculum. She also wondered, more cynically, if project work is simply a time-filler for many teachers, giving them a valuable breathing space in their otherwise busy lives. To use her assessment procedure, however, teachers would need to have a clear understanding of and commitment to Kilpatrick's first principles of the approach.

Summary

An integrated curriculum, fundamental to the progressive movement, is generally effected through projects. Kilpatrick first defined the methodology of such work as involving the four stages of purposing, planning, executing and judging. Many arguments are given in support of project work. Traditional subject boundaries are claimed to be artificial and to develop fragmentation in learning. Projects are also said to place the child rather than the subject at the centre of learning and to aid motivation.

Existing evidence indicates that approximately 17 per cent of the primary school curriculum is devoted to project work. However, research has been hampered by a confusion of terms which still need clarification. Such findings must therefore be treated with caution. If the practice is not as widespread as it should be, it is not surprising. Government publications and projects have repeatedly emphasised a compartmentalised curriculum. Pressure for the increased use of subject specialists has exacerbated the situation further. Teachers have also been confused over their role in the approach and have faced considerable criticism on the content and quality of project work in school. Leith hypothesised that helping teachers assess their effectiveness in the approach might be useful. In the past this has been fraught with problems and Leith's procedure received resistance from her trial group of teachers. However, it assumed an understanding and commitment to Kilpatrick's ideal project model that may not have matched the teachers' actual classroom practice.

Teachers obviously need help with the project approach. In the confusion and criticism over the years much has been lost. There is probably little project work in schools that is carried out in Kilpatrick's ideal form. And more criticism or, indeed, too much emphasis on evaluation could reduce such work in schools to a dangerous minimum.

Differences or Needs?

CHAPTER 17

Bomber

Older pupils often become heroes and heroines in the eyes of younger ones, and this was so with Bomber. From my first day in school I seemed to hear of no one else. James boasted that he was the only one in the class with a watch like Bomber's. Jean ate up all her liver 'because Bomber said it made you strong'. Did I know why you took a pencil to bed or what lay on the sea-bed shivering? Bomber had been telling jokes! I thought I had better get to know this charismatic character.

One playtime I asked Tony to point him out. He indicated that he was with a group of about a dozen boys playing marbles at the far end of the playground. I asked for more information. Tony thought for a minute and then came up with a solution.

'He's got a grey jumper on,' he said.

Such was the school uniform that most children wore grey jumpers or cardigans. It was no help.

'Has he got short trousers on?'

'No.' Oh dear. That would have left only two boys to choose from. Others in the class joined in.

'He's got curly hair,' offered Judith.

'He's got spectacles, too,' said Geoffrey.

There were still four boys with these characteristics.

'Is there nothing else about him?' I asked. 'Something that would help me pick him out.'

They all thought hard but were not particularly inspired. Bomber, like most of the others, had apparently got brown shoes with laces, a tie, a belt on his trousers . . . Suddenly Tony had an idea.

'I'll go and tell him you want him,' he said.

Running across the playground he pushed his way into the group of players. He emerged with Bomber, his face beaming with pride as the older boy placed an arm round his shoulders. They walked towards me, Tony and Winston 'Bomber' Dennison, the only non-white child in the school.

CHAPTER 18

Special needs

It was going to be a very hard choice. A new peripatetic reading teacher had been appointed to the school. One child from each class was to be chosen for special tuition. I looked around the class. Trevor, Andrew and George were all slow readers and would benefit from additional time and help. Sally, a fourth-year pupil, could do with extra support. Her speech problems were proving a handicap to her reading and writing. My eye wandered to Alan and Robin. Both could scarcely read, both had indecipherable handwriting, but two more different children you could never wish to meet.

Alan, with generally low ability, would sit quietly for most of the day, mouth open and tongue lolling over his lower lip beneath a vacant gaze. Occasionally he would have moments of bravado. He once punched an older boy for teasing his sister and once almost drowned himself by jumping in the deep end of the swimming pool. He could not fight or swim. I had to rescue him, smiling and unrepentant, on both occasions. In contrast Robin had an IQ of 132. He was lively and joined in everything with great enthusiasm. He was also cheerfully determined not to let his specific reading difficulty hold him back. His taped stories and accounts won all our admiration for their creativity and wicked humour. His art work was the best in the class. How could one choose one of these children for special attention? They all needed it. Unable to solve the dilemma I submitted a list of names to the headteacher. Robin was selected and attended a special class on two mornings per week. Alan and the others struggled on competing for my attention with the rest of the class.

By the end of the year both Alan and Robin had made some

progress. On open day I talked to their parents. Robin's laughed as they examined the drawings and cryptic comments in his books.

'He doesn't change!' said his father. 'Still can't read or write properly. Mind you, neither can I. It hasn't done me any harm and Robin will join the firm too when he leaves school. He'll be all right.'

I nodded my agreement. 'You have a talented son,' I replied. 'He is very bright and very successful socially. He'll be a great asset to your business.'

Alan's mum, a very large lady, approached tentatively. In her hand were his books. Mrs Taylor was a warm, good-hearted person with insurmountable problems. Mr Taylor, whom she loved dearly, was in prison again and she found raising two children on her own very difficult. Today she looked happier than I had seen her for some time.

'And how are you today, Mrs Taylor?' I greeted.

'Oh, I'm so pleased with our Alan,' she said. 'Sending home his reading book has been a good idea. I really do want him to read properly.'

I was touched. 'It's good of you to find time to help him when you have so many things to cope with,' I said. 'It's made all the difference, you know.'

She laughed. 'It's no trouble for me to do some reading, Mrs Stewart. I read all the time.'

To my surprise, Mrs Taylor was an avid reader. Her interest lay more with Mills & Boon than Mailer and Brontë, but she nevertheless read.

'It's my only escape,' she explained. 'If I didn't have my books I don't know what I'd do. That's why I want Sheila and Alan to read well. It might be all they have in life. Do you think Alan can have special help next year?'

I could not be sure. How could I explain that because of Alan's low IQ he was unlikely to be viewed as remedial (capable of having his problems remedied)? How could I tell her that only one child per class could receive special help? How could I explain that other children might be thought to have greater need than Alan? How was I going to sleep at night?

Alan was not selected for special reading attention during the next year. His sister came into the junior department and immediately joined the remedial class. However, Alan did learn to swim.

CHAPTER 19

Crossed by categorisation

Some children have always been selected out (by teachers or legislation) as requiring special treatment or even specialised schools. Differences in health, ability, handicap, culture and sex are amongst the many factors that have, over the years, been thought to require such attention. However, positive discrimination, though frequently necessary to effect change and ensure justice, always produces conflict. The quest to compensate and provide special help is always at conflict with the need to view people as individuals with equal rights and needs. Help for one group can also affect others. Equality for women has, for example, presented a threat to some men; equality for ethnic minorities is seen by some as threatening to the indigenous population.

There is also the problem of finance. Although the increase in money to one needy group does not necessarily mean its removal from another, a finite pool of resources is available (or so government would have us believe). Positive discrimination in favour of one group can therefore make others feel unequal. Unfortunately without direct action and even supporting legislation some groups remain less than equal. This chapter examines the problems created by recent moves to define and label children with special needs.

Problems with labels

A pervading theme in this book has been the danger of labelling schools, teachers, methods and other aspects of education. The practice, when applied to pupils, is fraught with problems. Most people dislike being categorised. Whether positive or negative, labels produce pressure and limit the possibility that we might vary or change our behaviour. Nevertheless we all label and are labelled as a means of making sense of a complex world. It is an almost essential part of the 'helping process', being the only way that common needs and problems can gain recognition and be catered for. Attempts to attribute certain traits and needs to women were frequently misguided attempts to protect them. The handicapped and disabled have particularly suffered from labelling. Originally precise legal definitions of their problems were necessary to draw attention to handicapped children and provided impetus for the development of special education. However, ultimately categorisation has proved a major obstacle to progress. It has initiated, for example, a breadth of separate provision for each group and the virtual isolation of some handicapped children in special schools.

Separating the handicapped

The education of handicapped children was originally specified by Part V of the 1921 Education Act which covered children who were blind, deaf, physically and mentally defective and epileptic.[1] Significantly the needs of these children were separated in the Act from those of normal children in elementary schools. Indeed, schools or classes for the separate categories had to be certified by the board as suitable. It was therefore to be expected that the LEAs would see their duties towards the two groups in equally separate terms. The 1944 Education Act extended the duties of the LEAs. They were now legally obliged to 'secure provision' for a child suffering from a disability, though this could be in an ordinary school as well as a special school. The Act, however, introduced the notion that children should receive 'treatment' (albeit educational) for their disabilities. The term is perhaps not surprising. Four out of five of the recognised handicaps at the time had a physical basis that might have required surgical or other medical treatment. To emphasise the importance of health aspects, the decision regarding both the categorisation of disability and the educational needs of pupils was given to a medical officer of the LEA. LEAs were empowered to establish special schools in hospitals and 'other' places including homes.[2]

Pressures for specialised treatment mainly resulted in an expansion of specialised schools, though provision in normal ones continued to be thought desirable. Thus, in 1954 the chief medical officer was to state that the handicapped should be kept 'within the normal environment, or as much of it as their condition allows, provided that within it they are treated with understanding and given the fullest opportunities'.[3] Equally the Plowden Committee could feel that 'segregation of the handicapped is neither good for them nor for those with whom they must associate. They should be in the ordinary school whenever possible.'[4] However, rules, regulations and separatism powerfully mitigated against this happening. The 1959 'Handicapped Pupils and Special Schools Regulations' laid down the maximum size of group allowed for the then ten recognised categories.[5] Classes for blind children were not to exceed fifteen pupils, and those for the deaf ten. By 1973 class size numbers were being replaced by regulations covering teacher/pupil ratios, again in the ten identified groups.

Changes and disadvantages in labels

The labelling practice was not only divisive; it did not work. Patterns of handicap are not static. They alter and broaden as a result of many factors. Thus societies such as the Invalid Children's Aid Association,[6] founded over a hundred years ago to alleviate the problems of tuberculosis, now meets the needs of children with asthma and language disorders as well as physical handicaps. Although poliomyelitis like TB has virtually disappeared, improved surgery techniques affected for a time a sharp rise in spina bifida children surviving to school age, a number that has now levelled out. Of greatest concern has been the rising number of children with multiple handicaps, as they are particularly difficult to place within separated facilities. In 1970 legislation made LEAs responsible for provision covering children who are both blind and deaf, indicating the inadequacies that existed at the time.

Between 1944 and 1959 the number of officially recognised handicaps doubled. Recent additions include autism, other forms of childhood psychosis and acute dyslexia, which eventually gained official recognition in 1970. In the 1980s understanding is broadening further. Dr Wisbey, for example, has gained significant media coverage on her new views and approaches to dyslexia.[7] Special language disorders are also gaining interest, and specialised provision and teacher training courses and materials are being devised.[8] Brennan feels that, in the future, the run-down in the health and social services and lowering standards in school meals may lead to a reappearance of nutritional diseases.[9] Each newly defined handicap needs not only recognition but also educational provision. Interestingly, since 1970 new categories have not been brought within the close legal definitions of the 1959 regulations. However, the tight categories of the past have encouraged a separatist attitude even to new problems as they, again, tend not to fit existing ones.

Labels have disadvantaged some handicapped children in other ways. Until 1970 school provision was thought inappropriate for the severely mentally handicapped. Instead they were placed in 'junior training centres' where their health rather than educational needs were met. Some, with no other provision available, were accommodated in the wards of mental hospitals. The term 'dyslexic' has presented problems since it was first conceived. Indeed, it is one of the most contentious handicap labels in use. In 1975, for example, the Bullock Committee considered that the term

> serves little useful purpose other than to draw attention to the fact that the problem of these children can be chronic and severe. It is not susceptible to precise operational definition . . . a more helpful term to describe the situation of these children is 'specific reading retardation'.[10]

Parents of dyslexic children, however, have tended to disagree. If the LEA is faced with spending several thousand pounds of its budget for specialised independent boarding school provision it is more likely to favour other than specific reading handicaps. Yet parents of dyslexic children tend to see such provision as their only means of overcoming the handicap. Parental pressure plus support from famous 'dyslexic' personalities such as Susan Hampshire and Oliver Reed have ensured continuing research and interest in the disability. Also, some GCE and CSE boards now allow extra time for dyslexic students to complete exams. The 'unwanted' label, therefore, is beginning to be applied usefully, though meanwhile some parents, like those in Cardiff, may have to pay for additional tuition (over and above that provided by the LEA) for this special need.

There has also been a tendency in the past for labels to become applied over every aspect of a handicapped pupil's behaviour. The title of the radio programme for the handicapped, *Does He Take Sugar?*, is an excellent illustration of the general prejudice. As Brennan points out:

> few disabilities generate all-round handicap, in the usual situation handicap is restricted to specific circumstances or activities. Many scholastic handicaps do not operate outside schools and some severe handicaps do not affect education . . . the effect of a disability may change as the child grows and develops.[11]

Concern about segregation in special schools and the lack of facilities in normal schools was amongst the reasons for the formation of an enquiry committee to review the whole field. The team was led by Mary Warnock. In 1980 they published their *Report of the*

Committee of Enquiry into the Education of Handicapped Children and Young People. It reflected a general feeling that the handicapped should be educated and live in the 'least restrictive environment possible'. It was followed by a White Paper, *Special Needs in Education*, which outlined the government's response to the Warnock Committee recommendations and set out a general approach to new legislation. In 1981 an Education Act on Special Educational Needs was passed to amend relevant aspects of the law.

The Warnock Report

Changes in provision
The Warnock Report introduced the idea of catering for handicapped children's 'needs' rather than providing 'treatment' in schools. It reflected practice in the United States where Federal Law 92142 requires LEAs to investigate the 'needs' – medical, social and educational – of the handicapped and to present a statement, agreed by the parents, as to how those needs should be met. Under the 1981 Act, instead of considering requirements under described categories they must be considered in total. Nevertheless, the Warnock Committee realised that broad descriptions of handicap would inevitably have to remain for groups of children with similar needs. They accepted retention of existing categories for sensory or physical disability.

However, the term 'maladjusted' was considered to cause problems. 'Maladjustment' has been as difficult a term to apply to pupils as 'adjustment'. It has covered in the past a range of conditions from hyperactivity to school phobia. The Report considered that it should continue to be applied but with the understanding that 'behaviour can sometimes be meaningfully considered only in relationship to the circumstances in which it occurs'.[12] The Warnock Committee nevertheless considered that the advantages of applying such a term would outweigh the disadvantages for the child.

The Committee did, however, reject the label 'educationally subnormal'. This has now been replaced by that of 'children with learning difficulties'.[13] It covers the sufferer of 'mild' difficulties whose needs might be met in the resources of a normal school; 'moderate', for those requiring placement in a special school or class; and 'severe', for those children previously termed ESN (severe). Brennan considers that the term 'delicate' may also now disappear; such children being capable of placement within the new categories according to the effects of their illness.[14]

The Warnock Committee made over two hundred further recommendations. They defined both 'special educational need' and 'special educational provision' in terms of resources. The former was seen as a need for one or more of the following:

(1) the provision of special means of access to the curriculum through specialist equipment, facilities or resources, modification of the physical environment or specialist teaching techniques;
(2) the provision of a special or modified curriculum;
(3) particular attention to the social structure and emotional climate in which education takes place.[15]

Similarly 'special educational provision' was interpreted as a need for one or more of:

(1) effective access on a full- or part-time basis to teachers with appropriate qualifications or substantial experience or both;
(2) effective access on a full- or part-time basis to other professionals with appropriate training;
(3) an educational and physical environment with the necessary aids, equipment and resources appropriate to the children's needs.[16]

Changes in assessment

The recommended changes in the assessment procedures for handicap demonstrated a deliberate attempt to bring more handicapped children into the normal school system. Although many handicapped children are diagnosed at the pre-school stage the described procedure needed to fit the school situation where most would be educated. It also needed to encourage co-operation between the various supporting services. Thus responsibility for advising the LEA was transferred from the medical officer to an educational psychologist or inspector/adviser for special education. There was also a recognition of parents' rights for more information and consultation on decisions made about their child in recommending the LEA to appoint a 'named person' for every handicapped child. They would help the parents understand what was happening to their child's case and be the parents' contact with the education department. Parents were also to be given opportunity to be present and express their views during any assessment.

Five stages of assessment were envisaged, the first three being school-based.[17] When the child first exhibited problems in school it would be the headteacher's responsibility to inform the parents and gather relevant educational, social and medical information. This would be examined with the class teacher, and potential changes in teaching discussed. Arrangements would also be made to review the child's progress. If other help is required stage two goes into operation. A teacher from the Advisory and Support Service (which would be set up to aid all the proposed changes) would be consulted. She or he may wish to carry out a personal assessment. As at stage one, colleagues review the information and decide whether to progress with a programme of work, possibly prescribed and supervised by the advisory teacher; if not, or if the programme of work is not successful, stage three goes into operation. This is a more rigorous investigation of needs, requiring a range of expert opinion. If outside support is available to continue the child's education within the school then this is arranged. If specialist or regular support external to the school is required the child progresses to stages four and five where a multi-professional assessment is carried out. This is then the LEAs responsibility and it is the authority's duty to gather the information and keep the parents informed through the 'named person'.[18] Having reviewed all the information, a 'statement' is then made setting out the child's needs and the most appropriate arrangements to meet them. The parents would have a right to express their views and appeal against any proposals. In this case the LEA would need to consider its decision. Once agreed by the parent, the LEA must legally provide the provision recommended. Every child for whom a 'statement' has been made must be reviewed annually and fully reassessed at least once in both their primary and secondary stages.

Through such an assessment procedure more children would be brought within the scope of special education. As well as those needing permanent special educational provision, any child causing concern, however temporary, could have their needs assessed in this way. Indeed, the Report considered that in a class of thirty mixed-ability children six may require some help of this kind during their school career, with the likelihood of four or five in need at any one time. To implement this new approach to special education the Committee outlined the range of provision that should reasonably be made by the LEA. This included:

- full-time education in an ordinary class with any necessary help and support;
- education in an ordinary class with periods of withdrawal to a special class or unit or other supporting base;
- education in a special class or unit with periods of attendance at an ordinary class and full involvement in the general community life and extra-curricular activities of the ordinary school;
- full-time education in a special class or unit with social contact with the main school;
- education in a special school, day or residential, with some shared lessons with a neighbouring ordinary school;

- full-time education in a day special school with social contact with an ordinary school;
- full-time education in a residential special school with social contact with an ordinary school;
- short-term education in hospitals or other establishments;
- long-term education in hospitals or other establishments;
- home tuition.[19]

Brennan, commenting on the list, felt it would also lead to more sensitive assessment, placement and review procedures through the need to utilise the range of provision.[20]

The list indicates the Committee's acceptance that some children would continue to need placement in a special school. Such children would be those with severe or complex physical, sensory or intellectual disabilities, who require special facilities, teaching methods or expertise that would be impractical in an ordinary school. Also included are children with severe emotional or behaviour disorders who experience difficulty in forming relationships and whose behaviour might seriously disrupt a normal school. Pupils with less severe difficulties but causing concern who might 'thrive in the more intimate communal and educational setting of a special school'[21] form the third group.

The Report not unreasonably proposed a range of teacher training for satisfactory implementation of the recommendations. This covered initial training and in-service courses for serving teachers. Three quarters of the profession were estimated to need retraining of some sort, and long courses would also be required for those who would be taking up special needs responsibility posts. Research and other developments were also considered necessary to ensure progress.

From recommendation to legislation

The Warnock Report ideals were hailed by many as crucial for effecting change in special education. However, ideas and recommendations in education need supporting legislation to be successful. On receiving the Report the government promised to maintain expenditure on special education against inflation at least until 1984. However, it firmly stated that no increased funds would be available. It was certain, too, that many of the recommendations would not 'entail significant additional resources' or legislation.

The resulting 1981 Education Act (Special Educational Needs) was, therefore, not surprisingly a damp squib. Neil Kinnock, Leader of the Opposition, described it as 'a Michelin guide to nowhere'.[22]

Certainly it disappointed many. Unlike the Warnock Report it narrowed the concept of special education, at least as far as LEA responsibility was concerned, by concentrating on those children who, under the old procedures, would have received 'special treatment', mainly in special schools. This was in direct conflict with the spirit of the Warnock Report. It left most children with special needs in the ordinary schools with no label to ensure LEA recognition of their right to help. It also meant that no minimum conditions were laid down for their relevant school facilities and curricula as would happen if they had been in a special school. This could lead to inadequate and ineffective provision through lack of appropriate resources.

Under the Act, pupils who have received a 'statement' from the LEA may be placed in a normal school. But this may happen only if the parents agree, if the required special education is available and if the placement is compatible with the efficient education of the other children and efficient use of resources. On placement of such a child in a normal school, responsibility again passes from the LEA to the governors. They must ensure that the recommended special education is available to the pupil and that the pupil's needs are known to all relevant teachers. The governors, too, must ensure that the child interacts as far as is practicable with the other pupils.

The Act has been equally criticised for failing to deal satisfactorily with assessment. No procedures for the 'in-school' assessments (stages on to three) recommended by the Committee have been set out. As most pupils with special needs will be assessed at these levels this is an unfortunate omission. The LEA is given responsibility for the inter-disciplinary assessment for children who progress to stage four for interactions with the parent and review procedures. Under the Act the secretary of state must provide regulations on the advice that the LEA must secure for its assessment. However, though this is defined as medical, psychological and educational the recommended status and qualifications of the advisers are not defined. There is a legal requirement on LEAs, however, that the assessment and statement will be highly individualised. Unfortunately, the Act assumes that assessment can be completed in a single examination. This is a rare occurrence even in a straightforward case. For most children it would be impossible and unwise to impose such a ruling.

Further criticism has been levelled at the Act's approach to parents. Brennan feels that the assumption that all parents requiring help will approach the LEA's 'named person' is unreasonable. He points out that the authority might well need to approach them. Also, the appeal procedure has been criticised. Under the Act the parents may appeal to the secretary of state if they disagree with the

LEA's 'statement'. They may also ask for a further assessment 'unless it is unreasonable' or 'inappropriate'.[23] The secretary of state, however, has the power only to ask the authority to 'reconsider', not reverse, its decision. Many think that this may undermine parents' rights. There are also no clear guidelines as to what 'unreasonable' or 'inappropriate' might mean, which could well lead to conflict between parents and the education authorities in the future. Finally under the Act LEAs are responsible for review procedures of the children for whom a 'statement' has been made, whether they are in a normal or special school. But there is no requirement for reviewing progress of other children with special educational needs in mainstream schools.

Implications for the primary schools

Remedial children
Apart from the 'statement' children integrating into mainstream schools, most pupils with learning difficulties, at least in Warnock terms, will be educated in ordinary classrooms with no legal obligation on the LEA to support them with special resources and provision. There is also some indication that the in-service training to help ordinary teachers may not be as broad and widespread as the Warnock Committee suggested. Indeed, there may well be a reduction in training. In 1984 ACSET (the Advisory Committee on the Supply and Education of Teachers), a government body, advised that special qualifications for teaching the blind, deaf and partially hearing should no longer be mandatory.[24] The proposal was rejected by the NUT, who stated that, on the contrary, from a certain date all teachers entering any sort of special education should have a mandatory qualification obtained through a recognised course of in-service training. However, the union did endorse the proposed abolition of current specialist courses because of the changing nature of special education, as long as they were replaced by something more suitable.[25]

At present there is a backlog of some 70 per cent of teachers in special schools who still have no 'additional qualifications'. Providing training for the ordinary primary school teachers may therefore be given low priority. Yet even with basic initial training, which should improve in the future, primary teachers seem to cope remarkably well with slow learners. The 1978 Report made special comment on 'the relative success that teachers have in matching the work in the basic skills for the slower children'.[26] Significantly, some help is likely to be organised for this type of child. Two fifths of the schools viewed by the Inspectorate had a teacher with responsibility for remedial work.[27] Approximately half of the schools withdrew groups or individuals for help. Sometimes this was arranged by providing additional support and sometimes by creating time through co-operative teaching. Generally, unlike in any of the author's schools, such children were integrated rather than separated in a remedial class.

All the same, the quality of provision may vary enormously. Remedial work tends to refer to help with reading rather than mathematics or, indeed, other subjects. The Bullock Committee found that help in reading might vary from

> an hour or two a week in a centre or clinic to a daily period in school. It can be closely related to the rest of the child's work . . . or it can be entirely dissociated from it, even to the extent of different orthography. It can range from unskilled treatment, based on inadequate understanding of individual differences, to expert help from a teacher with specialised training and long experience.[28]

Most designated remedial teachers in school are part-time.[29] They often work independently from the class teacher so that the 'special' work is removed from the normal. Many teachers rightly find such arrangements unsatisfactory. Where the part-timer is not a specialist it may be more profitable if she or he is used to release the class teacher to provide the special help. Others believe the part-timer should work in the classroom alongside the normal teacher. Certainly the remedial and normal work should be complementary.

The 1978 Inspectorate findings seem to indicate that in school the less able children are generally given work related to their existing knowledge and skills, carefully planned for progression in learning.[30] This is a much more positive picture than that presented by the Bullock Committee in 1975 and could well be a result of their recommendations. Certainly there is evidence that the long-term effects of specialist remedial teaching are negligible, although there may be short-term gains.[31] However, the problem could well be related to the quality of provision. The Bullock Committee stressed the need to integrate all the child's linguistic work. Remedial teaching is not for the indifferent and inexperienced as it demands combining 'a high level of teaching skill with an understanding of the child's emotional and developmental needs'.[32] Where experts in special needs are available to work alongside normal teachers there is more likely to be carry-over to the general class activities.[33] In 1978 the Inspectorate recommended extending such support.[34] In sharp contrast, faced with a period of financial stringency, many LEAs are having to reduce their remedial service. Such action could be particularly damaging in light of the 1981 Act.

Gifted children

One group of children for whom no support may be available in primary schools is the gifted. Unless suffering from behavioural or emotional difficulties, they are amongst those explicitly excluded from both the Warnock Committee recommendations[35] and the 1981 Education Act (Special Educational Needs). However, the Warnock definitions of 'needs' and 'provision' could well be applied to the gifted. Unfortunately, like dyslexia, there has been a general suspicion of the whole concept of 'giftedness'. Whilst recognising the existence of exceptional talent, educationalists find problems with identifying and providing for it. High intelligence may be only one indicator and tests of creativity which may be better predictors are still imperfect. Thus various LEA and research 'giftedness' check-lists tend to concentrate on indicators such as the ability to see a joke, or make analogies and use images. Many researchers have reported the difficulties teachers have in identifying the very able,[36] and one role of the check-list is to increase awareness.

Assuming positive identification of high ability, there are many indications that primary teachers are less able to provide satisfactory programmes of work for such children than for any other group. For example, the 1978 DES survey found that work for the most able pupils was too easy in almost half of the schools.[37] Significantly there was less likelihood that such children would have special provision in school. Some parents, of course, make their own by sending their child to certain private or specialist schools. Generally, however, whilst some countries such as the United States give much attention to the gifted, we in Britain offer them little. Occasionally a school may withdraw groups of children for special attention, but this is often for additional music tuition rather than general stimulus. The LEA may also identify a high ability group and provide enrichment experiences outside the school environment on one day a week.

There has been a disappointing failure of government reports to tackle the problem. The Plowden Committee recommended long-term studies on the needs of gifted children,[38] and much pioneering work has been done by educationalists such as Tempest.[39] Clearly this is one group of children for which primary teachers require particular support. It is perhaps unfortunate that the Warnock Committee did not include them in their definition of children with special educational needs.

Ethnic minorities

Whilst the 1981 Act, like the Warnock Committee, ignored the needs of gifted children, it specifically stated that a child is not to be taken as having a learning difficulty solely because the language, or the form of language, used for teaching is different from that spoken at any time in the home.[40] It is hard to understand why this exception should be made since many such children, like the most able, otherwise meet the Warnock Committee's requirements. However, they were anxious that a disproportionate number of ethnic minority children were already in special schools.

From the mid-1950s schools have received increasing numbers of children whose parents are of overseas origin. Many such families have now been settled in Britain for several decades. Their concentrations are chiefly in the inner-city areas. When the Plowden Committee commented on 'Children of Immigrants' they concentrated on 'needs', describing, like the Warnock Committee, actions and resources that were desirable. However, they considered that 'the purpose of the various measures . . . should be to eliminate, not perpetuate, the need for them'. They expressed concern that special measures inevitably identify children as 'different' and hoped that immigrant children would be quickly 'absorbed into the native population'.[4]

In the post-Plowden era many special measures have been adopted in schools. These have been partly stimulated by need and partly by outside pressure. There have, for example, been a number of specialist reports from bodies such as the Parliamentary Select Committee on Immigration and Race Relations and by organisations representing minority groups. In 1976 Parliament published the Race Relations Act in recognition of the discriminations that exist in society towards ethnic minorities. Changes in education have included improved nursery provision, an expansion of courses on teaching English as a Foreign/Second Language (EFL/ESL) and improved human and teaching resources in inner-city schools. There is now a considerable methodology developed for coping with EFL/ESL problems and a range of teaching materials.

There are still teachers outside inner-city areas receiving individual or small numbers of children from ethnic minority families coping without support. An LEA in the West Country might not plan for special provision because the children of Chinese, Spanish, Italian and Greek families, being mainly restaurant owners and employees, mingle in easily with the indigenous population. But wherever they live such children have 'special needs'. Of chief concern is the poor educational performance of some minority groups. The Swann Report makes particular reference to the relative under-achievement of West Indian children. Only 6 per cent of them achieved five or more higher grades in GCE O-level and CSE exams, compared with 17 per cent of Asian pupils and 19 per cent 'others'.[42] The Report has been criticised for its handling of the statistics involved. As Parekh states, in grouping races together it has overlooked some important issues. He particularly mentions the problems Asian pupils are experiencing in schools, which he considers provided for the Swann Committee 'an uncomfortable background against which the West Indian tragedy is enacted'.[43] He points out the under-achievement of Bangladeshi children and Turkish Cypriots (lumped with 'others' in the Report). He also points out the similarities between groups that were overlooked. Nineteen per cent of both Asian and West Indian children, for example, received no passes in such exams.

In establishing reasons for the differences in West Indian children, the Swann Committee ran into difficulties and had to rewrite their report. Their final conclusions that these children under-achieve through racial discrimination and social deprivation seem equally dubious since Asian children also suffer from these factors. Indeed, the Swann Committee found that Asian pupils are generally the group most frequently disliked and hated.[44] Parekh feels that a more subtle analysis of the factors is required, exploring common problems and abilities between groups.

The educational problems (and successes) of ethnic minority groups are as relevant to primary as to secondary teachers. Both must seek ways to break the cycle of failure in some families. Various theories have been proposed but they also tend to deal with groups in an undifferentiated way. There is some evidence that teachers are influenced by stereotypes, West Indians being seen as incapable of doing well whilst Asians are more highly regarded.[45] The self-fulfilling character of such views has been well researched. Resources may be also crucial. Sylvia Ashton Warner (see p. 174) certainly found that an alphabet with 's' for 'skellington' instead of 'snake' and books about life in the 'pah' were more powerful for her Maori children than 'Janet and John'. The ILEA Reading with Understanding project[46] examining the assumption that dialect in the home might interfere with acquisition of literacy found it to be unfounded. Their children of Caribbean origin were more adversely affected by the 'overwhelmingly "white English" content' of their reading materials. A new set of materials set in a multi-cultural British locality were devised. They drew upon folk tales from other cultures especially African and Caribbean and included stories of people with fine qualities who came from different parts of the world. The need for such special provision is well within the scope of the Warnock ideology.

'Colour blindness' in the classroom, whilst seeming to be less divisive and more conducive to the creation of a multi-racial society, is thought to be as negative as rejection.[47] Thus there has been a plea to develop multi-cultural education in schools. Woodroffe lists the issues as:

(a) assisting children to self-identity in a multi-cultural society;
(b) creating the basis of a wider world understanding through broader cultural sources and experience;
(c) combating racist ideas which are often supported in education by a narrow approach to values and by the development of stereotypes;
(d) fostering the development of inter-group relationships through the ethos of the school, curriculum and other activities;
(e) introducing the idea of linguistic diversity, in the world, in Europe, in this country.[48]

Primary teachers have shown themselves more disposed than most to accepting such aims. But there is still much to be done. Like eradicating sex stereotypes, the content of all books would need careful examination. Hill et al. in 1971, for example, found that many children's books revealed much inaccurate, thoughtless and sometimes thoroughly offensive writing about people from other countries.[49] History texts should present a balanced perspective on events affecting countries from which immigrant families have their origins. Books should also be available about these countries, the children's cultures and religions, and life in multi-cultural Britain.

Some have even suggested producing materials that would oppose racism. The ILEA's anti-racist team have developed examples of anti-racist mathematics texts. Secondary children, they say, could draw graphs illustrating unemployment among different ethnic groups in Britain and calculate the percentage success rates of discrimination complaints to the Commission for Racial Equality. This would provide meaningful mathematical work and promote greater understanding of problems between groups.[50] There may well be similar activities, but of a more subtle nature, devised for primary schools in the future.

The aim of promoting cultural identity in children has been variously interpreted. Some groups have expressed a desire to achieve this through separatism. In Bradford, for example, a small group of Muslim parents proposed to take over five schools and run them according to Islamic principles under the same law that allows the church schools in this country. The authority, like the Swann Commission, rejected the suggestion but made certain policy adjustments to meet the group's cultural needs. A middle school headmaster in the city, Ray Honeyford, criticised the authority's multi-racial policies, claiming they disadvantaged white children.[51] Certainly the Swann Committee have supported his view that multi-ethnic children should be taught in English. But for many his approach in a sensitive situation was offensive and inflammatory. The views of various private-sector school headteachers, claiming that their pupils are either Anglicised or wish to be so,[52] also indicate a lack of sympathy for the 'multi-cultural lobby'.

The main conclusion of the Swann Report is that attitudes must change. It sees the fundamental change required being a recognition that 'the problem facing the education system is not how to educate children of minorities but how to educate all children'. Some would hold that this is not entirely adequate. There is much work to be done in understanding the needs of ethnic minorities. Like the less able and gifted they deserve to have these needs assessed as individually as possible. Only then will understanding of different levels of performance in these and possibly under-achieving indigenous children begin to be developed.

Summary

Groups of children have always been singled out for special treatment. The Warnock Committee took a welcome broad view of special needs. It confined itself, however, only to certain types of child – in crude terms the handicapped and remedial. The Report reflected a developing view that many more such children should be educated alongside their peers in normal schools. Whilst being generally accepted by the government, the Report was not fully supported by legislation. Thus in the later legal translation it lost much of its original scope and purpose. The 1981 Education Act (Special Educational Needs) was disappointing in the limited responsibility it demanded of LEAs. Most children with special needs will, after all, be educated in normal schools. Under the Act, only children previously recommended for 'treatment' would be under LEA control. However, unlike the special schools the LEAs are not required to lay down minimum provision and curricula for special educational needs in normal schools. The educational and assessment procedures they adopt may be less adequate than those of the special schools children would have attended in the past.

This could lead to integrated special education on the cheap. One example may lie in the many 'special units' attached to normal schools. Accommodating eight to twelve children, these have been set up as a direct response to the Warnock Report. Some have been given a mere £500 for all equipment, a sum that would not purchase a suitable microcomputer system let alone the full range of equipment such an establishment needs. Their staff, too, do not always qualify for the normal special schools 'allowance'. As Winter says:

> Now I see the government actually intends to save money on our children several times over – no specialised equipment, no extra

resources in buildings, no concessions to their 'special needs' what-soever in terms of money . . . I've been conned. The harder we work the less help we get. The more children we send out successfully, the easier it will be for them to say that we are no longer needed. The more equipment I make the less they will spend on us.[53]

She also points out the other disadvantages of such provision, namely the lack of appeal to the public in contributing equipment to a unit for a few children as opposed to the local spastic society.

Special schools have been catering for children with special needs for many years. Indeed, the ILEA when advising the Warnock Committee pointed out that such schools could well be viewed as representing 'a highly developed technique of positive discrimina-tion' for the handicapped.[54] They have been generously resourced and staffed for years and these standards have not fallen as severely as in other sectors of education. In view of the present government's determination to expand and change special provision with no additional funds or courses, one wonders if the 'labelled' children may in the future have the advantage over their counterparts in mainstream education. Without sensitive interpretation of the 1981 Act, they could be the severely handicapped children of the future, at least in educational terms.

Teachers are also faced with many other children with special educational needs for whom they, rather than the LEA, are respon-sible. The remedial service, fortunately, is well established in some areas. Primary teachers also have been shown to cope well with the less able, though this could be a direct result of the support they have, until now, received. Evidence that financial stringency is bringing a reduction in the remedial services of some areas is therefore particularly worrying.

In contrast with the least able, high ability children have gained little recognition for requiring special needs. The Warnock Com-mittee excluded them unless they showed behaviour or emotional problems. There seems to be a certain prejudice against some labels given to children, and 'gifted' appears to be one. Talent is of course difficult to identify and provide for. Some authorities and schools, nevertheless, offer some provision, but compared with several other countries interest in meeting the requirements of these children in Britain is minimal. This is especially alarming since primary teachers find able children difficult to identify and teach adequately.

Considering its general vagueness the 1981 Act is remarkably precise over certain issues. One is its insistence that children whose home language is or has been different from the language used for teaching should not be counted as children with learning difficulties. It is an unfortunate ruling since many ethnic minority children cope inadequately in school and leave with less favourable qualifications than their indigenous counterparts. The causes are multiple, and researchers' inclinations to group such children into 'Asians' or, worse still, 'others' (meaning not West Indian or Asian) may indeed be cultivating stereotype views of traits and problems. Stereotyping has been found to disadvantage some groups. However, close research is needed as some previous assumptions about the learning of ethnic minorities have not been borne out in practice. Like sex stereotyping the materials presented for learning can have more effect on achievement than cultural traits.

If ethnic minorities are to gain equality, racial prejudice must be discouraged and children of all kinds helped to develop a meaningful cultural identity as well as an awareness of a growing multi-cultural world. For this, carefully selected resources and teaching strategies will be required. As such ideas are not acceptable to all members of the teaching profession there is still much to do to help overcome conflict in this area.

With so many groups singled out for positive discrimination, should not all children be seen as having special needs? Certainly there is a growing lobby in the United States that all schooling should, like that for the handicapped, be personally 'tailored'. It is an understandable claim. In an ideal world all would be 'equal'. There would be no conflicting demands for extra attention and resources. Teachers would have pupil quotas and a breadth of skills that would allow for 'common ground' and individual development. Without such conditions, individual differences can soon become 'special needs' and then the contrast between those 'without' quickly transforms into conflicts over rights, resources and relationships.

CHAPTER 20

Equal opportunity

When applying for a place in higher education I was careful to avoid the college whose rules stated that 'no female student should wear a forked over-garment in public'. Nevertheless, even in the 1980s the rule is still forced upon female staff and students in some schools. Normally one dresses conventionally in blouse and skirt, dress or suit until norms are realised. On joining Ford Farm I did exactly that but was not displeased to see Mrs Wilson arrive one morning in smart trousers and jacket. The weather was continuously cold and wet. Mrs Wilson and I were both housed in huts. We froze in the mornings and became wet and windswept with every trip to the main building. It seemed appropriate to don my own black velvet trouser-suit as protection against the elements.

The next day I appeared in full regalia. The children, as always, were quick to spot something new.

'Oo's just like my cat today,' murmured Daniel approvingly.

'I likes your blouse,' competed Natalie.

'And your ring,' cried Shaun.

'I like you in skirts,' said Jane, 'but my mum says you wear 'em too short.'

I firmly changed the subject. Nevertheless the children loved the different textures of lace and velvet. During reading, wet and sticky fingers slipped absentmindedly on to sleeve or cuff. A major struggle in 'together time' was averted only through a firm insistence that no one was going to be allowed to stroke my trouser legs.

After break a note was brought round by a pupil from the top class. It was from the headteacher. I read it with some embarrass-ment: 'Would all staff refrain from wearing trousers in future. It is setting a bad example to the children.' I acknowledged with a tick that I had read it and turned my attention to the children. An apology was obviously in order. I would see Miss Cribshaw at lunchtime.

The staff-room was tense during the midday break. The head-teacher was not on the premises but no one seemed to wish to discuss the issue. Finally the deputy headteacher broke the ice.

'Some of you women seem to be causing Miss a few problems,' he joked.

I winked at Mrs Wilson. 'It'll be you who'll have a few problems tomorrow.' I made my face as serious as I could.

'Why's that?'

'The note,' I said. 'Did you not read it properly?'

Mr Roderick took the paper from the notice-board and read it through. Puzzled by all our giggles he read it again.

'No trousers tomorrow,' I smiled. 'It's lovely to work in a school that takes equal opportunity so seriously!'

CHAPTER 21

No difference

Of all the differences between pupils that are of interest to teachers one that must be ignored and, indeed, actively rejected is that of sex. Since 29 December 1975 the Sex Discrimination Act has been operational. Its purpose is to eliminate less favourable treatment for any person (but particularly women) in society on grounds of sex. The Act covers all areas of life including practices in educational establishments.

There will always have been teachers believing in greater differences between the individual members of one sex than between the sexes. However, for generations society has held fixed and over-simplified views on the accepted behaviour of males and females. Women have frequently been reduced to secondary and inferior status through such beliefs. Typical are the views of the Hadow Committee. In 1931 they stated without question that the sexes inherit 'instincts' in differing degrees: 'the material, affectionate and submissive instincts are stronger in girls; the hunting, fighting and assertive instincts are more marked in boys'.[1] Such ideas have become so entrenched in our culture that it has taken legislation to force society to reconsider them. This chapter considers the origins of sex discrimination, its effect on schools and essential measures for its exclusion from society.

Are there any differences?

Research has, over the years, purported to show a range of differences between males and females. Specialists advising the Hadow

Committee claimed that girls were more liable to fatigue than boys.[2] Many researches apparently show that women have higher verbal and men higher spatial abilities.[3] Girls seem to perform best on short memory tests and be quicker and more deft in practical tasks. Conversely Hutt found boys frequently gain higher scores in arithmetic tests.[4] Galton *et al.* found girls more anxious though more content with school than their male counterparts. They also seemed more strongly motivated to do their best and please their teachers.

What causes differences?

As with IQ, researchers into sex differences cannot easily discover which behaviour results from nature and which from nurture. Corinne Hutt suggested in 1972 that the differences she observed between the sexes were innate. There was no doubt in her mind that men were physically stronger, less resilient, better at spatial, numerical and mechanical tasks and viewed the world in terms of objects, ideas and theories. For Hutt, women through their genetic make-up not only matured physically and psychologically earlier than men but were more verbally precocious, affiliative and nurturant in their attitudes and generally viewed the world in personal, aesthetic and moral terms.

Society has for generations socialised the different sexes according to stereotyped norms. Boys and girls have received different treatment from parents. Schools have perpetuated the practice, either overtly by offering different curricula and discipline, or more subtly, through inference – asking girls to wash up paint pots and boys to move heavy items. This can begin at an early age. For example, all nursery school pupils apparently show willingness to play with constructional toys, but boys are more likely to receive encouragement to use them from teachers. Beyond school, practices have been more overt. 'Vive la difference' has long been a cry of the church, employers and society in general. So indoctrinated are the public that even groups committed in principle to ideas of equality may, without realising, treat sexes differently. The Plowden Committee are an interesting example. Their Report is generally concerned with individual rather than sex differences. Apart from stating that 'possibly' the oldest pupils might be separated for craft and PE, different treatment for boys and girls is generally rejected. However, the Report photographs are illuminating. More boys than girls, for example, are included. Apart from some deliberate attempts to demonstrate the 'new equality' – boys sewing puppet costumes and a mixed painting group – boys are generally portrayed in more active roles. They are the ones testing leverage with pulleys and heavy equipment. They demonstrate 'agility' and aggression in drama whilst the girls' picture is labelled 'expression'. A boy sprawls with a book on the carpet whilst a girl sits neatly cross-legged and, of course, the doctor in the home area is a boy whilst girls play 'mother' and 'nurse'. These photographs are mirror images of findings on the balance of tasks in children's book illustrations.[5]

Are research findings, then, due to socialisation processes or innate biological factors? It is difficult to tell. Galton *et al.* comment that their findings on anxiety and attitude differences may well be caused by the former even though they support JEPI (Junior Eysenck Personality Inventory)[6] standardisation data.

> In considering sex differences in questionnaire responses, it must . . . be emphasised that the questionnaire is not a direct measure of anxiety, motivation and contentment, but rather a measure of the extent to which the pupils are willing or able to make their anxiety, motivation or contentment known. It could be that girls are more likely than boys to perceive some or all of the qualities under examination as socially acceptable.[7]

Studies comparing the academic achievements of boys and girls also emphasise that those differences which occur are susceptible to changes in content. Galton and Simon felt that this explained the variance between their findings in reading differences[8] and those of other researchers such as Douglas[9] and The National Child Development Study group.[10] The two latter, when testing word recognition, had found girls to be superior. But using tests of comprehension and vocabulary, Galton *et al.* found both sexes performed equally well. Content in tests of basic skills may also show sex bias. A problem about netball scores in arithmetic may be more interesting to girls than boys. Similarly a reading passage on space flight may have more masculine appeal. Illustrative test materials also need to be similarly examined.

Re-examination of test materials, therefore, may indicate similarities where differences were previously thought to occur. So might the examination of statistical data in general. As King points out:

> A small but consistent difference between the sexes in, say, a test of verbal reasoning, will undoubtedly reach statistical significance. The inference to draw from such a finding, however, may be the degree of similarity between the sexes, rather than a degree of difference. Although one sex may be significantly superior, on average, to the other sex on a certain type of ability, it may be that 45 per cent (or more) of the 'inferior' sex do better than 50 per cent of the 'superior' sex. There is a large and often huge overlap between the two sexes on all dimensions of human behaviour and functioning.[11]

Unfortunately, as the Equal Opportunities Commission point out,[12] research in the past that did not find differences, in sex or any other factor, tended not to be published. Only since the Sex Discrimination Act have researchers begun to show a deeper interest in the similarities between males and females. In 1973, for example, Good *et al.* showed that teachers gave boys more attention in class.[13] Yet in 1980, Galton *et al.* found there was no significant difference in the distribution of teacher attention across the class. The sex of the teacher also made no difference to class interactions or achievements.[14] This was in contrast to Douglas's 1964 finding that girls excel in subjects taught by women and boys in those taught by men.[15] Galton *et al.*'s findings on reading may also be a sign of the times. Of course, sensitive research techniques may be a factor. The ORACLE findings were based, unlike other studies, on direct classroom observation of activities and interactions. They conclude that many differences that were thought to exist between the sexes are 'more apparent than real'.[16]

The effects of the Sex Discrimination Act on schools

Whatever conflict exists over performance of the different sexes in the primary years, there is nevertheless a widening in attainment and orientation as pupils progress through school. Three times as many boys as girls take O-level physics; six times as many take it at CSE. Thirty-six times as many boys as girls study technical drawing at CSE. This results in part from stereotyped views of appropriate future occupations. Some pupils also consider it unfitting, in sex terms, to achieve highly in certain subjects. Such attitudes were often exacerbated in the past by separate curricula for the sexes. Under the 1975 Act a pupil must be given access to all the 'benefits, facilities or services' offered by a school.[17] Thus subjects such as home economics, woodwork and metalwork must be offered to all pupils equally. In addition they should not be timetabled against each other to restrict and force choice.

Separation of the sexes for curriculum purposes inevitably continues at primary and secondary level in physical education. Justifications have ranged from claims that boys benefit from gymnastics whereas girls prefer more aesthetic experiences[18] to the fact that certain games have long been reserved exclusively for one sex and thus it is pointless to make them available to the other. Performers such as Olga Korbut, John Travolta and the United States 'break dancers' clearly refute the first claim – and have many emulators amongst the young. Few sports need be the prerogative of one sex. Athletics, tennis, swimming and cricket are played by all and there are striking similarities between basketball and netball, rounders and baseball. It is therefore the boys' need to play football (and to a lesser extent rugby) that perpetuates the practice of PE separation. Considering it is disliked by many males and generates more anti-social behaviour than other sports, football receives fanatical support in and out of school. Even at primary level the members of the football team are given higher status than their counterparts in the netball team.

Some educationalists feel that the playing of adult games with young children is unjustified. More appropriate games – adaptations, perhaps, of their adult counterparts – could be devised. These allow essential skills to be developed and practised but allow greater individual participation. In contrast Whyte, however, would like separation of the sexes for sport to continue. She takes the view that the primary world is far too cosy, too like the Wendy House with its 'pleasant and reassuring experiences'.[19] Girls in particular, she feels, should be stretched and challenged rather than stultified as they are at present with its conventionalism:

> They could do with specific encouragement to become more independent, assured and intrepid, to take risks, to think and act for themselves. Perhaps while boys are in the classroom, catching up with the intellectual pace set by their female class-mates, the girls should be outside? Sports and venturesome physical activities will possibly help girls develop the healthy self-confidence, courage and independence they later seem to lack.[20]

For similar reasons a return to separate classes for some male-dominated subjects such as maths and physics is being argued for and even put into practice at secondary level.[21]

The separation of pupils for any activity, however useful in the short term, can only perpetuate old ideals rather than promote the new ones. Teachers and pupils must simply stop thinking in terms of boys and girls. Tann's findings on group work exposed the tip of an ominous iceberg. She found no mixed-sex groups formed by free choice. Where groups were allocated rather than chosen, single-sex groups worked differently but well together. Mixed-sex groups, however, repeatedly gave problems:

> the members at best tolerated each other and at worst swore at each other . . . the problems . . . became sharper with older pupils; indeed in only one instance was it possible to persuade a mixed-sex group, in the secondary school, to participate at all.[22]

The indications are that teachers must adopt positive strategies for persuading pupils to think of themselves and others as individuals. They could start with simple but important practices such as not

Girls and boys equally enjoying a primary school games lesson.

separating register names into boys and girls and not lining children
up separately (even for the school nurse). Sitting or working with the
opposite sex should never be seen as a punishment. Indeed, teachers
should show they approve of such practice. Stereotyped views
should never be attached to any activity, whether it be caring for a
young pupil or being untidy. Children should be actively encouraged to try equipment and activities that some parents would think
inappropriate for their sex. Sexist comments by pupils, demeaning
or ridiculing the opposite sex, should never be accepted or, worse
still, laughed at. All pupils should be expected to achieve the same
standards of behaviour. This includes allowing them (and their

teachers) to dress appropriately and comfortably for activities. If dresses or short trousers restrict play, are cold and uncomfortable or inhibit their wearers from dirty or active tasks, they should not be compulsory.

The list of such positive moves to equality is long and liable to continuous additions. Success will be unlikely, however, if the materials presented to children perpetuate stereotype views. Some early readers have been heavily criticised on this front. Lobban, for example, found six popular schemes, including 'Nippers' and 'Breakthrough to Literacy' rigidly divided activities into masculine and feminine. There were more male-type activities depicted and males had more fun. Indeed female activities were almost entirely domestic. Parents were frequently shown in 'conventional' roles, Dad instructing and Mum in the kitchen.[23] Traditional stories also do not help. As Frazier and Sadker point out, far too many of the heroines sit with fans in their hands and combs in their hair or lie in bed staring at the ceiling, wishing they had beautiful jewellery to wear at the ball.[24] Roald Dahl's *Revolting Rhymes*[25] has moved some way to counteracting such images. His Red Riding Hood certainly is not 'a girl bordering on mental deficiency'.

Textbooks can similarly be sex-biased. Walden and Walkerdine found many contained subtle clues about the masculinity and femininity of the activities to which mathematics relates.[26] Coote found that science books showed boys using torches and technical instruments whilst girls blew bubbles (presumably with their washing-up water). Few show women in a broad range of careers and tasks.[27] The language used can be equally sexist – describing 'a farmer and his wife', rather than 'a farm couple'; claiming that 'women were given the vote' rather than that they won it.[28] Weiner points out that publishers have been far too slow to realise the hidden assumptions in their books.[29] The Sex Discrimination Act makes it illegal to treat one sex less favourably than the other, and it has been suggested that if taken to court some books could be shown to be in breach of the law for their unfavourable influence. Certainly in Sweden a picture showing 'mother baking cakes' would not receive official approval.[30] Meanwhile it is up to publications such as *Spare Rib* and the *Children's Book Bulletin* to list and review non-sexist books.

Changes in attitude to the different sexes will not be easy. The increase in single parenthood, divorce and unemployment is effecting changing views in society. Fathers do now raise families or stay at home while mothers go out to work. Job sharing at home and in employment is increasing. However, many people, including teachers, still think in terms of sex stereotypes. To meet the requirements of the 1975 Act in spirit as well as kind will mean them reflecting, sometimes painfully, on their own attitudes. A recent survey of secondary teachers, for example, found half of male and one in three female staff were opposed to equal opportunity practices. Strong opposition came from over one in four men and one in seven women. Unless teachers are willing to eradicate sexism in their own and their pupils' lives it will persist. Whatever the legal requirement one cannot help others to feel equal whilst feeling unequal oneself. Equal opportunity is not a regular cause for concern in staff-rooms. Indeed, the subject gains little support on in-service courses and in the literature. Many consider that equal opportunity already exists, that sexism is not a problem or, if it is, there is little the school can do about it.[31] Research and experience show they are seriously mistaken.

Conflicts and Resources

CHAPTER 22

Eggsperiments

'Can we throw eggs today?'

It was a genuine question. We had explored just about every aspect of eggs: their structure, the different properties of yolk and white; the relationship between weight, size and the standard egg gradings. We had worked out ways of making a perfect boiled egg and telling a boiled from an unboiled egg. The edible products of our labours had been used to see if brown eggs were different from white. We had also stuffed them and made pancakes, real custard and meringues. The shells had also been used. Some crushed and dyed, had been used to make mosaics. Others, decorated with faces, grinned at us; their faces surmounted by hair of cress grown on cotton wool under different conditions. Then one member of the class reported seeing children throwing eggs on television to test their strength. We'd already mavelled at the weight an egg would support. The new test seemed a good way to conclude the project.

During break I examined the playing field. Conditions seemed favourable. The underlying soil was sandy and stone-free; the grass, thick and dry. Watched in amazement by my colleagues in the staff-room, I lobbed an egg with a gentle overarm bowl. It obligingly bounced several times before coming to rest some distance away unbroken. Things looked hopeful. We'd have a go!

Of the forty-two children hurrying onto the pitch a significant number considered that the six eggs I had dedicated to the activity would not survive long enough to give them a turn. We evolved a routine. Having chosen a number from a hat the pupils lined up across the pitch to observe the proceedings. Taking turns they were to throw the egg, count the bounces then retrieve it before joining the end of the queue. I agreed to tally the results.

With baited breath we waited while Martin, a sports enthusiast, demonstrated a perfect overarm. The egg bounced and rotated three times before coming to rest. It survived. We applauded the superb performance. Six throws later, and still unbroken, Jill passed the egg to Brian. I glowered fiercely along the line, suppressing the faint groan that had begun to run along it. Brian, left-handed and badly co-ordinated, hesitated. It seemed opportune to use his handicap to advantage.

'Have a go, Brian,' I encouraged. 'You might be the first to break the egg and give the seagulls a feast.'

Brian looked more cheerful. Lifting the egg behind his left ear he flung it forward. Bouncing once, it rolled to rest still whole. There were murmurs of surprise then applause.

Super Egg was to survive forty-one throws in all – the expert and the clumsy, the high, the low, the long and the short. Only Bobby remained. A small, very slight child, he had only recently been promoted from the remedial class. Shyly he received the egg from Brenda.

'Good luck, Bobby,' I encouraged. 'It's now up to you to break the egg.'

The rest of the class murmured support. 'You can do it, Bob!' 'Come on, Bobby.'

As he thrust his arm back there was silence. Hurling the egg as high as he could into the air he watched for a moment, then set off running below it like a fielder after a cricket ball. A cheer went up. Encouraged, Bobby quickened his pace. The egg bounced at his feet, once . . . twice . . . then, crash! Down on top of it fell our final contestant! We all dashed forward but need not have worried. Beaming with egg all down his jumper, Bobby was jubilant.

'I broke it! I broke it!' he yelled. 'I'm the greatest!'

CHAPTER 23

Even the kitchen sink: conflict over resources

Teachers have always used a variety of aids to enhance lessons. These have varied from concrete materials such as eggs to audio-visual equipment such as film and slide projectors. Some are more helpful to teachers than others. The number of cassette recorders, televisions and workcards in school are proof of this. The popularity of some products is not always a measure of their educational value. All resources are capable of use as well as abuse. Many primary school children regularly run the loneliness of the long-distance workcard. Indiscriminate use of television may provide a rest period for staff rather than a stimulus for further investigation and learning. Some apparatus also lies gathering dust on shelves.

School resources scarcely seem an area where conflict could arise. Nevertheless it does. Enforced use of media, the need for teachers to make apparatus and lack of funds for teaching aids have all produced conflict within the profession. Arguments have also raged over the most suitable content and appearance of books for children at both the initial and higher reading stages. This chapter describes some of the resources found in schools and the conflict that surrounds their use.

Objects as aids

In 1882 the government code stated that lessons on objects were to be encouraged in infant schools. By 1895 they became obligatory for all children.[1] 'Object lessons' had in fact formed a part of standard elementary school practice from the 1850s arising from the teachings of Pestalozzi. He believed that efficient learning involves the development of a set of images, concepts or sensory-motor patterns that form a model for further experiences.[2] Circular 369[3] to the Inspectorate maintained that the successful lesson had two parts to it: observation of the object itself and the imparting of information about it. The work was also intended to go beyond the classroom, with children bringing in items of their own and outside visits to museums and other educational institutions. At the time of the recommendation, schools contained jaded teachers battling with large classes and a widening curriculum.[4] Specialists such as Miall were running courses to try to improve practice,[5] and the Inspectorate were reprinting and distributing Circular 369.

In practice object lessons were not the 'interesting and often delightful feature of school work' that writers such as Forster would have us believe.[6] Good teachers certainly tried to make lessons interesting with pictures, blackboard drawings or relevant concrete materials. However, they often lacked cohesion and continuity, the camel being studied after a lesson on the clock, followed by work on coal. Concern was also expressed that object lessons without an object were not uncommon. Howard, HMI, reminded teachers that the aim was to develop children's observational powers and language. He suggested they prepare lessons carefully beforehand, considering the questions children might raise. Also at least one lesson per week should be conducted without a single utterance from the teacher. Observation sheets were to be used to record sightings from nature and items of social or political interest.[7]

By the turn of the century object teaching was on the decline, receiving its last mention in the 1905 *Handbook of Suggestions for Teachers*.[8] However, objects have continued to play an important role. Modern schools offer rich environments in terms of actual concrete materials although the emphasis today is on children handling rather than viewing at a distance. Collections of natural objects such as frog spawn, twigs and snowdrops may enhance work in art and science. Activity tables with items to explore and investigate can enrich topic work. Structured apparatus from Cuisenaire rods to Lego Technic has been developed to aid concepts in maths and science or the development of the senses. Specially designed equipment from giant callipers to hand lenses is available for observation and measurement.

Objects and apparatus alone, though, will not ensure learning. Primary school children indulge annually in 'autumn studies'. They collect leaves, and print with, rub and mount them on displays; yet at eleven years few pupils can identify any but the oak.[9] The 1978 DES survey found that children rarely drew or painted from careful observation of things around them;[10] also, that when such activities

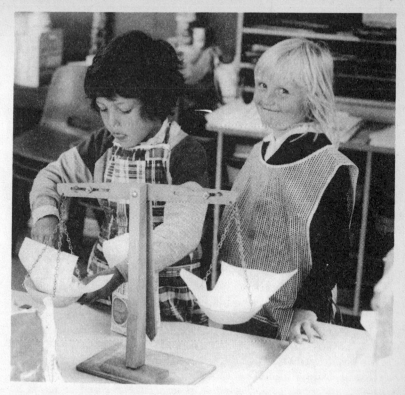

The modern primary curriculum benefits from provision of a wide range of specialist resources.

did occur there was insufficient observation or discussion before the work began.[11] Accurate or careful measurement in science, craft and social studies was just as rare.[12] Thus, work with objects still needs development in today's schools.

Home-made equipment

If effective use of equipment and apparatus is difficult for teachers, the situation is further exacerbated if pupils and teachers must make apparatus for themselves. Such items must compare favourably with their professionally produced counterparts if they are to have appeal to modern consumer-conscious pupils. They must also be used with caution, few being suitable for use from generation to generation.

The situation presents the 'Catch 22' that teachers must spend hours preparing items of equipment, such as workcards, which, by definition are intended to meet specific needs at specific times. Fortunately most primary teachers enjoy preparing some special or different sets of materials for their children. Pupils, too, often enjoy books, games and apparatus that they have written or prepared for each other more than the less personalised items from educational suppliers.

The making of apparatus can greatly add to studies. However, it can be demanding on teachers in terms of time, money and, more importantly, expertise. A useful example might be taken from the Schools Council 5/13 (SC5/13) unit, *Working with Wood*. This states that 'when children are reasonably competent at handling wood and tools, it's very exciting for them to make something of direct use to the school'.[13] Underneath is a picture of a nesting box, but no help is given with essential design features of such an item. For example, an ideal nesting box should have the inside left unplaned so that young birds can gain a footing on the surface. The entrance hole also needs to be bored at an angle from above or sawn obliquely with a coping saw and afterwards filed if rain is not to enter and soak the feathery occupants. The front wall needs to be removable for cleaning, yet the unit shows it firmly nailed in place. Finally, certain measurements must be strictly adhered to if a box intended for bluetits is not to be invaded by sparrows.

Thus to suggest blindly that children can be let loose with hammers and saws in a classroom is at least naïve and at worst a remedy for certain failure. The one subject where this is part of in-built philosophy is primary science. Indeed, the terms 'squeezy bottle science' or 'jam jar science' are often used to describe the approach. Traditionally everyday materials gained emphasis because complex equipment was thought to confuse young children and interfere with the principles being taught.[14] In 1961 the Ministry of Education claimed that the more homely the apparatus, the more telling the experiment,[15] and the Association for Science Education (ASE) saw such materials providing a useful link between home and school for the child.[16] Early recommendations excluded the use of any specialised equipment. By the end of the Nuffield Junior Science Project necessary equipment was being listed,[17] though many of the included items would not generally be called specialised. Although UNESCO have for some years produced a book of home-made apparatus for teachers in the Third World, the Nuffield team was the first to produce one for Britain. This emphasised the need for children to design equipment for themselves and contained ideas of what might be achieved. Having such practice as part of the essential philosophy of primary science could, because of the organisational and time factors involved, be one reason why teachers experience great problems with its teaching.

Books

Although concrete materials have been used by teachers for many years the oldest teaching aid of all is probably the book. Certainly the Bible has had an important place in British schools for centuries, forming the first reading material for many pupils including the young John Wesley. Books in primary schools were vital at the time of the Hadow Report as children below eleven years were then excluded from most public libraries. Even in the 1960s, 29 per cent of homes owned a desultory five books or less,[18] and the problems of the 1980s have ensured that such items remain a low priority for many families. A similar attitude is found in LEAs. In 1975 the Bullock Committee found the amount spent on books by authorities disappointingly small, some of them not even meeting the Association of Education Committees' (AEC) 'reasonable' expenditure recommendations.[19] Also criticised was the practice of linking books with non-teaching costs, which made them particularly vulnerable when competing with salaries of ancillary workers and maintenance or repair costs.[20] They recommended that, until new proposals could be made, AEC levels should be seen as minimum and be met by all authorities.[21] Rising costs in the 1980s have kept books low on the list of educational needs.

Even when adequate money is available for books they need choosing carefully. In times of financial stringency the need for control is even greater. The 1978 survey found that over half of the schools surveyed had teachers carrying responsibility for library provision.[22] The Bullock Committee three years earlier, however, had found that their duties tended to be simple and administrative. Few acted as guides to colleagues on sources of children's literature. Few had prepared guidelines for acquiring books or charted their dispersal throughout their institution.[23] There is therefore a lack of expertise in book selection in the primary sector. A valuable source of the required information is available from the Schools Library Association, although in 1975 only 12 per cent of primary schools were members.[24] Many authorities also arrange exhibitions to facilitate browsing. But attendance is sometimes difficult to organise and good choice often requires more than a brief skim of contents.

Some books, for example, contain serious inaccuracies. Pollard quotes the case where the captions to drawings showing edible and poisonous fungi were transposed.[25] Concepts may also be confused. Whittaker found that books with 'animals' and 'wildlife' in their title

generally contained only mammals or vertebrates.[26] Other books
may contain out-of-date information or views. Pollard found encyclopaedias notorious on these counts, long sales periods being
required to repay initial publication costs.[27] Research has also
shown that many books intended to support topic work with young
children contain inadequate information. Having embarked on the
observation of some nesting birds, Bainbridge listed the questions
raised; books offered no help on a third of them. He concluded that
the absence of good literature can mitigate against the full development of junior school projects. Furthermore, initial observations
that have a ring of originality in them may well be short-lived
because of lack of support material.[28]

Books and reading

Higher reading scores at nine are associated with effective use by
children of book collections or libraries.[29] It is therefore important
that children not only have a wide range of different kinds of book
available to them but that they are at the right level and designed to
aid research skills. One means of matching written materials to
children's abilities is to assess their readability level. Several formulae
are available for this. Once books are coded, pupils are able to choose
more accurately those at the right level for their needs. Non-fiction
books also need to aid rather than hinder research. Those for young
children might have page headings as in a dictionary to indicate
content. Where an index is present, it must be carefully designed for
young users. As Pollard points out, a child using a book on trains is
more likely to look up 'Rocket' or 'Stephenson' than 'Liverpool and
Manchester Railway'.[30] Similarly, a child interested in tap-dancing
does not wish to embark on a vast hierarchical search beginning at
'Leisure'. Pictures should be clear and directly related to adjoining
text. A range of books from dictionary to thesaurus and atlas to
anthology should also be available so that pupils may learn to search
for different types of information in different ways.

Early reading materials

One of the most costly items for infant schools and departments can
be the reading scheme. Whilst many educationalists would argue
that this is not a necessary tool for learning to read, most schools use
at least one of them. All schools visited during the 1978 HMI survey
used schemes. Grundin's research in the same year also showed that
typical infant practice was the use of one major scheme with two to

four supplementary ones.[31] In 1982 roughly twenty-eight schemes were in print with original publication dates from 1921 to 1982.[32] Over this period of time there have been vast changes in reading practice and in the style of children's reading materials. The early phonic primers have 'pigs in wigs dancing jigs'. The 'look-and-say' schemes drone with repetitious monotony, 'Look, look, look. Oh, oh, oh. Oh look. Oh look, Jane.' Neither style reflects real speech by real people. The books also often present outmoded attitudes to sexual or racial equality and authority. More modern schemes tend to begin with real stories. Some like Sparks are designed specifically to appeal to urban children with families living in flats and leading less than perfect lives.

Occasionally an older scheme will be updated. Ladybird restyled the clothes and hair of their children and added a multi-cultural flavour. Nisbets replaced Janet and John with Kathy and Mark when sales fell. New schemes such as Ginn 360 are sometimes produced to meet new needs. Schemes represent big business for publishers as they do not simply consist of reading books. Support materials range from puppets to flash cards, spirit masters and workbooks. The more dependent success is upon such additions, the greater the income. Thus schemes such as Ginn 360 provide a total approach to reading from reception to top juniors and beyond.

New ideas need support if they are not to fail. When Ford Farm decided to adopt the Initial Teaching Alphabet (ITA) as a medium for developing literacy it joined many others in a government-sponsored experiment. The simplified code did seem successful. The Schools Council, for example, came to the conclusion that 'the best way to learn to read in traditional orthography is to learn to read in the initial teaching alphabet'.[33] But many parents were cautious if not antagonistic to the idea. Few publishers printed in the new alphabet so that few books in ITA were available outside school. Schools themselves had to purchase reading materials in both ITA and TO. Some junior teachers, as at Ford Farm, were also unwilling to continue using the medium with pupils over seven. Consequently few schools now teach reading through ITA and publishers who invested in the alphabet will now have to cut their losses.

It seems therefore that teachers are attracted to the idea of reading schemes. They appear to provide a step-by-step structure in which they can operate. Fashions as to what form this structure should take have altered over the years. Indeed, by attempting to divide reading into steps it is possible that the total process – reading critically, habitually and for pleasure – is ignored. Many schemes have bored children and may well have contributed to literacy problems. A significant number of pupils have probably learned to read despite them.

Alternative approaches to reading

Because of the problems presented by schemes some teachers have opted to teach reading without them. In a 'language experience approach' the pupils themselves generate the ideas and materials for learning using their own interests as starting points. Sylvia Ashton Warner, who developed the approach, describes how it works:

> Primer children write their own books. Early in the morning this infant room gets under way in organic writing, and it is this writing that I use in relative proportions as the reading for the day . . . In this way we have a set of graded brand-new readers every morning, each sprung from the circumstances of their own lives and illustrated unmatchably in the mind.[34]

In their writing the children use what Sylvia Ashton Warner calls their 'key vocabularics' – words and phrases that have powerful, personal meaning for them.

Breakthrough to Literacy is a scheme that attempts to capture this highly individual approach and package it for general use. Unfortunately, the 'key vocabulary' provided is as stilted and artificial as that in many books despite allowing children to add important words of their own. The Bullock Committee pointed out that it has provided

> a stimulus to teachers to adopt the language experience approach and in offering them help. Whether or not the knowledgeable teacher needs this practical material once the approach is well established is open to question. And, of course, some teachers may prefer from the outset to use materials they have produced themselves for the same purpose.[35]

Yet Breakthrough does provide some useful support books and since its first publication in 1970 has produced several new titles and blank books for the children's own stories. Sylvia Ashton Warner had to write her own Maori scheme for the transitional readers in her class. It provided a bridge between their own writing and the available European reading materials. Many teachers adopting her philosophy are reluctant to revert to set schemes with the older children. Generally a system of 'individualised reading' is preferred. Here a wide range of fiction and non-fiction books – sometimes including some from schemes – are offered to the children. Like library books they are colour-coded so pupils can make choices at their own level. Supporters of the approach claim it offers a more attractive range of reading material than normal and that, in offering real choice to the children, rather than a paper rung in a pre-determined reading ladder, motivation is increased.

Individualised reading approaches are very demanding on the teacher, who must meticulously grade individual books within it and keep careful records of progress. Many teachers will continue to use schemes as they provide a step-by-step structure within which they can work plus a wealth of additional materials. Publishers will also strongly support the continuation of the practice, since any popular scheme has considerable earning potential.

Workcards and workbooks

Although sets of identical textbooks may not be found in most primary schools today, children still tend to follow published schemes in a range of subjects at their own level. These may be sets of books or workcards. Almost all upper junior classes in 1978 used commercial materials for reading, writing and mathematics. Over half also used them in geography and history. Science, too, has not escaped the phenomenon. Early projects such as Nuffield generally frowned on the use of workcards, seeing them only as a useful aid in organisation for teachers moving towards a freer approach in science. At the time, of course, many 'closed' investigations were suggested in the form of 'experiments to prove . . .'. The Schools Council Science 5/13 project (SC5/13) also produced materials for teachers rather than for children, considering that this was a better way of promoting a process rather than a content approach. However, in 1978 Albert James, a member of the SC5/13 team, produced a set of pupil workbooks called 'Active Science'. These closely reflected the content and ideas of the project. The Learning Through Science team also adapted ideas from the SC5/13 units to produce sets of workcards. Now such cards have support from the DES, recognition of the fact, perhaps, that teachers need support with this difficult subject.

Use of individual assignment books or cards illustrates the response by teachers to pressures for individualised learning. With these items they gain a security (which might be false) that they are both coping with individual differences and ensuring progress. Some claim that children are less aware of 'streaming' when assignment cards are used. In practice such claims are doubtful. Whatever the system adopted, children tend to identify an order of progress and thus the least and most able users. Many such materials also suffer the same problems as the early object lessons, in that new ground is covered on every page or card. Exercises, of course, may be connected into a theme. Indeed, Fletcher Maths produces a chart to encourage this.[36]

Exercises from books and cards may also result in concentration on unintended rather than intended skills. Some maths books, for example, have a high reading age in contrast to the level of mathematics covered. Activities such as drawing a chart may occupy more time than the analysis of results within it. Missing word exercises may be reduced to the matching of a set list to the text rather than the exploration of a range of possible inclusions. Individual tasks can be an inefficient means of teaching. As new ideas are introduced teachers have to deal with them individually rather than with a group or the class. Cards may contain too many or unrealistic ideas. History cards, for example, which contain activity sections suggesting that a child paint a frieze of 'transport through the ages' are bound to be unpopular, at least with teachers. The 'Learning Through Science' workcards have been criticised for containing too many activities on one card and being better resources for teachers than for children.

Some faults with schemes or workcards result from misuse rather than content. A good example is the SRA (Scientific Research Associates) Reading Laboratories. These form a graded scheme for the development of reading skills from pre-school child to student. The teaching of the higher skills of reading is not always adequately dealt with in the junior school. Three quarters of eleven-year-olds were not taught them at all and the others had no planned regular course. Packs such as SRA aid such skills and could therefore be a valuable resource. The SRA handbook clearly states, however, that the older pupils' cards should be used daily but only for one term. Few schools adhere to this advice, many forcing children to work through them weekly throughout their primary careers.

Fletcher Maths is also seriously misused. The books are designed to extend the work in informal classrooms. Children should first carry out a wide range of activities with real materials and then practise the new concepts from the book. One child using Fletcher Maths was in conversation with a friend from a neighbouring 'formal' school. The latter was heard to boast that they had regular maths tests. The Fletcher 'product' replied that every page of his book was a test of the practical work he had been doing. His teacher was suitably proud of the response. In practice, unfortunately, many users of the scheme omit the practical work and allow children to progress through page by page. The book is given total control of the syllabus.

Blenkin and Kelly totally reject the use of such schemes for teaching:

> Sequenced material of this kind in schools is unlikely to improve the teacher's practice. The evidence of those that have tried to do so suggests that good teachers become inhibited by the sequence and weak teachers become over-dependent on the materials. It would be a comfort if the activities asked of children by these books were at least a substitute for poor teaching, but many children . . . become confused

by the instructions . . . because they depend largely on two-dimensional sketches.[37]

If used correctly good workcards can prove effective. The 1978 DES survey, for example, found that higher average reading scores at eleven were associated with their use. At their worst they can produce lonely, isolated learners grinding through daily exercises with little opportunity to share experiences, recognise patterns and relationships, brainstorm ideas or collaborate to a given end.

Audio-visual aids

New audio-visual hardware is often treated with scepticism by teachers, who frequently have expensive unused items gathering dust in school cupboards. In 1976 it was estimated that some 200,000 filmstrip projectors had been bought by schools, a staggering seven per institution.[38] Whilst in the 1950s film was regarded as the medium of the future, teachers now seem to prefer slides and, indeed, often convert filmstrips to this form. Modern slide projectors allowing remote control or response to tape pulses have made this a more flexible medium. Teachers and children can also easily and cheaply produce their own tape slide sequences, perhaps presenting an audio-visual story or some information on a new project.

Cassette recorders are today one of the most widely used pieces of hardware in school. Connected to earphones, children can listen to stories accompanying written text or work through a programme of activities to develop listening skills. They can record interviews with people, produce plays or poems with sound effects or record their own creative music. They can also express their ideas in an alternative form to writing that can, if necessary, be typed up for them. This is particularly important for children who find writing difficult. At Eastlea, for example, the remedial class used the medium to produce a regular audial school magazine to which all classes contributed.

The Language Master is a specialised piece of hardware that uses cards with a strip of recording tape on their base. Recordings can be made on to the tape which the machine can then reproduce. Thus pictures, words or sentences can be drawn or written at the top of the card and a spoken accompaniment placed on the tape below. Children can therefore listen to words as they read them. Alternatively they can read cards aloud into the machine and then check their accuracy against the master voice. The Language Master is easy to use and prepare materials for. It gives children independence in their learning and immediate feedback on their reading efforts.

Tape recordings are also used frequently by teachers to monitor teaching and learning. This sometimes begins as part of an in-service course but can continue to be a valuable means of evaluation in school. They may listen to themselves in dialogue with a group of children. Alternatively they may tape children as they work to monitor the interaction and nature of discussion within a set task.

Television and radio

Radio programmes have been used in schools for about fifty years, and the first experiment in school television was tried out in the early 1950s.[39] A 1972 survey found examples of versatile and imaginative use of the two resources.[40] Some teachers, however, used too many programmes without adequate preparation and follow-up. The 1978 survey should the majority of classes using educational television but rather less using radio.[41] The most valued television programmes aided science teaching. The report found that they made a significant contribution to work in the subject and expressed surprise that 'in a subject where many teachers lacked confidence in their own abilities, more use was not made of this resource'.[42] The most popular use of radio was for music teaching. Again, the programmes made a fundamental contribution and were frequently followed up by teachers 'who made no claims to musicianship but felt it important that their classes should have the opportunity for this kind of work'.[43]

One of the greatest problems in using broadcasts in the past has been one of inflexibility. Programmes rarely followed an integrated sequence, and another programme in a series was often on the air before a previous one could be followed up adequately. Tape and video recorders have alleviated the problem considerably. Indeed, with their use, teachers need not now follow a series regularly, but integrate elements of several series into their own chosen project. This would seem to be a far better use of the medium.

Technological white elephants

Educational technology is accepted into schools when it is con-venient to use and when good materials are either supplied or readily produced by teachers and pupils themselves. Technology not offering these facilities tends to find more space on shelves than in the classroom. An example is the teaching machine. At the time of the Plowden Report this was the latest and most controversial teaching aid. Linear programmes for teaching machines broke tasks down into fine steps of learning and presented them to children in a logical sequence. Users were told at each stage whether their responses were right or wrong and progress was dependent on its mastery. Branching programmes gave children a choice of responses at each stage. Incorrect answers resulted in children being led to a sequence of activities that corrected their errors.

Teaching machines never became popular in Britain. Their use was more conducive to instruction than education and they therefore conflicted with philosophies of informal discovery method that gained support soon after their introduction. The technology was also inadequate. As one teacher found:

> The machine 'knitted' the programme . . . and the use of many in a classroom would have necessitated a full-time auxiliary with the sole duty of unjamming the mechanism and maintaining a smooth programme flow.[44]

The teacher finally designed his own machine and programmes. The latter in itself was no easy task. The analysis of stages of learning has been a popular tendency for some years. Unfortunately individuals vary considerably in the way they learn so that, even if stages can be worked out, a programme suitable for one individual may be totally unsuitable for another. Few published programmes were available for this reason and few teachers had the time, knowledge or skill to produce their own. When produced, use of a programme was then no guarantee of learning. The present writer once completed one on ohms yet at the end did not know what an ohm was. Dividing learning into fine steps actually sometimes confused children who would have benefited more from seeing the task or concept as a whole.

Teaching machines have not been the only technological white elephant. An attempt to introduce a machine offering 'talking pages' into the schools of one authority failed completely when the manufacturer went bankrupt. Many other pieces of equipment lie unused after an initial burst of enthusiastic experimentation. Eventually they become broken and too old or expensive to repair. Discarded equipment can also be evidence of an individual fad not shared by other colleagues. Frequently equipment is simply hoarded away by magpie-like owners and rarely used.

Summary

As compulsory education was introduced so were compulsory teaching aids. 'Object lessons' became common practice and at their best supported discussion and observation in school. However, lessons without objects predominated and emphasis on the approach declined.

Teachers still use concrete materials in school although the In-spectorate find a need to press for improved usage. Teachers also often have to make apparatus themselves. This can cause problems. The results must frequently match propriety counterparts in quality yet be dispensable, having been made to meet particular needs at particular times. There are also problems in requiring both pupils and teachers to make apparatus. Children often lack the necessary expertise, and teachers may find such requirements a deterrent. However, both teachers and children do enjoy producing materials for each other and they can often be richer and more personalised than published equivalents.

Books, the oldest teaching aid, are the source of many problems in school. Their provision has been seriously affected by financial cut-backs over the years. Choice of suitable reading materials for children is also not easy. Those for older pupils may hinder research and comprehension. Reading schemes for the initial stages may be boring or inappropriate, or bare little resemblance to real situations and speech patterns. Attempts at producing 'total literacy' packages have sometimes over-generalised the individual essence of their original inspirers. The appeal of apparent structure and pressure from publishers will nevertheless ensure the continued popularity of reading schemes in schools.

Workcards and workbooks continue to be prevalent in today's classrooms. They are often used as a response to pressure for more individualised learning. Many schemes are not only misused, they are positively abused. They can isolate children from the collabor-ation learning that Galton and colleagues (see p. 97) considered so essential for effective learning.

Audio-visual apparatus has had variable use in school. Some items such as the tape recorder and television have proved popular. Others lie on the shelf gathering dust. Sceptics have wondered whether microcomputers, the latest educational aid, may be added to this list in future years. There is good reason to think that they will not, though Chapter 25 considers some problems in their use.

CHAPTER 24

When is a rabbit not a rabbit?

Teachers use many aids to support their teaching. The 1980s, for example, have seen a major influx of rabbits into schools. Educationalists have, of course, had contact with and experience of rabbits since the 1950s through behaviourist research. Their shortage and expense, however, made them a rare presence in school until the late 1970s when a new bread of rabbit (cheaper and smaller) plus a new type of lettuce (Cos 3.0 and the later Cos 3.4) made them a new and viable educational tool.

The French were the first to recognise the political implications, announcing that they would aim to provide two free rabbits to every secondary school in the country. In Britain enthusiasts saved carefully to purchase one of their own. Even primary teachers 'bit the carrot', many gaining rabbits through contacts in the field. The work and opinions of these pioneers rapidly became the basis for articles, media interviews and films. Great claims were made as to their effectiveness as a learning and teaching tool. Mrs Bunny Hutch, Watership Down Primary School, for example, said:

'Since we have had our rabbit the children are enjoying school more. They now arrive early and there is a never-ending supply of willing hands to feed it. The rabbit has solved all our behaviour problems.'

Rabbi T. Pie, writing in the *PTA News*, Warren Bank School, stressed the difference it had made to his own child:

Young Sam was poor at maths. Since measuring and weighing the rabbit, counting its whiskers and working on sums such as, 'If one rabbit has four legs how many do three have?', his interest has been captured and he is now almost up to the standard of the rest of the class.

Early users were surprised to find that no particular specialism was required for the new resource, though some claimed that one expert per school would be necessary even at primary level to encourage good use. Course and development groups formed to consider 'rabbits across the curriculum'. Finally the government, seeing an opportunity to boost British agriculture, launched a 9 million programme to examine the 'Rabbit Involvement Potential' (RIP). Through this, every secondary school was given opportunity to purchase a half-price rabbit provided it was of British stock. This was finally extended to primary schools after protests that their needs were equally great. Now most schools possess at least one – BBC rabbits (who have had both breeding and selling problems), Research Rabbits and Sinclair Bunnies being the most popular types.

The presence of so many rabbits in schools is now causing some problems. They are, for example, proving costly to feed and maintain. Suggestions have been made that they might be undermining the very foundations of our schools. Are the rabbit enthusiasts' claims justified, or would the same effects have been achieved with donkeys (the famous Buckthorn effect)? Already one survey has found a significant number of teachers using rabbits for routine and mundane tasks. Indeed, fears have been expressed that children may simply end up running the loneliness of the long-distance rabbit rather than being involved in the exciting problem-solving tasks we know that these creatures can provide. Projects like RATS (Rabbits and Teaching in School) are asking teachers, 'What are you doing with your rabbit in school?' 'Are your children simply sitting down and watching it or are you using it for active learning?' 'Is your rabbit solving teaching problems or is it a problem waiting for a solution that is not forthcoming?' If readers find that this is the case they should probably pop their rabbit in a pie and buy a microcomputer. At least we know what to do with them.

CHAPTER 25

The micro: another white elephant?

Into the vast arena of resources used by teachers there has recently appeared the microcomputer. This particular teaching aid deserves special attention; for not only is it the most recent, but its widespread application allows a review of many aspects of education. Even before initiatives to support schools with half the cost of such a machine, primary teachers were providing them out of their own pockets. In 1978 Jones found that over thirty primary schools owned microcomputers and many others had occasional access to them for teaching.[1] In the 1980s their use is widespread, most primary schools having at least one machine at their disposal.

To justify such a major commitment there has emerged a plethora of arguments and rationales for a microcomputer's inclusion into a school's resources. These range from utilitarian claims – that acquaintance the technology will help prepare today's children for tomorrow's world – to educational arguments, that micros enhance classroom interaction and problem-solving. At worst such arguments are spurious. At best they have to be tempered with scepticism, since certain necessary pre-conditions are required for their achievement. This chapter examines some of these claims and conditions to evaluate whether the new technology will be just an expensive rabbit, perhaps another white elephant or a completely new species of resource for education.

Limitations of utilitarian justifications

The Department of Industry (DoI) initiative was launched with the sole aim of giving computer experiences that would help pupils and

Britain in the future. Baroness Young was careful to state when launching the scheme that 'It will ensure that the shortage of trained people is no longer a constraint on Britain's use of micro-electronics.'[2] Similarly Prime Minister Margaret Thatcher hoped, when officially announcing the 'Micros in Primary School' phase of the DoI offer in July 1982, that having microcomputers would mean that 'by the end of 1984, every primary school . . . will be giving young people the experience they need with the technology of their future working lives'.[3]

Educationalists such as Obrist also see 'preparation for the future' as a fundamental aim of their use in the classroom:

> Computers will undoubtedly come into ever wider use throughout the world, and this is an important reason why they should be brought into the educational environment. Children are growing up into a computer society and it is vital for them to become familiar with computers at an early age and to learn how to control computers rather than be controlled by them.[4]

Similar justifications are given for subjects such as 'computer studies' in secondary schools, plus a genre of software purporting to develop computer literacy skills and various schools' radio and television programmes. Such an argument might seem plausible to a country whose commitment to the new technology has resulted in the largest ownership of home computers in the world. However, are they merely words?

The term 'preparation for the future' seems to have at least three meanings: learning to run a computer and use the keyboard; learning to program; and learning about computers and how they work. That children will learn 'keyboard skills' may be a valid reason for supporting the use of computers in school. Recent research at Exeter University, for example, revealed that for employment potential with computers 'the most important skills a child could acquire were keyboard skills'.[5] Stated crudely, this means 'learning to touch-type'. Most efforts in school, however, have interpreted 'keyboard skills' as training children to recognise the position of keys on the keyboard visually. The 'Welcome Pack' provided to all schools receiving a BBC machine, for example, has programs requiring children to find letters of the alphabet and certain computer keys, such as 'delete', on command.

Similarly, the 'keyboard literacy' section of 'Passing our Test on the Micro', in the magazine *Primary Teaching and Micros (PTM)*,[6] requires children to remember the position of keys on a blank keyboard diagram and to type strings of letters and numbers (including a sentence containing words such as 'atmospherically' and 'ozone'!) in a set time. Both tasks seem at least a waste of time. At worst they might provide a whole generation of two-fingered typists since future transfer to touch typing might be extremely difficult. A significant number of schools have happily wasted hours putting children through the motions of these experiences. Had they, instead, launched pupils into some appropriate educational software demanding keyboard use, they would have seen recognition (though not typing) skills appear without training or prompting.

PTM considers that other skills are important enough to be monitored and recorded by teachers. Launched in 1985, it consists of a series of structured tests designed to provide primary teachers with a means of introducing 'the class to the computer whilst keeping a useful [*sic*] check on pupil progress'.[7] Badges and certificates are provided for the successful. The whole activity seems either to reduce the use of the micro to the lowest common denominator of skills – 'What is "micro" short for? Can child switch on power?' – or to concentrate on those that are completely irrelevant, asking, for example, whether the child can demonstrate how to LIST a program page by page or two ways of clearing the micro of a loaded program without switching the computer off. I confess to having used microcomputers for seven years without ever having to do either of these things. Again, using the micro regularly will help children learn certain management aspects. But they will be achieved incidentally and in context, not transposed into isolated exercises.

'Learning about computers' is another aspect of 'preparation for the future'. Schools television programmes for young children such as *The Micro at Work*[8] are specifically designed to give children insight into the role of computers in society and their potential impact on life in the future. Some of this information might well interest children, some might even be relevant to their understanding of the computer's potential and, hopefully, its limitations. But such courses may not prepare children for tomorrow. Will the technology of the future be similar or very different to that found in the present? Will it be programmed and utilised in similar or very different ways? Or is it likely that future users of microcomputers will no more think about their programming and functioning than readers think about the writing, typesetting and printing of books? Such forecasts are always difficult. The only fact that has emerged about teaching in general and computers in particular is that forecasts have been too conservative. For example, it was popular in the 1970s to present graphs showing ever increasing curves relating to computer compatibility.[9] Supporting text tended to refer to the ridiculous results if such curves were extrapolated. However, in the 1980s such extrapolations have proved to be hardly steep enough.

Can this constant emphasis on computers be justified? Televisions, telephones and even the wheel are all discoveries that have altered and permeated human lives, yet schools have never introduced such equipment for studying *per se*. Better than 'computer awareness' courses might be 'information technology courses' or 'media studies' which cover a wide range of information sources, their use and misuse.

There remains the teaching of programming in schools. Here conflict exists over whether programming as an activity is good preparation for future use of microcomputers. 'Programming' can have different meanings. To universities and employers it can mean learning to use specific languages such as Basic or Pascal. At another level, as Chandler points out, programming can be simply defined as 'an attempt to make a computer do what you want it to do in the language it allows you to use'.[10] Thus an infant child who makes the electronic toy tank Bigtrak move under a table to her friend's feet, stop and fire three times through pressing arrow and number keys can be said to be programming. At this level primary children can be regularly practising and developing programming skills. They can even 'program'. Papert's famous 'turtle' – a dome-shaped robot controlled by a computer language called Logo – provides children with a set of commands such as 'forward' and 'pen down' through which they can control the turtle's movements. As it can also leave a trail of ink from a strategically placed pen, a picture of the movements can be made. Thus the turtle can draw if given instructions by the child – a highly motivating task! Moving a turtle on the floor or on the screen with Logo commands is programming, and the sets of instructions (procedures) built up for specific moves, programs.

There is much evidence that, even using a narrow concept of programming, the activity can be a powerful educational tool. It has already been shown to be an effective way of establishing certain difficult mathematical concepts in children. Twice as many pupils learn algebra successfully through programming, for example, than through the standard alternative routes.[11] Apparently programming a computer provides structured activities that form crucial stepping stones leading children from concrete to formal reasoning and abstract skills. For algebra, programming tasks provide 'a semi-concrete model of the algorithmic processes involved'.[12] This leads to the formal reasoning skills characteristic of the subject.

The proposal to help children grasp abstract ideas through practical tasks is not new. It also need not involve programming on computers. Seymour Papert[13] was fascinated by the possibility for many years before developing Logo, and originally used 'gears' for modelling certain abstract mathematical concepts. The 'gears', he said, formed a micro (meaning small) world in which children could explore and control their own learning. Logo, a full programming language, of which turtle graphics are only a part, is also a micro-world. Logo as an educational tool has gained fanatical support across the world. An extreme view takes Logo to be the only computer microworld that exists for children. However, Fraser holds that the concept can apply to a wide range of computer software, particularly programs that allow children to design and control content. She uses several examples including a program called SLYFOX.

SLYFOX is a program that involves a search for something hidden in a scene. In the farm scene (figure 2) the children search around the regions, areas and objects for a fox; however, it could equally be a galleon scene with a search for a treasure map. The program aims to develop logic and language skills. According to Fraser SLYFOX can be called a microworld because it allows children to create scenes of their own. All scenes can be presented on SLYFOX provided the designer can conceptualise them in an appropriate way. You can see in the farm scene, for example, that the scene is split into a number of regions and wholly enclosed sub-regions (figure 3). The farm therefore consists of the farmyard, backyard and fields. The farmyard, in turn, consists of the garden, cowshed and garage. Each of these contains objects. Children must draw up scenes with a similar structure; they must also design warm, neutral or cold secret messages to help the searcher. The design of such scenes could also be defined as programming. The final result, rather than being a picture, however, is a game that can be played in a variety of ways at different levels.

For Fraser the key characteristic of programs such as Logo and SLYFOX is that, like many non-computer microworlds, they bring children into 'active learning modes'.[14] Both have a structure that confines and restricts children to a certain extent. Classes all over the world produce houses and gardens of flowers drawn by turtles and environment-based scenes with SLYFOX. Both programs, how-ever, give children control over their learning and confidence to learn from mistakes. In allowing children to incorporate their own ideas they are motivating for children.

Fraser has been interested in the way such programs 'impose shape' on children's thoughts and can 'offer back the same informa-tion in a range of shapes'.[15] Papert emphasised that they encourage a new relationship between pupils and teachers because of the 'real intellectual collaboration' the task involves.[16] This is supported by Shiengold's research[17] (which showed more interaction and col-laboration between pupils programming than in other classroom tasks) and by Stewart, who found more purposeful discussion arising from classification with the SEEK microworld than with similar activities on worksheets.[18] For these reasons turtle antics and

Figure 2   Drawing of the farm scene for SLYFOX

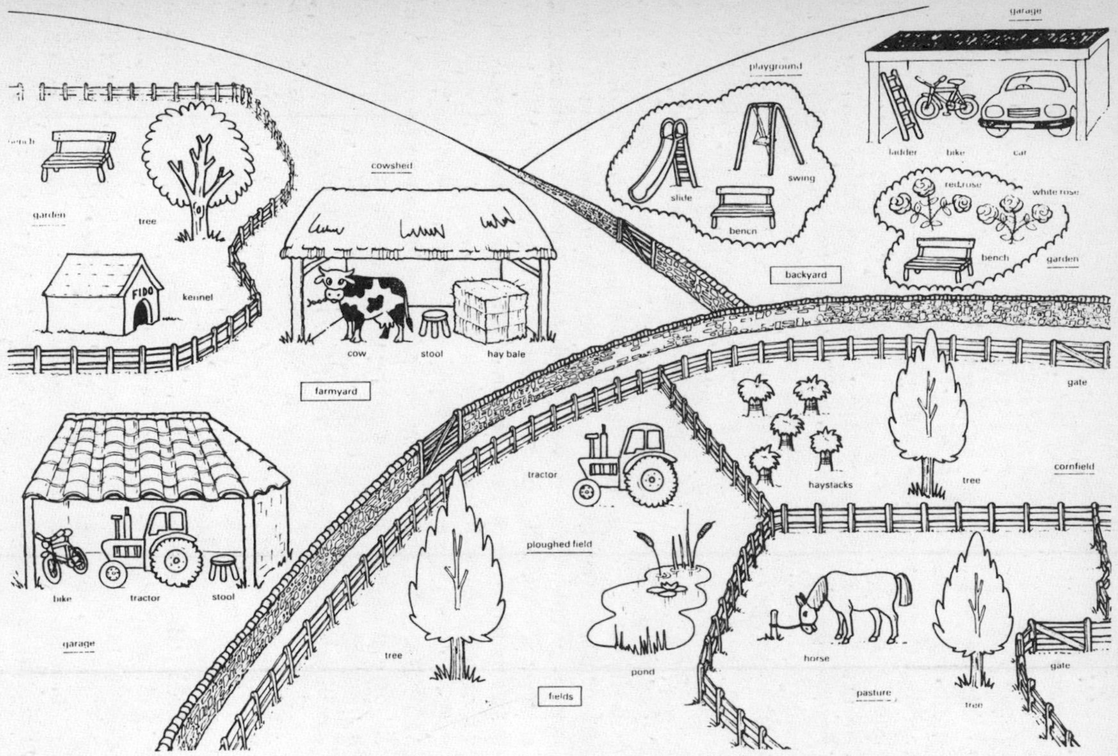

garage
ladder
bike
car
teeter-totter
white-rose
bench
garden
playground
swing
bench
slide
gate
cornfield
tree
gate
tree
pasture
haystacks
horse
backyard
cowshed
stool
hay bale
cow
tractor
ploughed field
pond
fields
farmyard
tree
bench
tree
kennel
garden
gate
pipe
stool
tractor
lake
garage

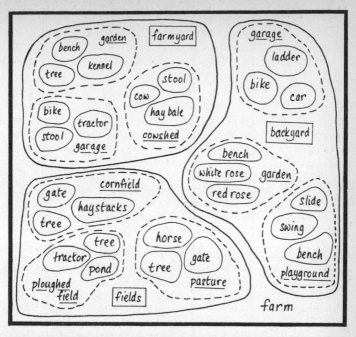

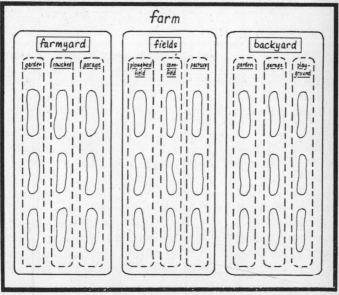

Figure 3   The Structure of the SLYFOX farm scene

pupil-designed hunts have become more popular in primary schools than learning languages like Basic.

Programming at all levels can therefore be justified in educational terms. Should they, however, be learning Basic or all applications of Logo? This topic causes great conflict between schools, universities and employers. A-levels in computing are not a prerequisite for entrance to university computing courses. In the past they complained that schools taught pupils to program in Basic. Employers in turn sometimes criticise university degrees in computing because most concentrate on programming in Pascal. Ball gives an amusing comment on the conflict:

> I have a colleague whose six-year-old son writes computer programs at home in Logo. He runs these programs, however, on a computer which is using a simulation of the screen-turtle aspect of Logo . . . written in Basic. Unfortunately my six-year-old will not write programs in Logo, not even when I offer him a computer loaded with real Logo . . . He prefers Basic, because the games programs he uses are written . . . in Basic. This is bad news, because Basic is a bad language and my six-year-old has no business wanting to use Basic . . . Prolog is not a bad language like Basic. On the other hand it is not a good language like Logo, because Logo is easier to teach to young children and generally easier to use, or so I am told. There are other languages such as Pascal (which is too hard), Fortran (which essentially is bad like Basic) and Smalltalk (which is good but even less available than Logo).[19]

The languages used to program computers today are unlikely to be used tomorrow. Fashions also change. Logo has recently gained respectability by being used to design business software.[20] Programming must therefore be carried out, in all its senses, for educational rather than utilitarian reasons.

Limitations on educational claims

Functionalist views of microtechnology in schools have fortunately subsided as educational software has improved. Now teachers are turning their attention, as Papert and Fraser did years ago, to the teaching and learning potential of the new technology. A popular trend is to claim that programs can promote individualised learning or the development of processes and skills such as discussion or problem-solving. Again, such global claims must be treated with caution. Like television, the technology is only as good as the programs available for its use. Computer programs include the equivalents of both *The Ascent of Man* and *Crossroads*. They range from the creative to the convergent; the accurate to the misleading; the magic to the tragic.

A personalised learning program?

Many teachers consider that computers can offer individualised tuition generally for mechanistic exercises in the basic skills. An extreme claim has been that this application will provide all children of the future with 'the personal services of a tutor [who is] well informed and responsive'.[21] Advocates see the advantages as the personalisation of learning (that is, they can ask for children's names and appear to converse with them); the individualisation of the work set (which usually means setting different levels of the same task for different children and allowing children to work at their own pace); and the monitoring of activities (children being told when they are either right or wrong, and computer acting as 'big brother', keeping records of pupil's responses).

The power of personalising computer programs is shown in Bernard Weizenbaum's ELIZA. This program, which is sometimes called DOCTOR, sustains a dialogue with users in the manner of a psycho-analyst, raising the user's consciousness of problems that are troubling them. Weizenbaum named the program after Shaw's heroine Eliza Doolittle, as 'although it could be taught to speak exceedingly well, like Miss Doolittle, it was never quite clear whether it could become smarter'.[22]

Weizenbaum did not seriously consider that his experiments with 'personalising' should become generalised. ELIZA's very personal response with the user is also well removed from standard programmers' tactics of asking children to put in their names for the computer to use occasionally. Rather than an intimate dialogue, this tends to result in the 'Jan got three right; Bill got twenty-five right. Well done, Bill; tough luck, Jan' style of software. Such 'personalised' responses might well elicit negative reactions in pupils rather than motivate them.

The individualisation of content?

Logo and SLYFOX show how computers can become powerful educational tools when children incorporate their own ideas and set their own problems within a task. It is rather different if someone else defines limited ideas and problems for the pupils and, worse still, makes them battle through the programmer's chosen stages for their completion. Attempts at programmed learning revealed the problems of defining the stages of instruction (for it cannot be called education) within a skill without forcing children through unnecessary stages of learning. It is doubtful whether learning can ever be broken down usefully in this way except for the most mundane of tasks. Howe and Boulay have complained that in computer programs it tends to mean each pupil acquiring 'individual access to the program rather than specific teaching that takes his individual strengths and weaknesses into account'.[23]

Teachers have generally rejected and criticised excessive use of drill in school for many years. Yet such ideas have been commonly converted into computer programs, which then appear to provide 'respectability' for classroom use. Staff who have moved to a language experience approach suddenly see an attraction in isolated phonic and word recognition drills. Those who have fought to encourage problem-solving in mathematics are seduced by programs offering low levels of shape recognition or tasks with 'hundreds, tens and units'. As Chandler says:

> The most imaginative and sensitive teachers may easily become so overwhelmed by the pressure to use computers, or so mesmerised by the technology, that when they use the computer in the classroom they may come to inflict on their charges mechanistic exercises which they would otherwise have condemned with vigour.[24]

The problem with such programs is that they may not in practice teach what they are supposed to teach. Matching a shape or colour on the screen does not mean that a child knows its name or essential characteristics. Recognising a word on the screen as being the same as one on a 'concept keyboard' will not ensure that the word has been read or will be recognised in a different context. Some drill programs may be capable of completion only by children who have already learned the skills. For example, children who can match letters on a screen with those on a QWERTY keyboard (even with lower-case sticky labels applied) can probably recognise letters anyway. Those who cannot might be better using less complicated and less expensive equipment for the task. Similarly, most young children can group objects according to colour, yet colour recognition is a theme of many programs. Careful monitoring of children's progress is therefore required when using this genre of software.

Appeals that children can choose the speed at which they work with the computers are also suspect. Galton and his colleagues (p. 90) have shown well the evasive tactics employed by some pupils when offered boring tasks and the willingness of others to work at anything. The researchers may have found different results if they had observed children's use of microcomputers. As many observers have noted, there is something about computers that makes children stick at even the worst-presented and dreariest tasks.[25]

The limitations of monitoring procedures

The 'monitoring' aspect of using computers as a 'mechanical

instructor'[26] has two facets: encouraging and correcting the child and recording responses. The first generally consists of 'happy' and 'sad' faces, ticks and crosses or, worse still, happy jingles or electronic 'raspberries'. The latter not only tell you of your failure, they relate it, embarrassingly, to the whole class! Although such responses can indicate an error and even state what the correct response should be, the isolation of such drills from real problems often prevents children learning from their mistakes. The positive and negative reinforcements they give can also affect attitudes to learning, boring the competent and dispiriting the incompetent. Many drill tasks are also best completed without any active thought.

Top of this category are those programs that give more satisfying rewards for incorrect errors than for correct ones – a person falling into a pool and being eaten by a shark, for example, as opposed to standing safely on the diving board. What encouragement for a bored child to press incorrect keys, for this not only brings greater rewards, it solves the problem of having to do any work. It is the sabotaging strategy of the creative who refuse to be drilled and bored. Fortunately most drill and skill programs are vulnerable to such sabotage.

The 'big brother' role of computers monitoring performance and keeping records of results sounds very attractive to some teachers in this age of accountability. Records must, of course, provide useful information for teachers; information from which they monitor learning and improve their own teaching. This is possible. WOR-DAMATICS, an ILEA language program, asks children to guess and type in the missing words in texts. The program is flexible in its response to answers differing from the original words and tolerant of imperfect spellings. At the end, a record of children's varied guesses and omissions is kept. Any words that have been spelled incorrectly can be saved on a file and practised by the child. Help is given with recognising the shape of the word and order of the individual letters. Again, efforts are monitored. The resulting records of comprehension and spelling are extremely detailed. The only disadvantage they might offer to teachers could be the time taken for their analysis.

Few programs attempt to monitor in as detailed a way as WOR-DAMATICS. Most simply offer the number of correct and incorrect responses within a task. Such a score, unfortunately, does not necessarily tell teachers how such responses have come about. Just as incorrect responses might simply indicate boredom, correct responses can occur by chance or through being told by a friend. Children can also get the right responses for the wrong reasons and the wrong responses for the right ones. Unfortunately the computer can give individual scores with such ease that Smith has predicted it could result in an actual increase in testing and record keeping in school 'no matter how significant the mistake or irrelevant the learning task'.[27] The disadvantage of this for children might be their isolation in tasks so that records might be kept. The dangers of a 'one child, one machine' approach to learning are unknown but, with the lack of collaborative group work in primary schools, even more individual work seems highly undesirable.

Suspicions about software

The factually incorrect

Claims on learning become particularly invalid if programs are factually incorrect or an activity could be learned better with another medium. Factual inaccuracies, as opposed to 'bugs' in a program, unfortunately do exist. Neither programmer nor user may realise the inaccuracies. The Mathematical Association (MA), for example, created something of a scandal by questioning the quality and accuracy of mathematics programs in the schools' Microprimer packs. These were produced in conjunction with the DES and subsidised by the Department of Industry. As the MA said, for this reason alone 'primary teachers and parents . . . would assume that "official" packs supplied to schools are mathematically correct'.[28] In fact, the MA considered that out of the twenty-two programs, four contained serious mathematical deficiencies. They also thought that a further eight needed to be used with caution if children were not to develop incorrect concepts. Errors included a shape program that assumed all shapes with four equal sides were squares, and a logic program indicating that a set and member of a set were one and the same thing.

Many other programs contain comparable inaccuracies: the anagram program that rejects perfectly correct words from the original group of letters; the shape program that says a triangle will not fit into the bottom section of a diamond shape even though the child has been able to position it there; and the 'concept keyboard' money program that asks a child to point to 5p but rejects pressure on the group of coins containing two 2p's and 1p, accepting only the single coin. The examples are, regrettably, endless and even include programs rigorously trialled in school.

Unwanted by-products

DRILLS AND SKILLS

Certain programs, though not unsound factually, have raised suspicions because of the possible hidden outcomes that might arise. Chandler, for example, quotes a program that gives four written versions of 'commonly misspelt words'. Children are asked to identify the ones spelled correctly. As he says:

> Aside from the bad practice of presenting (and thus reinforcing) misspelt words, it is extraordinary that any set of pre-selected words should be regarded as 'common errors of children' en masse. The declaration (in a review) that 'the author has chosen his words well' would appear to mean that it is hoped that children will spell most of them inaccurately.[29]

WORD PROCESSORS

Respectable types of program such as word-processors and information retrieval packages have also come under criticism for the learning problems they may give to children. They tend to reinforce the argument that specific claims for specific programs are more reliable than general claims. Grand, for example, presents a plausible argument that writing both on paper and on conventional word-processors can reinforce incorrect spelling habits, restrict writing vocabulary and result in a poor self-image for the less able child.[30] This is interesting since many teachers make strong claims to the contrary.[31] Grand details the basis of the problem:

> First the child will produce many spelling errors. The alternative is to repeatedly ask the teacher for words, which not only interrupts his train of thought but . . . advertises his failure. These incorrect spellings become impressed on the child's mind by the mechanical act of forming (or typing) the letters before a teacher can correct them. They are further reinforced by the child reading and re-reading what has already been written to enable him to decide on the next word . . . Poor spelling often limits a child's language development. Unable to confidently guess the appearance of a new word in the vocabulary a familiar one is often chosen . . . all word processors suffer from the limitation that they only enable the correction of words after they have been made . . . What is needed is a program that will correct spelling at a time of writing.[32]

Grand has produced two specialised word-processors, WRITERIGHT and STORYBOX, for this purpose. These can be programmed to cope with an individual's idiosyncratic spelling errors. On typing, a warning 'ping' and the appearance of the correct word in the text provide a patient and persistent reminder. Unknown words can be traced by typing the first three sounds. In this way the program acts as both interpreter and dictionary tracing unlikely pronunciations to likely spellings. Only such a tool, says Grand, can really help the slow learner improve writing and reading.

INFORMATION RETRIEVAL PACKAGES

Information retrieval, like word-processing, is generally seen as a

Figure 4 A DATAPROBE map of the worst litter levels in Billingham

```
DATAPROBE Enquiry

File name          :LITTERL
Description        :Litter levels in Billingham

Enquiry            :total>140
Printing           :MAP
```

TCENTRE

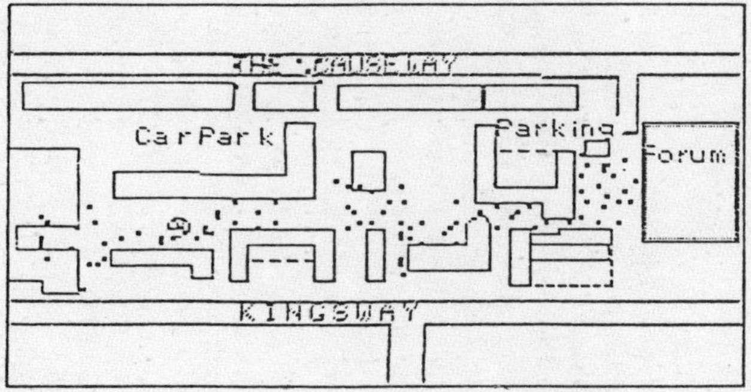


```
Records Matched : 98
Records Read    : 306

Finished
```

useful activity to carry out with a microcomputer. The computer provides facilities for storing large quantities of data which it can rapidly sort, subdivide and select. Information placed into an information retrieval package can be easily corrected and extended. This means that children can collect and sort through much more information than they could manually. Thus children can frame intelligent hunches or hypotheses about what they have observed and then quickly use the microcomputer to check the idea. Information retrieval packages, however, can vary enormously. Some can produce only lists of the required details. As Ross points out, these can be difficult for children to use.[33] Others, such as DATAPROBE, can produce many different forms of iconographic output including bar charts and maps. Figure 4 for example, shows a DATAPROBE map of the dirtier areas of Billingham from children's records of little levels in the town.[34] SEEK (figure 5) prints information in the form of a biological key.

	Question	YES	NO
1	Has it a collar?	Shirt	2
2	Is it worn on the legs?	3	4
3	Are they worn on the feet?	Socks	Trousers
4	Is it worn on the head?	Hat	Jumper

Figure 5   A key printed out from the SEEK information retrieval program

The creation of files on most packages is generally straightforward. Census information is popularly used. Figure 6 shows the sort of details that might be fed into the machine. They concern John Perkins, who lived on Mutley Plain, Plymouth, in 1871. The information is divided into 'fields' such as the surname or place (of birth) which remain the same for all people entered. When a large file has been gathered, children then form a hypothesis and decide what information they need from the file. They might wonder if all households on Mutley Plain had servants or whether most people in the street came originally from Plymouth. Most conflict in information retrieval surrounds the querying demands made on children for finding such information. Some, such as QUEST, are extremely

SURNAME: PERKINS

NAME: JOHN

STREET: MUTLEY PLAIN

NUMBER: 9

AGE: 43

CON: MARRIED

OCCUP: GENERAL SERVANT

PLACE: PLYMOUTH

COUNTY: DEVON

Figure 6   Detailed record from a QUEST file of 1871 Census data on Mutley Plain, Plymouth

powerful tools but their interrogation demands the learning of a specialised 'language'. To find details of all the Perkins family in a QUEST file, the child would have to ask:

QUERY SURNAME IDENT "PERKINS"

'IDENT' here means 'identical to'. In order to find people whose occupation contains the word 'servant' and who are over forty-three, the child would have to ask:

QUERY (OCCUP SUB "SERVANT") AND (AGE GT 43)

With such a complex language it is sometimes easy to see achievement in terms of the mastery of the querying technique, rather than in the quality of hypothesising and subsequent analysis of supplied information.

Programs such as QUEST have been useful for indicating to teachers the value of information retrieval in school. Now new programs are being developed that remove these querying problems. Coupland, for example, has developed INVESTIGATOR, which handles coded data. The enquiry system is extremely simple, using only the arrow keys on the keyboard to select fields and entries. No words are typed in at all. The initial enquiry frame presents the user with a list of headings. For traffic accident information this might resemble figure 7a. Any number of headings can be selected by simply moving an arrow up and down and pressing the computer RETURN key. Once a choice has been made, FINISH is selected in the same way. Each heading is then displayed with its associated entries. Again, any number of entries may be selected. It is very easy to search for all the accidents involving taxis being driven in wet weather between 8 a.m. and 6 p.m. When accidents are found to match the enquiry, full details are displayed, as in figure 7b. A simple count is kept of the records searched, the number that match the enquiry and the corresponding percentage. On completion of an enquiry it can be repeated, altered or replaced by a new one. In this way the concentration is on interpretation of results rather than enquiry skills and it becomes more an exercise in road safety education than information retrieval.

The wrong medium

Inevitably there are programs that introduce ideas more suited to other media. This does not include some of the drill-and-skill programs that would not even be acceptable on paper. Rather it encompasses useful ideas that would be better taught in another way. The logic activities on the Microprimer GATES program, for example, were thought by the MA to be less useful than similar tasks with real multi-attribute blocks. Science simulations imitating

INVESTIGATOR: Accident detail

Pedestrians aged 0–15 : Devon 1983

Time of day: 0845   Grid Ref:
Day of week: Thursday   SS5632
Month: March 24
Weather: Fine
Road surface: Dry
Light: Daylight
Road type: Single track road
Vehicle: Car
Vehicle manoeuvre:
  Going forward
Sex of driver or rider: Male
  Aged: 18
Sex of casualty: Male
  Aged: 15
Injuries to casualty: Slight
Pedestrian location:
  Unknown
Pedestrian movement:
  Walking facing traffic

Searched: 4   Matched: 4   100%

Figure 7b Investigator: accident detail

INVESTIGATOR: Choice page

Pedestrians aged 0–15:
  Devon 1983

Time of day:
Day of week:
Month:
Weather:
Road surface:
Light:
Road type:
Vehicle:
Vehicle manoeuvre:

Sex of driver or rider:
  Aged:
Sex of casualty:
  Aged:
Injuries to casualty:
Pedestrian location:

Pedestrian movement:
** FINISH **

Figure 7a Investigator: choice page

practical work such as floating and sinking or simple electrical circuits seem misguided if the activities can actually be performed with everyday equipment readily available in primary classrooms. Some even provide more tedious experiences and fewer decision-making opportunities than real-life tasks. Many teachers simply use such programs to supplement their practical work. However, there remains the temptation to substitute computer experience for real experience. In some teachers' eyes logic games on a microcomputer remove the problems of all those little blocks falling on the floor and creating a mess; experimental simulations avoid the requirement of messy substances such as water.

The human dimension

Finally, one limitation on claims of computer potential is the human one. As Fraser says:

> the strengths and weaknesses of people and computers are so different that to combine their strengths is no mean task. The dream child of an ugly genius and a beautiful moron is a beautiful genius; it would be a tragedy if reality produced an ugly moron.[35]

Software is open to abuse as well as use. Logo can easily be reduced to a series of boring exercises, QUEST to an 'eleven-plus' in querying technique. Simulations on the one hand may provide opportunities for observation, the development of concepts, logical thought, the posing of questions and the selection of answers, plus opportunities to note patterns and relationships. On the other hand they can result in a mechanical convergence towards the discovery of right answers; a mere game in which children develop winning strategies but fail to see the significance of the events simulated. As Whalley and Stewart point out, 'Treated as a strategy game they can be less exciting than arcade games and have about as much educational value.'[36] One teacher may use a program for an exciting project lasting a whole term; another can use it as an activity for wet playtimes. In contrast some fairly unpromising programs have been known to be used imaginatively by talented teachers.

What then are the conditions that might encourage the correct use of the new technology? First, programs should be produced that aim to have a qualitative influence on the educational process. As Fraser says, 'There are very few (~100) different programs teaching units to have effect on the whole 5–18 curriculum (~50,000 hrs). It is an effort for teachers to use them – the mediocre is not worth the effort.'[37] Mathematics will serve as a useful example. The Cockcroft Report on mathematical education asserted that:

Mathematics teaching at all levels should include opportunities for: exposition by the teacher; discussion between teacher and pupils and between pupils themselves; appropriate practical work; consolidation and practice of fundamental skills and routines; problem solving, including the application of mathematics to everyday situations; investigational work.[38]

As with other subjects, teachers have tended to emphasise exposition and drills at the expense of discussion, practical work, problem-solving and investigational work. It is therefore to these problem areas that programmers should turn their attention.

A further positive move for programmers should be away from a view of the computer as an individual tool for single or very small group use. Originally the example from the United States and the incorporation of small fixed monitors into microcomputer designs exacerbated this view. The ITMA (Investigations on Teaching with Microcomputer as an Aid) project has for years emphasised the importance of whole class investigations with children. Phillips describes the possibilities with the ITMA program EUREKA. As figure 8 shows, this uses the example of a man having a bath to help children with graphical interpretation:

In one lesson, the whole class viewed the program on a large television monitor. The teacher introduced EUREKA by taking the man through the usual sequence of events when having a bath and then got the class to point out these events on the graph. 'When did the taps go off? When did the man sing?' . . . the graph for example 2 [was shown] without any pictures. A number of pupils attempted to explain the graph and there was some argument about what it showed.[39]

This lesson proceeded with children looking at other EUREKA examples and trying to interpret them. A second teacher switched off the computer and asked children to develop their own stories about having a bath, representing them as pictures, words and a 'story line' or graph. Phillips describes one result:

Suzanne created her own version of events [see figure 9]. After writing the story and drawing some pictures, she sketched the graph. After folding the paper above the graph it was given to Jonathan to interpret. Suzanne's comments on his version of the story are very perceptive. She not only sees how graphs communicate, but sees their limitations.[40]

The procedure is remarkably similar to Galton *et al.*'s recommended approach for effective teaching: a class lesson, leading to collaborative work.

The EUREKA example illustrates that whole class teaching can be

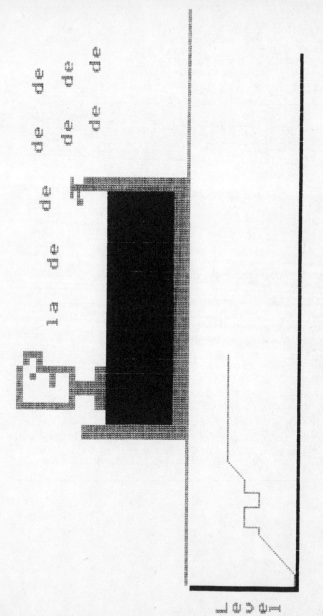

Figure 8 The EUREKA program

Son I thought I would have a bath so I ran the
water. I let it run untill it was half full with
hot water no cold. I jumped in and at
once jumped out. I was to hot, so I let
the water run out untill it was a quater
full and filled the quater I had let out
with cold water then I got in and had my

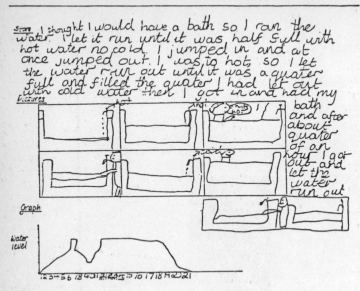

Pictures

bath
and after
about
a quater
of an
hour I got
out and
let the
water
run out

Graph

Water
level

I this the story of my graph Puts the plug in, turns water on, rises and then
g d in stays for a little while and then gets out, and it goes
down, and gets in again, then it rises, and then stays in
for a long time and pulls the plug out.

My comments
This was quite good but Jonathan
said that the first time I stayed
in for a little while but I was meant
to have jumped striaght out again
but my graph may have deceived him.

Figure 9   Suzanne's story after using Eureka

undertaken with a microcomputer if programs are flexible enough to allow all styles of teaching. Whilst initiating interest, either further work could be computer-based or, as with the second teacher, the machine could be switched off and non-computer tasks developed. Using computers to initiate rather than totally dictate all activities is an important aspect of design and use. Fraser complains of programmers suffering from 'designer lust', where the computer is made to carry out activities that are best left to the pupil. She quotes the example of PIRATES, a program in which you hunt for treasure on a grid using a variety of clues. The program can provide five types of clue from compass direction to vectors, and 120 different types of game are possible which can be levelled at a seven-year-old class or students in higher education. The program, however, does not draw a grid on the screen. As Fraser says, 'this program is all about plotting points, lines and regions but it never displays a graph or plots a point. This is to be part of the desired pupil activity and therefore is not taken over by the computer.'[41]

Such 'omission design'[42] is an important encouragement for teachers to allow pupil activity with paper or apparatus with a computer program. It can also encourage teacher to switch the machine off. Both are important, since there is a common feeling that writing, apparatus and recording are not necessary when you use a computer. Phillips also points out the common attitude 'that the school's computer should perpetually be the centre of frenetic activity'. Arranging non-computer activities that are related to a program, however, seems an important facet of effective use of the technology in teaching and is a strategy used regularly by the best users in school.

Summary

The original reason for introducing microcomputers into school was utilitarian: to prepare a new generation competent in handling the technology of the future. 'Preparation for the future', however, seems to have several meanings. Some define it as keyboard skills, which have been shown to be useful for employment potential. Computer programs and tests for keyboard skills tend to concentrate on key recognition, which is best achieved through using the technology. All ignore touch-typing and encourage skills might inhibit its learning in the future.

Television or radio programmes and courses about computers also aim to prepare children for the future. No other item of everyday equipment is singled out in this way, and as future generations might simply use the technology without knowing anything about its functioning (as we do telephones and televisions), utilitarian aims for such courses should be treated with caution.

Preparation for the future can also include teaching programming to children. Programming is a broad concept that at one level can mean making a computer do what you want it to do in the language it allows and at another level being taught languages such as Basic. Both activities can be justified in educational terms. In utilitarian terms conflict exists between schools, universities and colleges as to the appropriateness of training in one particular language.

There are limitations to the educational justifications that are made for microcomputers. Whether programs can develop problem solving, or encourage discussion and learning, depends on many factors. Claims about individualising learning depend on aspects of computers such as the way programs can be personalised, individualised, or made to monitor and respond to performance. Personalisation at a crude level can be boring if not irritating. Planning fine stages of learning is also difficult, and though children can work at their own pace with some programs the technology can seduce them to concentrate on the most boring and useless tasks.

Monitoring and responding to children's responses seem attractive but are fraught with problems. Most reinforcements for children bore those who can and dispirit those who cannot. Some rewards also actively encourage negative learning strategies. Records of progress can be made but they must give useful information and be capable of accurate interpretation by teachers. An emphasis on monitoring, however, could result in undue isolation of children in individual tasks.

Claims about learning are rendered invalid if software is inaccurate or has unseen and undesirable by-products. Even well-accepted categories of software can be criticised on this count depending on the program used. Some programs also present ideas to children that might be explored more effectively in other media.

Finally there is the human dimension, which can turn the exciting into the boring, or add quality to the unpromising. Conditions for effective use would seem to include programming curriculum aspects that teachers do not readily utilise with other media, allowing flexibility of teaching styles and encouraging the use of additional materials and other activities both with and away from the screen. Should such conditions be met, the computer should add greatly to the level of educational activity in the classroom and should achieve more than a rabbit without becoming a white elephant.★

★ A note on software and hardware mentioned in this chapter follows the notes and references on p. 250.

Beyond the Teacher's Day

CHAPTER 26

Food for thought

Everyone was shocked when Jeffrey started school – the teachers, the social workers, even the neighbours who only now knew of his existence. All were shaken by his frail form, lack of speech and general poor level of development. It did not take long, however, for us to realise that we had quite a character on our hands. Jeffrey may have been locked away in one room for four years but now the world was his. Heading straight for the Wendy house, he donned a long dress, red woollen bonnet and climbed into the dolls' cot. The continuous stream from his pinched nose trickled down his lip and curled around the edges of an endearing smile. He was thoroughly pleased with himself. For half an hour two fellow newcomers joined in the game – feeding him imaginary meals, tucking him up to sleep and, much to our amusement, even wiping his nose. The first of several messages then began to arrive: 'Jeffrey wants to go on the slide'; 'Jeffrey's too hot'; and, more importantly, 'Jeffrey wants to go to the toilet!' How our four-year-old translators deciphered the range of grunts and noises with such skill remains a mystery, but they were never wrong. This child was an effective communicator!

At 10.30 a.m. a new problem arose: milk. Good teachers are known for their ability to exploit every situation for its maximum learning potential. The milk break is no exception. Bottles and straws can be counted or matched by one-to-one correspondence. Further matching and counting – singly or in groups – can accompany their distribution. Rudimentary concepts of area and multiplication arise from noting the numbers in a row and the number of rows in a crate. Empty bottles form the basis of such diverse activities as music and science. Today's task, however, was simply to establish a routine for milk consumption.

Children were seated and bottles distributed, mouths sucked on straws and milk descended. All except for one. Clearly, this was Jeffrey's first use of a straw. Lowering his open mouth over it he tried vainly to imitate the others. Then, grasping the bottle and upturning it above his head, he aimed. Teacher rushed to the rescue. Milk splashed over sweater, shorts, legs and chair. But the beaming smile told all. Some at least had reached the required target. As staff stripped him down he chattered away, and our translators announced with glee that Jeffrey wanted more.

Giving Jeffrey more became a problem for several weeks. He was unable to drink from anything but a bottle and required full-time assistance at meals. Gradually he progressed from a feeder-cup to a mug and then to a straw; from hand-feeding of mashed food to using a spoon, then a fork and finally a full set of cutlery. He learned steadily, and during that time so did we. Jeffrey's feeding problem provided many occasions when staff could wash both child and clothes. Ensuring the latter were still damp at home-time provided opportunity to supply the mother with extra garments for her child without 'loss of face'. Indeed, I recall how she helped us over the years by making use of perfectly sound items of clothing that blocked up our store cupboard after a jumble sale.

CHAPTER 27

Deals on meals

The story of Jeffrey illustrates some of the problems, outside academic ones, that teachers face. The school is concerned with far more than the intellectual development of children. For example, it is one place where positive intervention can improve their total health profile. Children like Jeffrey who are victims of poverty, ignorance or neglect need such intervention most. For them a healthy school environment is essential. Over the years a battery of legislation covering buildings, services and facilities has evolved to provide it. But the underlying rationale and goals, whether altruistic, economic or even military, have, like most aspects of education, been more easily formulated than achieved. The teacher is an agent in the front line of implementing health ideologies. No matter how willing and concerned, as the case of Jeffrey shows, they strive in their task against a battery of problems not always apparent to the lay person or legislator.

Supervising school feeding, whilst supported by many teachers, has caused persistent problems in school. Ensuring standards of diet and adequate provision of meals and dining areas have all produced conflict. Meal supervision also means that teachers do not enjoy the midday break enjoyed in other professions. This chapter examines the background to the facility, its range and the conflicts it has engendered.

Why school meals?

Few people would argue about the importance of an adequate diet. Providing food in school aims to supplement home feeding with at least one good balanced meal per day, to teach children, through example, good manners and the importance of proper diet[1] and also to support working parents.[2] Achieving these aims is by no means easy. For many years only poor or undernourished children were allowed to partake of school meals. These were children with

> pale and haggard faces, lank and bony figures, children with the countenances of old men, deformities with irons upon their limbs, boys of stunted growth, and others whose long meagre legs would hardly bear their stooping bodies.[3]

Provision was through charitable organisations whose work is documented in the literature of the past. A favourite meal was porridge. Nicholas Nickleby's 'brown composition which looked like diluted pin-cushions without the covers'[4] was, on balance, more appetising than Jane Eyre's, which was burnt.[5] Portions were often inadequate, as Oliver Twist was quick to point out,[6] and Miss Temple was probably not the only teacher secretly to provide extra rations and luxuries for her pupils.[7] But empathy for such action was not necessarily widespread. Mr Brocklehurst's view was that putting 'bread and cheese instead of burnt porridge into children's mouths . . . may indeed feed their vile bodies but . . . starve their immortal souls'.[8] And, as everyone knows, Oliver Twist's request for more was greeted with apoplexy.

Even the London County Council of 1906 claimed that providing lavish school meals for children might demoralise parents and charities. The 'lavish' meals to which they referred were savoury suet pudding followed by ground rice pudding or vegetable pie and cornflour moulds.[9] Nevertheless this was still an improvement on what many children ate at home. 'Tea sops' (bread soaked in tea) or 'kettle broth' (bread, dripping and hot water) formed a typical country breakfast. A general diet of bread, jam, cake and potatoes was quite common.[10] A 1907 investigation in Bradford confirmed that children lost weight in their school holidays.[11]

As the diet of the population improved, school meals became more open to criticism for being monotonous and unbalanced. In the Great Depression of the 1930s a typical meal consisted of soup, potatoes, bread, milk and jam. Today, as enlightened families turn to a diet of whole-foods, Britain faces yet another economic crisis and schools are turning to 'junk' food. Thus children's midday meals might be less well balanced and nutritious than those provided at home.

Like economic crisis, the world wars have been important in school meal terms. In the First World War the number of children eating at school was reduced ten-fold in the interest of economy, and by 1918 two thirds of authorities offered no meal provision at all.

Malnutrition remained a common problem. The Second World War, however, produced a contrasting attitude. The public were better informed on nutrition and there was a suspicion that starvation had contributed to Germany's defeat. The British government was determined at least to keep the nation's children well fed. Extra grants, rations and facilities swelled the school meal service. Consequently the six-year war produced no decline in the physique and health of pupils, and for the poor there was a positive improvement.

Problems with finance

Problems of finance have always plagued the service. That such provision was a 'burden' was frequently emphasised. Some worried where it all would end:

> Already the question is being asked why necessitous children are not fed in the holidays . . . and moreover, if from five to fourteen, why not from birth, onwards?[12]

Because of the enormous scale of provision, meals had to be cost-effective. This situation has frustrated teachers, health workers and canteen employees whose ingenuity at providing balanced meals on minimal budgets has to be acknowledged. Before the 1906 Education (Provision of Meals) Act transferred responsibility from the Poor Law to the education authorities, a charitable meal cost approximately ½p. It was therefore surprising that the 1906 Act limited costs to half of this amount per child – and this only if private funds ran out!

Such constraints, as has been noted, undermined provision early in the century. By 1920 the cost of a school meal rose to 3p. However, the 1921 coal strike required authorities in mining areas to spend more on meals than anticipated. Therefore the cost had to be reduced to 2p to meet available funds. The financial state of the country was causing serious concern. In 1922 the Geddes Commission proposed saving millions of pounds on education by raising the school-entry age to six and cutting both teachers' salaries and the school meals grant, claiming:

> We have been accused of starving the minds, and indeed the bodies also of the children . . . The only thing that matters in this country is to get down taxation or we die.[13]

The chief medical officer of the time claimed that no ill-effects were caused to children as a result of such economies. Yet a 1926 comparison of public schoolboys and elementary school pupils showed the former to be fifteen to twenty pounds heavier than their under-weight state counterparts.[14]

Restrictions on meals have persisted to the present day. The improved financial climate of the 1960s briefly brought standards closer to imagined ideals. Jeffrey, for example, experienced 'home cooking' of the highest order in his school. By the 1980s, however, circumstances necessitated most schools adopting a self-service cafeteria system. Chips, pasties and beefburgers became a common choice. Justifications for the change have ranged from arguments that children enjoy such food to claims that they receive a good diet at home. Many teachers have not simply expressed concern at this change; like Miss Temple they have intervened. With support from ancillary staff, a 'traffic light' system, common in adult slimming diets, has been organised. Food is arranged under red, yellow and green labels. Red represents the least desirable elements of a diet and green the most. Children must choose their meal from elements in

Lunch-time in the school hall doubling as a dining room.

each section. Under the system no child can choose a 'double chips and doughnut' diet and many are persuaded to try, and gain a taste for, healthy foods. However, any child wishing to take only 'green' foods is sometimes prevented from doing so because of cost. Thus, some children may be forced to take a food from each section, including the harmful ones, and so eat less desirable foods than they would normally.

Ensuring meal provision

If providing meals has constantly caused problems, so has ensuring that children like Jeffrey actually receive them. At first it was difficult for the Board of Education to force authorities to meet the Provision of Meals Acts. Consequently many did not provide meals. When they were available a plethora of rules and regulations caused stigma for child and parents. In 1905 legislation enabled boards of guardians to help the needy but proceedings were then taken against parents to recover costs. This, in effect, rendered them 'paupers' – a category of person not allowed to vote. Rules were equally punative in the 1930s. As one frustrated medical officer stated:

> When you have starved sufficiently to show signs of actual malnutrition, 'however slight', come back for meals. Then you may have meals until malnutrition is cured, but only until then. After that you must have another period of starvation.[15]

But meals could not be provided without necessary buildings and equipment. Indeed, this was one reason why free meals for all were not provided in the post-war period (an official aim of the time). Thus, in 1946 children received free milk but paid for their meals from the new family allowances. The stigma for children still deemed to require 'free' meals persisted and the organisational burden of collecting the money was placed upon the teaching staff. I well remember those Monday mornings collecting, counting, checking and rechecking the piles of coins – so often the first task of the week! Bringing the service into schools from the 'feeding centres' also produced organisational problems that even today have not been fully resolved.

Problems with buildings

The provision of school dining areas aimed to make mealtimes more central to school life. It also removed the stigma of attendance at a free-meal centre. But the supply of facilities tended to be spasmodic.

In the three primary schools I attended in the late 1940s and early 1950s meals were taken in the local secondary school. A 1955 survey by the NUT showed that many meals were still served in buildings ranging from parish rooms to the annexe of a public house.[16] The overwhelming demand for resources of the 2,500 schools surveyed was for a dining room of their own. I well remember lunchtimes at High Rise School. Meals were served in a church hall some distance away. Children were lined up and walked in a crocodile along one of the busiest roads in the city, a journey of some ten minutes' duration. On dry days a full accompaniment of staff, in front, aft and along the crocodile's length, was required to ensure safe arrival. On wet days we often sat throughout the afternoon damp and cold from our midday tramp. That staff could never have the 'lunch break' enjoyed by other professions was not considered. Most felt that untrained ancillary helpers would have been overtaxed even had they been available.

In many schools the hall was and is now used for dining. Separate dining areas tend to be a luxury easily requisitioned in times of economy. The more 'open' architectural styles of the 1960s and 1970s demanded flexible use of most areas. If a dining room was built it had to function as a music area (as at the 1958 Amersham school – see p. 42) or even a classroom (as at the 1965 Eastlea school). Dining space was also limited. The Amersham plans clearly show ninety-four places in the area for an eight-class school. If all children wished to stay for meals, at least three sittings would be needed. The 1966 Delf Hill purpose-built middle school was provided with a generous net area cost of 58 sq ft compared with the 41 sq ft 1965 average. No dining room was planned, however. Meals were instead to be taken at one end of the hall (which was also used for PE, music and drama) and in a corridor outside the head's study, facing onto a central courtyard. Seventy-two places could be accommodated in this way, which in a school for 420 pupils was not over-generous. The supervision required in this L-shaped space looks impractical, but was achieved until two years ago through 'family service' whereby staff sat with the children and meals were served at the tables. Since then a cafeteria system has been introduced. All four meal sittings are taken in the hall only.

The dual function of school areas such as halls and dining rooms causes many problems. Their use for meals necessitates positioning near the kitchens. Thus all other activities – music, PE or general class use – operate against a background level of noise that is often unacceptable. From approximately 11.30 a.m. no use can be made of dining areas. Activities must be left, and apparatus cleared. Children using the area as a classroom must be resited, often in a corridor or cloakroom. This can create a feeling of insecurity and demand

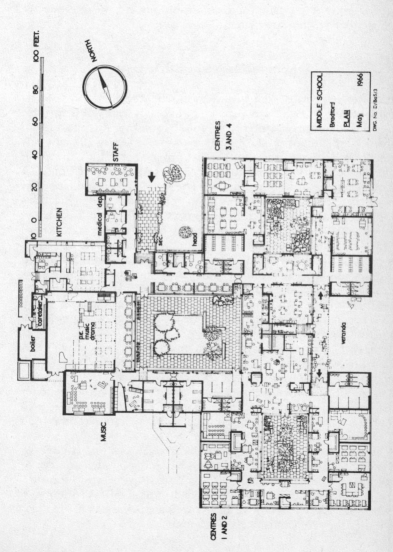

Figure 10   Plan of Delf Hill Middle School, 1966

considerable organisational skill to maintain a good working atmosphere.

A further problem is the need to plan several meal 'sittings'. If facilities are some distance from the school, 'second sitting' children and staff may need to queue in all weathers if the first meal is prolonged. Eating in sittings also tends to be a rushed affair, adding stress to what should be a relaxed social occasion. Younger children such as Jeffrey need more time for their eating than older pupils; time for persuasion to try new foods or simply finish a meal. Not only food is wasted if they are rushed.

School meals as a health hazard

Whilst school meals were originally introduced to improve children's health, there is a real danger that they can result in food poisoning or even dysentery. In 1984, for example, 800 French children and 150 of their teachers became violently ill with salmonella enteriditis after eating a school dinner. Both the fresh mayonnaise garnishing the hors-d'oeuvre and the minced meat of the main course were contaminated. The problem is a familiar one in large-scale catering, as occasional food-related tragedies in hospitals and old people's homes testify. Yet in 1955 the NUT reported that in Britain more food poisoning outbreaks occurred through school canteens than in all the hotels, cafés and restaurants put together: sixty out of eighty-four outbreaks.[17] The outbreaks were attributed to conditions ranging from overcrowding to the use of pupils for washing floors and teacloths. However, the NUT suggested that the most likely source of contamination was from containers, many meals travelling several miles and then standing, warming, in a playground or corner of a building.

Interestingly, the suspect French mayonnaise may have been contaminated because it was not refrigerated. Being 'fresh', cool storage was crucial and though the company delivering the hors-d'oeuvre denied responsibility its contract was cancelled under pressure from parents who suspected negligence. Had the firm adopted the British practice of using bottled preparations of this food the problem would not have arisen.

The tightening up of regulations on refrigeration, storage or reheating in both France and Britain has reduced such sources of infection. Some school kitchens now resemble operating theatres, though in others staff suffer outmoded buildings and equipment. Unfortunately, where thousands of meals are being prepared in vast quantities the problem is likely to continue.

School milk

School meals could not be considered without reference to school milk. For Jeffrey it was the one food he recognised, in spite of his problems in drinking it. Milk supplies to schools have a history almost as long as that of meals. Just as teachers and workers across the nation have their morning cuppa, so children have their 'bottle'. The practice partly has its origins in a 1922 project when the National Milk Publicity Council provided a free pint to certain Birmingham children – some undernourished, other not. After some months the children were shown to display 'a notable improvement in their mental and physical vigour and alertness, in the haemoglobin content of their blood and by an increase in weight and nutrition'.[18]

This experiment, possible because of milk surpluses at the time, was to have repercussions up to the present day. In the 1920s research into the advantages of dairy foods became popular. Corry Mann, who evaluated the Birmingham research, and Orr[19] both produced studies confirming the value of milk. In 1935 the government provided £500,000 for the Milk Marketing Board to supply school children with a third of a pint per day at half the normal price. The suggestion came from the Board, again to deal with surpluses. By 1938 half the school population was drinking milk during the mid-morning break, one fifth of them having it free.

Up to this point any researcher could view the government's interest in milk provision with scepticism; but by the Second World War milk was perceived by the nation as necessary for a balanced diet. Now it was in short supply; traders complained that the profit margin from the third-of-a-pint bottles was too small and requested bulk provision. The government refused – each child was to have their own bottle where possible. Nevertheless, when the supply of third-of-a-pint bottles was discontinued in many areas it was teachers who had to organise the bringing, filling and cleansing of cups for the increased number of children drinking milk. Leff and Leff made the point that clearly this 'seriously inconvenienced' them.[20]

By 1941 children were given special milk priority, receiving half a pint for consumption at home and one to two thirds of a pint at school. Needy children were allowed free 'as much as was considered necessary for their health'.[21] From September 1946 free milk, but not meals, was available for all – a practice that was continued until the 1970s when the government attempted to remove the concession. Up to that time school milk provision had again proved a useful means of reducing surplus supplies. The 'Drinka pinta milka day' and current 'Milk's gotta lotta bottle' campaigns have both attempted to persuade the adult population to consume the remainder. Some health specialists have expressed concern at the growing milk consumption of Britain, particularly those interested in reducing the fat content of the nation's diet. Nevertheless the indoctrinated public produced such an outcry at the proposals that a compromise was reached: 'Thatcher the Snatcher', as she was misguidedly dubbed, allowed provision to continue for infants and older children in need. Pleas from some nutritionists to substitute skimmed milk were ignored. The EEC, which supported the move, now has an outlet for some of its 'milk lake', and provision thus looks likely to continue for some while. For children like Jeffrey this could well be beneficial. For others it could be harmful. As a country with one of the highest per capita fat consumptions in the world, a reduction in fat sources such as dairy food would be beneficial. For the many children allergic to dairy food, abolition of school milk would be even more desirable.

School 'tuck'

Arriving simultaneously with the provision of milk in school came the habit of the morning snack – a practice, again, common with adults. During the 1922 National Milk Publicity Council experiment, a Birmingham firm made its own contribution of a biscuit per day for each child involved. This was said to have contributed to the measured increase in health. The milk-and-biscuit practice became, and still is, a habit. At first children took food from home to consume during the morning break. As food supplies recovered and rationing ceased many were given small sums of money to purchase snacks such as penny buns, Oxo cubes, Horlicks tablets or sweets from shops in the vicinity.

Many schools saw an opportunity to supplement their allowances by selling 'tuck' in school. It was, once more, something teachers had to organise, this time in their break periods. However, extra equipment and books were thus funded – though often at the expense of children's health. Biscuits, for example, remained a common choice in spite of rising concern over the effect of sweet foods on the nation's health and teeth. I remember in particular 'Jammy Dodgers', a sweet sticky concoction that clung around pupils' mouths for hours after consumption. Restricting purchases to crisps or peanuts was no improvement. As knowledge increases of the danger caused by a high-fat diet in early childhood, it would seem that only schools that supply apples, or ban tuck eating altogether, are acting responsibly.

Cookery in schools

Whereas cookery, food science and nutrition have long been an essential part of the secondary curriculum, their teaching in primary school has been spasmodic and often supervised by parents. That this can be an opportunity for educating children and, indirectly, their parents in nutrition is clear. Take, for example, one school in a poor area of Cornwall. Here a lesson on fruit culminated in the making of fresh fruit salad. The teacher was surprised at how many parents requested the recipe! From then on, the school introduced children to home-made recipes of foods such as soup, brown bread and lemonade which so often came, expensively, ready prepared. Dedicated staff not only researched the most economical, nutritious versions but carefully adapted recipes so that each pupil could prepare and take home their own 'mini-product'. Whole-foods were encouraged, and sweet items, common in school cookery, were kept to a minimum. The children also learned basics of food science and, incidentally, mathematics.

Conflict over meal supervision

Teachers' support for and dedication to school feeding has, since the 1960s, become the cause of major conflict between them and the employers. Under the 1968 School Meals Agreement teachers are no longer required to supervise mealtimes. The agreement was generated because of deep resentment in the later 1960s over low pay in comparison with other professions.

It resulted in LEAs having to provide school meals supervisory assistants, though it was always hoped that teachers would continue to support them in the supervision. Teachers could, for example, volunteer for 'dinner duty' in return for a free meal. However, teachers have increasingly claimed their right to the midday break enjoyed in other employment. They began to enjoy the freedom to carry out other tasks, sometimes chatting socially to a colleague but frequently carrying out other more important aspects of teaching such as resource preparation, or the display or marking of work. The job has seen increased extra-curricular demands over the last few years. As salaries again deteriorate in relation to those of others with whom, in 1974, teachers were given parity, attitudes harden. 'Withdrawal of goodwill' in trade union action generally affects mealtime supervision. As each battle over pay is fought, dinner duty volunteers decrease.

British parents have, unlike their continental counterparts, come to expect and depend upon a school meals service. If secondary

schools close at lunchtime due to union action, many parents allow
children to roam the streets rather than organise home feeding.
Teachers' pay deals now tend to include a requirement for mealtime
supervision. The agreement of December 1984 suggested two half-
hour supervisory sessions a week. But the NUT has firmly held to
the view that teachers are there to teach, stating that they 'cannot
give of [their] best if they are teaching all morning, working all
lunchtime and teaching all afternoon'.[22] Clearly ideologies of the
past have become the battleground of the present. School feeding is
now becoming increasingly expensive to implement. Children left
unsupervised by parent or teacher at lunchtime can be restless or
even disruptive in the afternoon. A 'continental day'[23] would provide a solution to all problems, but until the British public are ready
to accept this there may be many more deals on meals.

Summary

School feeding has a long tradition. Originally it was introduced for
poor and undernourished children. The meals were lavish in relation
to the home diet. This cannot always be said of modern provision.

The two world wars played an important part in school feeding.
The first saw a massive reduction in the service; the second an
expansion of provision. School meals, however, have always been
limited by available finances. When the education authorities first
took the service over from the charitable trusts they halved the trusts'
cost limit per meal. For years elementary school pupils were under-
weight in comparison with their well-fed private-sector counterparts. Even today children enjoying whole-foods in the home may
have only 'junk foods' available in school.

There has also been conflict over ensuring that meals are available
for the most needy. Authorities in the past did not always meet their
statutory requirements under the Provision of School Meals Acts.
Those that did often had punitive rules that perpetuated malnutrition
amongst the poor. Buildings in which the service could operate were
also lacking, a factor preventing a totally free service being provided
after the Second World War. Today, with the emphasis on multi-use
of school facilities meals may be served in halls, corridors or
classrooms – disrupting the organisation of educational activities and
causing considerable tensions within schools.

Although introduced to increase the nation's health, a school meal
may also be something of a health hazard. The consumption of milk
and the provision of high-fat or sugary foods as 'tuck' in school can
also threaten the balance of a child's diet. Unfortunately the one
subject where education on healthy feeding could take place –

cookery – is either left to parents or produces yet more buns and sticky cakes to rot the children's teeth and pervert their tastes.

The major conflict over school feeding today, however, lies in its supervision. In the late 1960s teachers, overworked and severely underpaid, developed an agreement with the LEAs that lunchtime supervision should not be compulsory. The authorities appointed supervisory staff but hoped that teachers would continue their support on a voluntary basis. Increasing extra-curricular demands combined with decreasing salaries have reduced the number of these volunteers. School meal supervision is provided only on a basis of goodwill between employer and teacher. In the 1980s this goodwill has also decreased. A continental day would remove the conflict entirely, though the British public with their current reliance on the meals service would be unlikely supporters of such a change.

CHAPTER 28

Overpaid and underworked?

It was the vacation and I was on my way to a conference in the North. There was a long train journey ahead so I settled down with reference books and paper to complete a research report. I had two companions in the compartment, both strangers. After a while one of them leaned across and asked if I knew anything about teaching. Her daughter was apparently keen to enter the profession but was concerned about the problems she might experience in school. I had just begun to outline the pros and cons of teaching when the train pulled into a station. Fixing his bowler hat firmly in position, the third member of our group rose. He picked up his briefcase and umbrella, then leaned forward as close as possible.

'If you ask me,' he said, his breath and saliva blasting aggressively across my face, 'you teachers are underworked and overpaid.'

CHAPTER 29

And what did you do at school today, Teacher?

Many people accuse teachers of being underworked and overpaid. Even at best teaching is viewed as an easy nine-till-four job that has long holidays and fits in well with family life. Everyone has at some time been to school. Although no one would claim that being ill qualifies you to be a doctor, the experience of school seems somehow to render everyone an expert on the teacher's role.

The 1980s have seen teachers' salaries and esteem sink to a worrying low. Being paid from public money, the situation is not new. Pestalozzi's assistant, Herman Krusi, had his pleasure at gaining a teaching appointment somewhat reduced when his competitor eight days later became the local policeman. Much attention in the local community was

> excited by the fact that . . . he received three gulden a week, while the schoolmaster, who was obliged to furnish his own school-room, had to satisfy himself with two and a half.[1]

Had Krusi taught in a British state primary school in 1974, his salary would have been similar to not only a policeman's, but also an accountant's. Now both these occupations enjoy significantly greater rewards for their work. An average policeman earns more than twice the salary of his counterpart in teaching with additional generous allowances for overtime.[2] Krusi and his competitor at least had similar abilities in that 'both candidates knew little'![3] Now potential teachers struggle on grants for three or four years to achieve their relevant degrees whilst their police-force counterparts enjoy high salaries after two years' training.

As Wilby states, teaching is one of the few professions where the 'private rate of return' (salary advantage after sacrificing loss in training) approaches zero.[4] The various reasons for this sad state of affairs must include a failure to accept the importance of teaching governed in part by a genuine lack of understanding of what the job involves. This chapter attempts to provide an insight into what lies within and beyond the teacher's day.

Studies of teaching

In 1971 Hilsum and Cane carried out a detailed study of the teacher's day.[5] Arriving totally unannounced, so as not to distort the findings, they recorded everything teachers did from going to the lavatory and marking books to disciplining and teaching children. Teachers also kept a diary of their activities in the evenings, at weekends and in their infamously long holidays. The average primary teacher worked a 44.25-hour week. Adjustments for the holidays converted this to 38.2 hours, which cannot be regarded as a short working week.

A more recent survey of teachers' hours shows no decrease in teacher commitment, and in many ways the job has become more demanding and difficult.[6] Teaching itself has always been a high pressure task. Any parent knows what it is like having two children in the house on a wet Saturday. Imagine three friends being invited for the day. Would not this add to the pressure? Then think of a child you would rather not have to tea. In your mind's eye, picture identical twins with the same characteristics turning up to join the group. Think of organising and disciplining them for a whole day. Are you becoming tired just contemplating it? A teacher does not have twice as much to cope with, her or his pressure is at least four times as great from Monday to Friday, week in week out. There is also the added stress of not just containing and occupying the group, but educating them. Add to this the preparation, marking and presentation of children's work; then the vast list of incidental tasks such as issuing toilet paper and collecting dinner money. In my time I've been asked to do just about everything from cutting pupils' fringes ('Me mam has no scissors') to giving them breakfast ('Our dad says crisps'll do' – but he knows it won't).

In a *Sunday Times* good careers guide[7] teaching was given the highest stress rating, 6.2, compared with 4.3 for a solicitor. In 1985 the NUT reported a significant increase in teacher resignations on health grounds. They found that nearly 6 per cent of teachers may be out of the classroom at any one time because of ill health.[8] As David Hargreaves said, 'Other professions get tired, teachers get exhausted.'[9] Some, particularly those with marketable talents, seek less stress and more remuneration elsewhere. In one school alone four teachers left simultaneously. The loss to the school was significant but the community gained a new travel agency, law school and sports instructor.[10]

An easy job?

Emotional stress

So what causes stress in this amenable job which can earn appreciable 'pin money' in sociable hours? Hochschild[11] claims that it is because the task demands a high level of 'emotional labour' – personal contact with people in whom teachers must induce a state of well-being through their own cheerfulness. This can sometimes mean enforcing a sense of bonhomie for hours at a time. Hochschild considers this to be as demanding as the intellectual labours of the task but largely invisible and unrewarded.

Wilby claims that further stress results from controlling the unwilling presence of many pupils. 'Only they and prison officers,' he says, 'have to base their professional lives on dealing with unwilling conscripts.'[12] The argument may have some grounds but, due to the efforts of teachers, many children would actually prefer to be at school than at home! Children, however, have become more demanding in school. Three out of four headteachers responding to an Assistant Masters and Mistresses Association questionnaire[13] believed there had been a marked deterioration in children's behaviour; 64 per cent said that aggression towards other children had increased; 53 per cent thought defiance towards teachers was more common, and half reported more destructive attitudes. A growth in obscene language and temper tantrums was also noted. It is not unknown for such behaviour to be blamed on the schools themselves. Indeed, 'poor discipline in schools' is claimed to be behind a range of social ills. As one infant headteacher stated, 'We must be a remarkable profession. After learning nothing during their five years at home, we can teach them on their first day to swear, fight and flick peas at each other.

Pressure for teacher accountability

If children are changing, even more so is the nature of the job. Increased accountability means a school must produce 'guidelines' for each subject area. These vary but may include aims and objectives for the different stages of learning, outlines of exemplar activities and lists of useful texts and resources. Unlike the old syllabuses presented to the author at all three of her schools, these are much broader documents. Though there will be a leader, they are generally designed by the staff as a group during lunchtime and after-school meetings. Every subject must be covered in this way and as ideas change so the policies must be reviewed and improved.

Teachers also have to keep an increasingly complex range of records to be available for headteachers, parents, other staff, schools and local authorities. The demands of such record keeping can vary, but at its extreme it may involve completing a whole book of details for each child covering concepts and skills, processes and personal traits.[14] There are also the informal assessments carried out by teachers as aids to their own teaching and the preparation of remedial activities where necessary. Under the Warnock recommendations, considerable attention will also be needed for the assessment and review procedures concerning children with special needs.

The responsibility for guidelines generally lies with the post of responsibility for the subject. These management positions qualify for extra allowances over and above the basic scale. The amount of additional work generated from such posts varies. In the past, a teacher may have had responsibility for welfare demanding no more than maintaining the first-aid box. Today's responsibility allowances generally demand 'value for money'. Requirements are stated in writing and may be examined by parents or other outside agencies.

Multiple responsibilities are not uncommon. Mrs Appleby, a teacher in a South West primary school, for example, has six components to her Scale 3 post: the school library, educational technology, humanities, girls' welfare, community contacts and gifted children. Every year there is £1,000 allowance for books within the school. Mrs Appleby consults with staff as to library and school needs. She attends exhibitions, browses bookshops and gathers up-to-date catalogues. She then lists books and discusses her decisions with the head and staff. Books are also chosen from the local book library service so that the library is actively changing to meet new needs. To train children for more effective use of local libraries, the books have been organised by Mrs Appleby on the Dewey system. Classification and the development of an index have been part of the post's requirements, as is library maintenance and care. Facilities are usually checked daily and each evening.

Mrs Appleby has been interested in the use of microcomputers in school for many years. She was one of the first teachers to help develop primary computer materials in the country and has been actively involved in the research of the ITMA project (see p. 202). She has attended many courses on the subject. The school has also invested considerable money in software and hardware. These have been carefully catalogued by Mrs Appleby with helpful ideas for use. Again, she offers staff advice on appropriate supporting resources, and new software is chosen and ordered according to needs. Staff are also kept up to date about new programs on the market. During Monday lunchtimes she runs the computer club.

Mrs Appleby's school operates an integrated curriculum. Staff plan their projects, normally in year groups, in the term before implementation. They use the school guidelines for each subject to ensure a balance of activities is achieved. Mrs Appleby collates the results and gives advice on content and supporting resources for the humanities aspects of the projects. She has recently completed a course on world studies involving seven 'day' sessions and two residential weekends; naturally, she paid part of the course fees herself.

On Wednesday evening there is the youth club to organise and run. Mrs Appleby has trained in youth leadership. The club is part of the community contact of the school. It is therefore open to any children in the area regardless of school attended. There are also good contacts with a local home for the elderly. Children visit the old people, who in turn attend sports days and other school functions. Mrs Appleby organises and co-ordinates the respective visits.

Then there is the responsibility for welfare. This involves keeping a general eye on standards of behaviour, in and out of school. Any female child whose behaviour is causing concern is directed first to Mrs Appleby, then, if necessary, to the headteacher. Academic problems of any girl in school are also Mrs Appleby's concern and she has special responsibility for all high ability children in the school. These children receive extension activities in language on one afternoon per week. She simultaneously organises group work for her own class which is supervised by parents. In summer a week's camp is organised. All arrangements for the holiday are included in the post of responsibility, as is supervision of female pupils during the camp. Beyond this Mrs Appleby manages the school accounts – from tuck sales to fund-raising. She also teaches a class of thirty-two children!

Such a description of one teacher's additional responsibilities gives some impression of modern teaching. Gone are the days when books were distributed and children told to 'get on with it'. Mrs Appleby is not unique in her responsibilities. Indeed, some teachers have a similar work-load on a lower scale. However, to the lay person and even pupils such responsibility is unseen. It is another hidden aspect of teaching that needs greater recognition.

Pressures for professional development

Like Mrs Appleby, all teachers are regularly required to go on courses. Unlike some professions who travel in work hours to luxury hotels in salubrious parts of the country, teachers trudge in the evening to their local teachers' centre, often at their own cost. To cut travelling expenses and improve the relevancy of INSET, school-based courses are common. The whole staff join together in their own or a neighbouring institution for discussions, lectures and practical activities. The teachers themselves help design the course so that it is tailored to their particular needs. In this way the school as a whole benefits from the exchange of views and ideas plus additional resources that can be generated. Schools, too, may be used as exemplars for courses, the staff demonstrating through displays or talks their ideas and approaches to teaching a certain curriculum area.

However, the procedure has been criticised by the teachers' unions as being a means of providing in-service on the cheap and allowing authorities to escape from their responsibilities to continued teacher education under 1972 agreements. The National Association of Schoolmasters and Union of Women Teachers, for example, stated in 1981:

> It is easy to see why [the school-based or focused course] . . . was becoming a fashion much advocated by local authorities; the approach combined the virtues of low cost (possibly no cost) with the high probability that there would be no question of release time for teacher participants . . . It would be . . . unacceptable if local authorities were to seek to evade their responsibilities for providing adequate resources and time off for in-service training by promoting a prostituted concept.[15]

Additional 'training' pressures on schools also come from the colleges of education or other initial training establishments. Student teachers have always spent a significant part of their course 'on the shop floor'. The practice is demanding on teachers. Even fitting visitors into some staff-rooms can be difficult, but staff must also absorb, encourage, help and supervise the trainees in class. Like allowing a child to bake or sew it is usually quicker or easier to do the task oneself. However, that is no way to gain expertise. Added to this, many B.Ed. courses now seek greater relevance by being school-focused. At its best such work takes considerable planning by school and college. If it can meet the school's as well as students' needs this is ideal, but a further burden in the classroom.[16]

Part of the community

A blue notice with white lettering can still be found outside many French schools. It prohibits anyone who is not a member of the teaching profession from entering the building. Since the 1960s British schools have been increasingly involved in the community. Few playground gates, like those at High Rise, forbid entry. Indeed, parents are generally welcomed within schools. They are, after all, important. Today all schools produce a prospectus for parents on their aims and activities.[17] Many reception class teachers visit homes of potential newcomers and operate a 'mums and toddlers' group during the day, utilising any spare room and equipment. Furthermore, they often prepare a list of useful activities parents might undertake before their child enters school. Other help might be given to parents – from advice on diet and discipline to marriage guidance and family planning assistance.

Parents in turn can help teachers by raising funds and carrying out a range of tasks from covering books to supervising group work. Many themselves are trained teachers either raising a family or unable to gain employment. Indeed, there is growing concern that many qualified staff are supplementing LEA provision by working voluntarily in this way.[18]

Any helper in school, whether ancillary or parent, needs organising and supervising. Where parent helpers are used in school, activities must also be carefully planned and prepared so that the non-professional can cope. Often this means training them by observing their performance carefully and feeding back suggestions for improvement. As Theresa Ireland states:

> It is no use giving a parent three children and a board game made for a specific teaching purpose and then not keeping an eye open to see that purpose achieved. It does make for more preparation, but, once good practice is established, I'm not left trying to teach rules, see they're kept, listen to children read instructions, check they've followed them, as well as deal with the rest of the class.[19]

Helping parents, though, can be a subtle and sensitive task. I remember well Lisa's mum. Mrs Walker was a strong character and wished to follow a career when the last of her six children entered school. She thought she would enjoy teaching. Although doubtful of her potential I explained the required entry qualifications for both the profession and nursery nursing. I also invited her in to work with a group on one afternoon per week. On the first occasion, she arrived prompt at 1.15 p.m. in good time for me to explain what I wanted her to do. She was to join a group of children painting and I suggested she talk with the children both socially and about their work. At first I hovered close at hand but, when all seemed well, continued with my own teaching. Some time later June carried her painting towards me, giggling uncontrollably.

'Mrs Walker says to show you what I've done.' June lowered her mouth to my ear, and whispered with a chuckle, 'She says its bloody lovely!'

Involving parents in the general life of the school can also be done through a parent/teacher association (PTA). There are always, of course, parents who need a certain amount of persuasion even to set foot inside the establishment. Teachers have to use a variety of strategies with them. The PTA can serve the interests of the others. The Plowden Committee did not generally support PTAs. In their opinion they were not necessarily

> the best means of fostering close relationships between home and school. They may do harm if they get into the hands of a small group . . . a smaller portion of manual workers attend PTA meetings than any other function . . . [and] in some schools, at some moments in their history, particularly if heads cannot delegate to others the administrative work of running a PTA, it may absorb too much of their attention.[20]

Now many LEAs strongly encourage them and themselves meet representatives of the county or city federation of PTAs. One of the major roles of parent groups is fund-raising. However, it is often teachers who ultimately organise and co-ordinate the annual Christmas fair and the sponsored swims.

As well as general involvement in school, parents may also need encouragement to concern themselves further with their own child's education. Alan's mother (p. 134) willingly listened to him read at night. Home reading of this kind has been given more formal structure at Belfield Community School, Rochdale, with great success in improved reading standards.[21] One of the writer's local schools has also just spent considerable time making a video of staff listening to children read to help and encourage parents to participate more effectively in the task at home.

Primary teachers, generally under pressure from parents, may also set homework for children. As at secondary school this can supplement class activities and encourage pupils to direct their own learning. Homework, however, can take considerable organisation in its planning and marking. It may also reduce time for pupils' hobbies and other valuable leisure activities. Interestingly, when the Secretary of State for Education, Sir Keith Joseph, attempted to increase homework as a means of broadening the curriculum of schools, both parents and teachers reacted angrily; the former because they could not see how they could cope with the extra work-load, and parents because they felt that 'homework should not be a substitute for what the educational service should provide'.[22]

Parents' involvement can also be achieved by sessions updating and broadening their understanding of the curriculum. At Eastlea, a series of practical mathematics lessons was held in the evenings to demonstrate what the school hoped to achieve by increasing its range of practical work in the subject. When 'sex education' gained new attention in the late 1960s parent/teacher discussions were held and materials demonstrated. 'Open days' or 'science fairs' can also extend understanding in an enjoyable way. However, such occasions are an organisational burden similar to that of, say, a business conference.

Finally, both parents and teachers may spend evenings meeting together as governors of the school. At present there is an equal partnership of both groups on governing bodies. In 1985 the National Confederation of Parent/Teacher Associations rejected a move by the secretary of state, Sir Keith Joseph, to effect a balance in the favour of parents. They said that 'the "majority" concept conjures up impressions of vested interests taking "suspect" decisions and arriving at policies without a neutral debate'.[23] They were also concerned that the move would place even more reliance on parents for financial contributions.

Summary

Although the public generally see teaching as an easy job with short hours and long holidays the multifarious hidden demands within it make teaching stressful and exhausting. Studies of teachers' days indicate perhaps surprisingly that, on average, staff work long hours, like most professions, yet their salaries are regularly allowed to fall behind others with comparable responsibilities. These also may be less stressful than teaching. Life in and outside the classroom involves considerable intellectual and emotional labour for the teacher. There are the problems of remaining cheerful even with the most disturbed pupils and fending off constant attacks from politicians, inspectors, employers and even strangers on trains. Add to this the evidence that children are becoming more badly behaved and challenging in school. Ironically teachers are frequently blamed for the poor behaviour of young people in society, yet pupils normally behave better in the classroom than they do at home.

The changes in teaching itself have also generated additional pressure and work in and out of school. Increased accountability and new approaches to children with special needs have resulted in a plethora of assessment, recording and review procedures in school. Continued professional development is also demanded, which teachers often undertake in their own time and at their own expense. School-focused courses, whilst drawing attention to the importance of tailoring in-service work to particular needs, have been condemned for undermining teachers' rights and the responsibility of authorities to provide full-time release for in-service training.

Schools must also increasingly involve themselves with their surrounding communities. B.Ed. courses are now frequently school-based, with students, teachers, lecturers and children working together for mutual benefit. Parents need encouragement to involve themselves not only in the general life of the school but also in the education of their particular child. Strategies for such encouragement can be satisfying but time-consuming. Add to all this the other pressures on teachers that have been indicated in this book: teachers doing as they are told and then being regularly criticised for doing it; the problem of carrying out tasks in ways that seem to defy definition and assessment.

Despite frequent claims to the contrary, there is a definable end product of primary teaching. This is the legacy of adults who view this as the happiest time of their education. Despite, rather than because of, our society, British primary schools and teachers are also the envy of the world. Politicians, parents and the general public should sit up, recognise, support and reward such efforts; otherwise morale, which is extremely low, will sink even further. The very talent that has produced this phenomenon will be lost to less stressful, better paid jobs, and society might well get the primary teachers and schools it deserves.

Notes and references

1 First impressions

1. Hoggart, R. (1963), *The Uses of Literacy*, Harmondsworth/London: Penguin, pp. 19, 21, 24, 46.

2 Contrasting types of primary school

1. Board of Education (1933), *Infant and Nursery Schools*, London: HMSO, p. 3.
2. Ibid., p. 4.
3. Rogers, P. (1887), *Reminiscences*.
4. Bartley, G. C. T. (1871), *The Schools for the People*, p. 107.
5. Board of Education (1933), op. cit., p. 6, n. 1.
6. *Penny Encyclopaedia* (1841), Vol. XXI.
7. Arnold, M. (1920), *Reports of Elementary Schools, 1852–82*, London: HMSO, p. 14.
8. Board of Education (1854), *Committee of Council on Education: Minute on Education of Mistresses for Infant Schools*, London: HMSO.
9. National Education Union (1870), *A Verbatim Report of the Debates in Parliament on the Elementary Education Bill*, pp. 441–2, 551.
10. France, Germany, Sweden and the United States favour a starting age of six. The USSR only recently began experimenting with a reduction of the entry age from seven.
11. *Minutes of School Board for London, 1*, pp. 155–61.
12. Board of Education (1871), *Rules to be Observed in Planning and Fitting Schools*, London: HMSO, Rule 12.
13. Board of Education (1904), *Rules for Planning and Fitting up Public Elementary Schools*, London: HMSO, Rule 18.
14. Board of Education (1918), *Education Act* (The Fisher Act), London: HMSO.
15. Board of Education (1926), *Report on the Education of the Adolescent*, London: HMSO.
16. Board of Education (1931), *The Primary School*, London: HMSO.

17. Ibid., p. 63.
18. Ibid., p. 63.
19. Ibid., p. 67.
20. Ibid., p. 66.
21. Ibid., pp. 65–6.
22. Central Advisory Council for Education (CACE) (1967), *Children and their Primary Schools* (The Plowden Report), London: HMSO, par. 262.
23. Ibid., par. 368.
24. Ibid., par. 372–374.
25. Ibid., par. 384.
26. Ibid., par. 344–359.
27. Ibid., par. 361.
28. Ibid., par. 362.
29. Ibid., par. 368.
30. Taylor, B. (1983), *A Parent's Guide to Education*, London: Hodder & Stoughton for the Consumers Association.

4   Contrasts in primary school organisation

1. Arnold, M. (1920), *Reports on Elementary Schools, 1852–82*, London: HMSO, pp. 14–15.
2. Board of Education (1931), *The Primary School*, London: HMSO, p. 77.
3. Board of Education (1933), *Infant and Nursery Schools*, London: HMSO, pp. 138–9.
4. Somerhill, H. J. and Clark, E. (1971), 'Variations on Family Grouping in an Infant School', in Walton, J. (1971), *The Integrated Day in Theory and Practice*, London: Ward Lock, p. 83.
5. CACE (1967), *Children and their Primary Schools*, London: HMSO, par. 802.
6. Somerhill, H. J. and Clarke, E. (1971), op. cit., p. 83.
7. CACE (1967), op. cit., par. 349.
8. Ibid., par. 794.
9. Ibid., par. 802.
10. Department of Education and Science (DES) (1978), *Primary Education in England*, London: HMSO, p. 21.
11. Ibid.
12. Ibid.
13. Board of Education (1931), op. cit., pp. 77–9.
14. Isaacs, S. (1932), *The Children We Teach: Seven to Eleven Years*, London: University of London Press (ULP).
15. Galton, M. *et al.* (1980), *Inside the Primary Classroom*, London: Routledge & Kegan Paul, p. 54.
16. Ibid., p. 54.
17. Ridgway, L. (1976), *Task of the Teacher in the Primary School*, London: Ward Lock, p. 101.
18. DES (1978), op. cit., London: HMSO, par. 3.6.
19. Galton, M. *et al.* (1980), op. cit., p. 69.
20. Yates, A. and Pidgeon, D. (1959), 'The Effect of Streaming', *Educational Research*, Vol. II, No. 1, pp. 65–70.
21. Daniels, J. C. (1961), 'The Effects of Streaming in the Primary School', *British Journal of Educational Psychology*, Vol. XXXI, Part 1, pp. 69–78.
22. Jackson, B. (1964), *Streaming: An Education System in Miniature*, London: Routledge & Kegan Paul.
23. NFER (1967), *The Organisation of Junior Schools and Effects of Streaming*, in CACE (1967), op. cit.

24. Jackson, B. (1964), op. cit., pp. 125–6.
25. Morrison, A. and McIntyre, D. (1969), *Teachers and Teaching*, Harmondsworth/ London: Penguin, p. 101.
26. Board of Education (1931), op. cit., p. 78.
27. Fraser, R. (1981), 'Driving Turtles Can Be Fun', *Education*, 15 May 1981.

6   Within these walls

1. CACE (1967), *Children and their Primary Schools*, London: HMSO, par. 1094.
2. Seaborne, M. and Lowe, R. (1977), *The English School: Its Architecture and Organisation; Volume II 1870–1970*, London: Routledge & Kegan Paul, p. 3.
3. Curtis, S. J. and Boultwood, M. E. (1966), *An Introductory History of English Education since 1800*, London: University Tutorial Press, 4th edn, p. 10.
4. Ibid., p. 122.
5. Board of Education (1872), *Committee of Council on Education Report 1871–72, CXIX*, London: HMSO.
6. Board of Education (1898), *PRO Ed. 21/12065*, London: HMSO.
7. Board of Education (1872), *PRO Ed. 14/1*, London: HMSO.
8. Quoted by Seaborne and Lowe (op. cit.) from Board of Education (1898), op. cit.
9. Kirby, R. G., in *Journal of the Society of Architects*, September 1909, p. 403.
10. In *Public Health*, November 1907, p. 87.
11. In *Journal of the RIBA*, XXIX, 1921, p. 42.
12. Board of Education (1914), *Building Regulations for Public Elementary Schools*, London: HMSO.
13. Board of Education (1931), *Report of the Consultative Committee on the Primary School*, London: HMSO.
14. Board of Education (1936), *Elementary School Buildings*, London: HMSO.
15. Seaborne, M. and Lowe, R. (1977), op. cit., p. 83.
16. Board of Education (1933), *Yearbook of Education*, London: HMSO, pp. 330–1.
17. Seaborne, M. (1971), *Primary School Design*, London: Routledge & Kegan Paul, p. 51.
18. DES (1960), *The Story of Post-War School Building*, London: HMSO, p. 2.
19. The Amersham school in Buckinghamshire was built in 1956. It was the Ministry's development group's interpretation of junior school requirements for a more progressive type of education. It was followed in 1958 by a village school in Finmere, Oxfordshire, designed to reflect the family character of a village community.
20. CACE (1967), op. cit., par. 1094.
21. Ibid.
22. DES (1972), *Education Survey 16: Open Plan Primary Schools*, London: HMSO.
23. NUT (1974), *Open Planning: A Report with Special Reference to Primary Schools*, London: NUT Publications.
24. Bennett, N. *et al.* (1980), *Open Plan Schools*, Windsor: NFER for the Schools Council, p. 51.
25. Bennett classified open-plan schools according to the number of teachers the unit was designed for and the amount of shared space. The four categories for the teacher numbers were Pairs, Triples, Quads and Multis. Schools could either have shared teaching space and shared practical or enclosed areas such as quiet rooms (Type 1), or shared practical and enclosed spaces but no shared teaching area (Type 2). Combinations of these variables provided the eight basic types.
26. Rattenbury, P. (1978), 'More or Less Open: The Present Day Design of Primary Schools', *Aspects of Education*, 21, pp. 28ff.
27. Bennett, N. *et al.* (1980), op. cit., p. 231.

28. Hagedorn, J. (1984), 'After the Walls Came Tumbling Down', *Guardian*, 8 May 1984, p. 11.
29. Ibid.

8   Design matters

1. Kirkman, S. (1985), 'Ten-Year Wait for a Staff Toilet', *The Times Educational Supplement*, 7 June 1985, p. 10.
2. CACE (1967), *Children and their Primary Schools*, London: HMSO.
3. Bennett, N. *et al.* (1980), *Open Plan Schools*, Windsor: NFER for the Schools Council, p. 225.
4. Ibid., p. 79.
5. Seaborne, M. (1971), *Primary School Design*, London: Routledge & Kegan Paul, p. 7.
6. Board of Education (1931), *The Primary School*, London: HMSO, p. 118.
7. Pearson, E. (1972), *Trends in School Design*, London: Macmillan for the Schools Council, p. 23.
8. Ibid., p. 23.
9. Dean, J. (1972), *Room to Learn: Working Space*, London: Evans Bros.
10. Pearson, E. (1972), op. cit., p. 21.
11. Bennett, N. *et al.* (1980), op. cit., p. 225.
12. Ibid., p. 226.
13. Pearson, E. (1972), op. cit., p. 30.
14. Bennett, N. *et al.* (1980) op. cit., pp. 225–30.
15. Manning, P. (1967), *The Primary School: An Environment for Education*, Liverpool: Pilkington Research Unit, University of Liverpool.
16. Bennett, N. *et al.* (1980), op. cit., p. 174.
17. CACE (1967), op. cit.
18. DES (1972), *Open Plan Primary Schools*, London: HMSO.
19. NUT (1974), *Open Planning: A Report with Special Reference to Primary Schools*, London: NUT Publications.
20. Bennett, N. *et al.* (1980), op. cit., p. 174.
21. Ibid., p. 170.
22. In Bennett, N. *et al.* (1976), *Journeys into Open Space*, Lancaster: University of Lancaster.
23. Kruchten, P. M. (1971), *Survey of Teachers' Perceptions in Open Area Schools*, M.Ed. thesis, University of Calgary, USA.
24. Bennett, N. *et al.* (1975), *Enquiry into Cumbria's Open Plan Schools*, Lancaster: University of Lancaster.
25. Strathclyde Regional Council (1976), *Primary School Buildings Report*.
26. Pritchard, P. and Moodie, A. G. (1971), *A Survey of Teacher Opinions regarding Open Areas* (ED 157 102), Vancouver, Canada: School Board of School Trustees.
27. SEF (1975), *E6 Academic Evaluation*, Toronto, Canada: Metropolitan Toronto School Board.
28. Brunetti, F. A. (1971), *Open Space: A Status Report. Memo No. 1, School Environment Study*, Stanford, California: Stanford University.
29. Bennett, N. *et al.* (1980), op. cit., p. 177.
30. NUT (1962), *The State of our Primary Schools*, London: NUT Publications.
31. Quoted in Seaborne, M. (1971), op. cit., p. 7.
32. DES (1962), *The School Building Survey*, London: HMSO.
33. CACE (1967), op. cit., par. 1113.
34. 'More Hurt in School Accidents', *The Times*, 16 April 1984.
35. Durham, M. (1985), 'The Least of their Concerns', *Guardian*, 18 January 1985, p. 6.

36. DES (1985), *Report by HM Inspectors on the Effects of Local Authority Expenditure Policies on Education Provision in England, 1984*, London: HMSO.
37. Maclure, J. S. (1970), *One Hundred Years of London Education*, London: ILEA, p. 31.
38. Northumberland Education Committee (1905), *Minutes, 30th June*, pp. 145–6.
39. Seaborne, M. and Lowe, K. (1977), *The English School: Its Architecture and Organisation; Volume II 1870–1970*, London: Routledge & Kegan Paul, p. 81.
40. Ibid., p. 81.
41. Board of Education Departmental Committee on the Cost of School Buildings (1911), *Report and Abstracts of Evidence*.
42. Ibid., p. 5.
43. See Board of Education (1933), *Infant and Nursery Schools*, London: HMSO, p. 181.
44. Board of Education (1918), *Circular 1051*, London: HMSO.

10   Pressure from the progressives

1. Lawrence, D. H. (1921), *Women in Love*, Harmondsworth/London. Penguin, p. 27.
2. Salmon, D. (1898), *The Art of Teaching*.
3. Rousseau, J. J. (1750), *Discourse on the Arts and Sciences*, p. 147.
4. Rousseau, J. J. (1762), *Émile*, London: Dent, 1911 edn, p. 1.
5. Ibid., p. 131.
6. Quoted by Curtis, S. J. and Boultwood, MEA (1960), *An Introductory History of English Education since 1800*, London: University Tutorial Press, p. 127.
7. Ibid., p. 128.
8. Ibid., p. 247.
9. Ibid., p. 251.
10. In the late 1960s Cheadle Grammar School reorganised on the basis of the Dalton Plan but the organisation was discontinued when the school amalgamated with the neighbouring secondary modern to form a comprehensive school.
11. Board of Education (1918), *Handbook of Suggestions for the Consideration of Teachers*, London: HMSO, preface.
12. Board of Education (1931), *The Primary School*, London: HMSO, par. 75.
13. Ibid., par. 83.
14. Ibid., par. 67.
15. Ibid., par. 67.
16. Board of Education (1933), *Infant and Nursery Schools*, London: HMSO, p. 141.
17. Ibid., p. 125.
18. Ibid., p. 125.
19. Ibid., p. 143.
20. Ibid., p. 133.
21. Ibid., p. 142.
22. Selleck, R. J. W. (1972), *English Primary Education and the Progressives 1914–1939*, London: Routledge & Kegan Paul.
23. Daniel, M. V. (1947) *Activity in the Primary School*, Oxford: Blackwell.
24. CACE (1967), *Children and their Primary Schools*, London: HMSO, par. 9.
25. Ibid., par. 753.
26. Ibid., par. 531.
27. Ibid., par. 530.
28. Ibid., par. 530.
29. Ibid., par. 549.
30. Bruner, J. S. (1961), in *Havard Educational Review*, Vol. 31 (1), pp. 22–32.
31. Hendrix, G. (1961), in *Mathematics Teacher*, 54 (5), pp. 290–9.

32. Kersh, B. Y. (1962), in *Journal of Educational Psychology*, 53 (2), pp. 62–75.
33. Keisler, R. (1962), in *Science Teacher*, Vol. 29, pp. 18–25.
34. Ausubel, D. B. (1963), in *Science Education*, Vol. 47, pp. 278–84.
35. CACE (1967), op. cit., par. 529.
36. Ibid., par. 761.
37. Ibid., par. 761.
38. Ibid., par. 755.
39. Ibid., par. 757.
40. Ibid., par. 757.
41. Ibid., par. 758.
42. Ibid., par. 759.
43. Ibid., par. 553.
44. Blackie, J. (1967), *Inside the Primary School*, London: HMSO.
45. Bainbridge, J. W. (1977), 'Basic Concepts as a Common Core', Natural Science in Schools, Vol. 15 (2), pp. 274–83.
46. CACE (1967), op. cit., par. 536.
47. Brown, M. and Precious, N. (1968), *The Integrated Day in the Primary School*, London: Ward Lock, p. 12.
48. Ibid., p. 13.
49. Ibid., p. 13.
50. Ibid., p. 13.
51. Ibid., p. 14.
52. Ibid., p. 14.
53. Rintoul, K. A. P. and Thorne, K. P. C. (1975), *Open Plan Organisation in the Primary School*, London: Ward Lock.
54. Strathclyde Regional Council (1976), *Primary School Building Report*.
55. Ibid., p. 41.
56. Bennett, N. *et al.* (1980), *Open Plan Schools*, Windsor: NFER for the Schools Council, p. 61.
57. Seidman, M. R. (1975), 'Comparing Physical Openness and Climate Openness of Elementary Schools', *Education*, 95 (4), pp. 345–50.
58. See, for example, Charters, W. W. (1978), *The Effects of the Team Organisation of Elementary Schools on Teacher Influence and Work Attitudes*, Toronto: Research Association.
59. Arkwright, D. *et al.* (1975), *Survey of Open Plan Primary Schools in Derbyshire*, Derbyshire Education Authority.

12 Effective teaching

1. See, for example, Dearden, R. F. (1976), *Problems in Primary Education*, London: Routledge & Kegan Paul.
2. Ibid., pp. 88–93.
3. Foss, B. (1969), 'Other Aspects of Child Psychology', in Peters, R. S. (1969a), *Perspectives on Plowden*, London: Routledge & Kegan Paul, pp. 49–50.
4. Dearden, R. F. (1969), 'The Aims of Primary Education', in Peters, R. S. (1969a), op. cit., pp. 21–41.
5. Peters, R. S. (1969b), 'A Recognisable Philosophy of Education: A Constructional Critique', in Peters, R. S. (1969a), op. cit., pp. 1–20.
6. Peters, R. S. (1969a), op. cit.
7. Naish, M. *et al.* (1970), 'Ideological Documents in Education: Some Suggestions Towards a Definition', in Hartnett, A. and Naish, M. (1970), *Theory and the Practice of Education, Vol. II*, pp. 370–8.
8. Moran, P. E. (1971), in *Educational Research*, Vol. 14 (1), November.
9. Dearden, R. F. (1976), op. cit., p. 97.

10. Gagne, R. M. (1963), in *Journal of Research in Science Teaching*, Vol. 1, pp. 27–32.
11. Bruner, J. K. (1961), in *Harvard Educational Review*, Vol. 31 (1), pp. 21–32.
12. Gagne, R. M. (1963), op. cit.
13. Ausubel, D. P. (1963), in *Science Education*, Vol. 47, pp. 278–84.
14. Bainbridge, J. W. (1971), 'Science in Primary Schools', *Schools Science Review*, Vol. 53, p. 277.
15. Board of Education (1921), *The Teaching of English in England*, London: HMSO.
16. Cox, C. B. and Dyson, R. E. (eds) (1975), *Black Paper 3: Goodbye Mr Short*, London: Critical Quarterly Society, editorial.
17. Quoted by Cox, C. B. and Dyson, R. E. (eds) (1969), *Black Paper 1: Fight for Education*, London: Critical Quarterly Society, 'Letter to Members of Parliament'.
18. Maude, A. (1969), 'The Egalitarian Threat', in Cox, C. B. and Dyson, R. E. (eds) (1969), op. cit.
19. Start, K. B. and Wells, B. K. (1972), *The Trend of Reading Standards*, Windsor: NFER; Burke, E. and Lewis, D. G. (1975), 'Standards of Reading: A Critical Review of some Recent Studies', *Educational Research*, 17, pp. 163–74.
20. Gardner, K. (1968), *State of Reading* in Smart, N. (1968), *Crisis in the Classroom*, London: Hamlyn pp. 18–30.
21. Root, B. (1969), in *The Times*, 5 July 1969.
22. Bantock, G. H. (1969), 'Discovery Methods', in Cox, C. B. and Dyson, R. E. (eds) (1969), *Black Paper 2: The Crisis in Education*, London: The Critical Quarterly Society, p. 6.
23. Auld, R. (1976), *William Tyndale Junior and Infants Schools Public Enquiry*, London: ILEA.
24. Ibid., pars 247–56, 467–9.
25. Bennett, N. (1976), *Teaching Styles and Pupil Progress*, London: Open Books.
26. Bennett, N. (1974), 'Plowden's Progress: Informal One in Six', *The Times Educational Supplement*, 18 October 1974, p. 21.
27. Bennett, N. (1976), op. cit., back cover.
28. Morrison, A. and McIntyre, D. (1969), *Teachers and Teaching*, Harmondsworth/London: Penguin, p. 73.
29. Anderson, R. C. (1959), 'Learning in Discussions: A Resumé of the Authoritarian–Democratic Studies', *Harvard Educational Review*, 29, pp. 201–15.
30. Gage, N. L. (ed.) (1963), *Handbook of Research on Teaching*, Chicago: Rand McNally, p. 13.
31. Flanders, N. A. (1965), *Teacher Influence, Pupil Attitudes and Achievement*, Co-operative Research Monograph, Washington, DC: US Office of Education, p. 29.
32. Flanders, N. A. (1970), *Analyzing Teacher Behaviour*, Reading: Addison Wesley.
33. Bennett, N. (1976), op. cit., p. 38.
34. Ibid., p. 32.
35. Taba, H. and Elzey, F. F. (1964), 'Teaching Strategies and Thought Processes', *Teacher College Record*, 65, pp. 524–34.
36. Ibid.
37. Elliott, J. (1976), *Developing Hypotheses about Classrooms from Teachers' Practical Constructs – An Account of the Work of the Ford Teaching Project*, University of North Dakota: North Dakota Study Group on Evaluation.
38. Galton, M. (1982), 'Strategies and Tactics in Junior School Classrooms', in Richards, C. (ed.) (1982), *New Directions in Primary Teaching*, Lewes: Falmer Press, p. 251.
39. Ibid., p. 251.
40. Galton, M. *et al.* (1980), *Inside the Primary Classroom*, London: Routledge & Kegan Paul.
41. in Wright, N. (1977), *Progress in Education*, London: Croom Helm, p. 49, n. 40.

42. Gardner, D. E. M. (1966), *Experiment and Tradition in Primary Schools*, London: Methuen.
43. Wright, N. (1977), op. cit., p. 49, n. 40.
44. See Galton, M. and Simon, B. (1980), *Progress and Performance in the Primary Classroom*, London: Routledge & Kegan Paul, p. 11.
45. Bennett, N. (1976), op. cit., p. 188.
46. Galton, M. and Simon, B. (1980), op. cit., p. 188.
47. Romberg, T. A. (1980), 'Salient Features of the BTES Framework of Teacher Behaviours', in Denham, C. and Lieberman, A. (eds) (1980), *Time to Learn*, Washington, DC: Department of Health Education and Welfare, US National Institute of Education.
48. Wragg, E. C. (1979), 'Superteach and the Dinosaurs', *Guardian*, 9 January 1979, p. 9.
49. Grouws, D. A. (1981), 'An Approach to Improving Teacher Effectiveness', *Cambridge Journal of Education*, 11, i, pp. 2–14.
50. Galton, M. (1982), op. cit., p. 251.
51. Ibid., p. 251.
52. Galton, M. *et al*. (1980), op. cit., p. 118.
53. Ibid., p. 119.
54. Aitken, M. *et al*. (1981), 'Teaching Styles and Pupil Progress: A Re-Analysis', *British Journal of Educational Psychology*, 51, p. 184.
55. Gray, J. and Satterly, D. (1981), 'Formal or Informal? A Re-Assessment of the British Evidence', *British Journal of Educational Psychology*, 51, p. 191.
56. Rosenshine, B. (1970), 'Evaluation of Classroom Instruction', *Review of Educational Research*, 40, pp. 279–300.
57. Gray, J. and Satterly, D. (1981), op. cit., p. 192.
58. See Gray, J. (1975), 'The Roots of Reading: A Critical Re-Analysis', *Research in Education*, 14, pp. 33–47.
59. DES (1978), *Primary Education in England*, London: HMSO, p. 75.
60. Gray, J. and Satterly, D. (1981), op. cit., p. 192.
61. Ibid., p. 191.
62. See, for example, Carver, R. P. (1978), 'The Case against Statistical Significance Testing', *Harvard Educational Review*, 48, pp. 378–99.
63. Aitken, M. *et al*. (1981), op. cit., p. 184.
64. Gray, J. and Satterly, D. (1981), op. cit., p. 187.
65. CACE (1967), *Children and their Primary Schools*, London: HMSO, par. 270.
66. See Bennett, N. *et al*. (1980), *Open Plan Schools*, Windsor: NFER; and Bassey, M., (1978) *Nine Hundred Primary School Teachers*, Windsor: NFER.
67. In de la Mare, W. (1913), *Peacock Pie*, London: Faber, 1969 edn, p. 30.
68. Board of Education (1931), *The Primary School*, London: HMSO, p. 129.
69. Galton, M. and Simon, B. (1980), op. cit., p. 29.
70. Wragg, E. C. (1976), 'The Lancaster Study: Its Implications for Teacher Training', *The Times Educational Supplement*, 15 September 1976, p. 285.
71. Galton, M. and Simon, B. (1980), op. cit., pp. 36–9.
72. Moran, P. E. (1971), op. cit.
73. Galton, M. and Simon, B. (1980), op. cit., p. 202.
74. Ibid., p. 199.
75. Ibid., p. 205.
76. Ibid., p. 205.
77. DES (1978), op. cit., par. 6.13.
78. Southgate, V. *et al*. (1981), *Extending Beginning Reading*, London: Heinemann.
79. Galton, M. and Simon, B. (1980), op. cit., p. 207.
80. Bennett, N. *et al*. (1980), op. cit.
81. Galton, M. and Simon, B. (1980), op. cit., p. 207.
82. Ibid., pp. 204–5.

83. Ibid., p. 212.
84. Acland, H. (1976), 'Stability of Teacher Effectiveness: A Replication', *Journal of Education Research*, 69, pp. 289–92.

14   **Battles over basics**

1. Cox, C. B. and Dyson, R. E. (eds) (1969), *Black Paper 1: Fight for Education*, London: Critical Quarterly Society.
2. Froome, S. (1977), 'The Bullock Report', in Cox, C. B. and Boyson, R. (eds) (1977). *Black Paper* London: Maurice Temple Smith, p. 30.
3. Lyness, R. C. (1969), 'Modern Maths Reconsidered', *Trends in Education*, 14, April 1969, pp. 3–8.
4. Cox, C. B. and Dyson, R. E. (eds) (1970), *Black Paper 2: The Crisis in Education*, London: Critical Quarterly Society, p. 4.
5. See, for example, Jencks, C. *et al.* (1972), *Inequality: A Reassessment of the Effect of Family and Schooling in America*, New York: Basic Books.
6. Cox, C. B. and Dyson, R. E. (eds) (1969), op. cit., p. 4.
7. Walker, D. (1970), 'William Tyndale', in Cox, C. B. and Dyson, R. E. (eds) (1970), op. cit., p. 40.
8. Reported in *Education*, 22 October 1976.
9. DES (1977), *Education in Schools: A Consultative Document*, London: HMSO, p. 8.
10. DES (1979), *Local Authority Arrangements for the School Curriculum*, London: HMSO, p. 6.
11. Ibid., p. 7.
12. DES/Welsh Office (1980), *A Framework for the School Curriculum*, London: HMSO.
13. Golby, M. (1980), 'Perspectives on the Core', in Golby, M. (ed.) (1980), *The Core Curriculum*, Exeter: School of Education, pp. 3–10.
14. DES/Welsh Office (1981), *The School Curriculum*, London: HMSO.
15. Richards, C. (1980), 'Demythologizing Primary Education', *Journal of Curriculum Studies*, p. 78.
16. DES (1978), *Primary Education in England*, London: HMSO, par. 8.28.
17. Bassey, M. (1978), *Nine Hundred Primary School Teachers*, Windsor: NFER.
18. The ORACLE Project (Observational Research and Classroom Learning Evaluation) was the first large-scale observational study of primary school classrooms to be undertaken in Britain. It was funded by the Social Science Research Council over the period 1975 to 1980 with the major objective of studying the relative effectiveness of different teaching approaches in primary schools. The results are published in Galton, G. *et al.* (1980), *Inside the Primary Classroom*, and Galton, G. and Simon, B. (1980), *Progress and Performance in the Primary Classroom*, both titles London: Routledge & Kegan Paul.
19. HMI (1980), *A View of the Curriculum*, Matters for Discussion series, London: HMSO.
20. Ibid., p. 2.
21. DES Welsh Office (1985), *The Organisation and Content of the 5–6 Curriculum*, London: HMSO.
22. HMI (1985), *The Curriculum from 5 to 16*, Curriculum Matters series 2, London: HMSO.
23. Ibid., p. 4.
24. DES/Welsh Office (1981), op. cit.
25. Kelly, A. V. (1977), *The Curriculum: Theory and Practice*, London: Harper & Row, p. 167.
26. Bryce, J. S. (1868), in *Schools Inquiry Commission*.

27. Brown, R. (1980), 'A Visit to the APU', *Journal of Curriculum Studies*, 12, pp. 78–81.
28. Ibid., p. 79.
29. Quoted by Blenkin, G. and Kelly, A. V. (1981), *The Primary Curriculum*, London: Harper & Row, p. 150.
30. Ibid., p. 154.
31. Ashton, P. *et al.* (1975), *Aims into Practice in the Primary School*, London: ULP, p. 15.
32. NFER (1977), *Areas of Discussion for Teacher Groups: Record Keeping*, Windsor: NFER.
33. Blenkin, G. and Kelly, A. V. (1981), op. cit., p. 159.
34. Harlen, W. *et al.* (1977), *Match and Mismatch*, Edinburgh: Oliver & Boyd for the Schools Council.
35. Goodman, K. S. (ed.) (1973), *Miscue Analysis: Applications to Reading Instruction*, ERIC, Clearinghouse on Reading and Communication Skills, Urbana, Illinois.
36. Chandler, D. (1984), *Young Learners and the Microcomputer*, Milton Keynes: Open University Press.
37. ILEA (1977), *Keeping the School under Review*, London: ILEA.
38. Barker Lunn, J. (1984), 'Junior School Teachers: Their Methods and Practices', *Educational Research*, Vol. 26 (3), November, Windsor: NFER.

16   Problems with projects

1. Quoted in Board of Education (1931), *The Primary School*, London: HMSO, p. 101.
2. CACE (1967), *Children and their Primary Schools*, London: HMSO, pars 540–2.
3. DES (1978), *Primary Education in England*, London: HMSO.
4. Kilpatrick, W. H. (1930), *Foundations of Method*, New York: Macmillan, pp. 204–5.
5. Board of Education (1931), op. cit., pp. 102–3.
6. Barnes, R. and Dow, G. (1982), 'Looking at Topic Centred Teaching', in Daw, G. (ed.) (1982), *Teacher Learning*, London: Routledge & Kegan Paul, p. 22.
7. CACE (1967), op. cit., par. 535.
8. Dearden, R. F. (1976), *Problems in Primary Education*, London: Routledge & Kegan Paul, pp. 72–4.
9. CACE (Wales) (1967), *Primary Education in Wales*, London: HMSO, par. 10.3.
10. See any SC5/13 unit, rear section on 'Broad Aims'.
11. Ausubel, D. B. (1963), in *Science Education*, Vol. 47, pp. 278–84.
12. CACE (1967), op. cit., par. 541.
13. Leith, S. (1981), 'Project Work: An Enigma', in Simon, B. and Willcocks, J. (eds) (1981), *Research and Practice in the Primary Classroom*, London: Routledge & Kegan Paul.
14. Blenkin, G. M. and Kelly, A. V. (1981), *The Primary Curriculum*, London: Harper & Row.
15. Rance, P. (1968), *Teaching by Topics*, London: Ward Lock, pp. 13–20.
16. Bassey, M. (1978), *Nine Hundred Primary School Teachers*, Windsor: NFER, p. 21.
17. Alexander, R. J. (1984), *Primary Teaching*, London: Holt, Reinhart & Winston.
18. DES (1978), op. cit., annexe B, p. 212.
19. Ibid., foreword, p. vii.
20. Bennett, N. *et al.* (1980), *Open Plan Schools*, Windsor: NFER.
21. Ibid., p. 234.
22. Ibid., p. 205.
23. Ibid., p. 240.
24. Ibid., p. 240.

25. Strathclyde Regional Council (1976), *Primary School Building Report*.
26. Galton, M. *et al.* (1980), *Inside the Primary Classroom*, London: Routledge & Kegan Paul, p. 192.
27. Leith, S. (1981), op. cit.
28. NUT (1979), *Primary Questions: The NUT Response to the Primary Survey*, London: NUT Publications.
29. Rance, P. (1968), op. cit.
30. Blenkin, G. M. and Kelly, A. V. (1981), op. cit., p. 107.
31. Bassey, M. (1978), op. cit.
32. Bennett, N. *et al.* (1980), op. cit., p. 141.
33. DES (1978), op. cit.
34. DES (1982), *Education 5–9: An Illustrative Survey of Eighty First Schools in England*, London: HMSO.
35. Richards, C. (1982), 'Curriculum Consistency', in Richards, C. (ed.) (1982), *New Directions in Primary Education*, Lewes: Falmer Press, pp. 47–61.
36. Board of Education (1931), op. cit., p. 104.
37. Blenkin, G. M. and Kelly, A. V. (1981), op. cit., p. 108.
38. DES (1975), *A Language for Life*, London: HMSO, pars 6.40, 8.13.
39. DES (1978), op. cit., par. 5.129.
40. Ibid., p. 619.
41. Ibid., p. 861.
42. Leith, S. (1981), op. cit., p. 56.
43. Buckley, R. *et al.* (1975), *PE7271 Technology for Teachers, Block 5, Unit 16, Curriculum Change and Organisation III, Syllabus Building and Assessment*, Milton Keynes: Open University Press.
44. Leith, S. (1981), op. cit., pp. 60–1.

19   Crossed by categorisation

1. Board of Education (1921), Education Act, London: HMSO.
2. DES (1944), *Education Act*, London: HMSO, section 8.2C.
3. MOE (1954), *Report of the Chief Medical Officer of the Ministry of Education, 1952–1953*, London: HMSO.
4. CACE (1967), *Children and their Primary Schools*, London: HMSO, par. 837.
5. For a summary, see Brennan, W. (1982), *Changing Special Education*, Milton Keynes: Open University Press, appendix 1, p. 110.
6. The ICAA is at 126 Buckingham Place Road, London, SW1W 9SB.
7. Wisbey, A. (1980), *Learning through Music*, Lancaster: MTP.
8. Thomas, G. (1984), 'Finding Meanings', *The Times Educational Supplement*, 14 September 1984, p. 52.
9. Brennan, W. (1982), op. cit., p. 13.
10. DES (1975), *Language for Life*, London: HMSO, par. 18.5
11. Brennan, W. (1982), op. cit., pp. 10–12.
12. DES (1978a), *Special Needs: Report of the Committee for Enquiry into the Education of Handicapped Children and Young People*, London: HMSO, p. 42.
13. Ibid., p. 43.
14. Brennan, W. (1982), op. cit., p. 59.
15. DES (1978a), op. cit., par. 3.19.
16. Ibid., par. 3.40.
17. Ibid., pars 4.35–4.47.
18. Ibid., par. 4.28.
19. Ibid., par. 6.11.
20. Brennan, W. (1982), op. cit., p. 52.
21. DES (1978a), op. cit., par. 8.8.

22. Quoted in the editorial, *Special Education*, Vol. 8, No. 1, March 1981.
23. Brennan, W. (1982), op. cit., p. 107.
24. Reported by Lodge, B. (1984), 'NUT Accepts Loss of Special Training Courses', *The Times Educational Supplement*, 19 September 1984, p. 1.
25. Ibid.
26. DES (1978b), *Primary Education in England*, London: HMSO, pars 6.13–6.17.
27. Ibid., pars 2.16, 5.29.
28. DES (1975), op. cit., par. 18.11.
29. Ibid., par. 18.13.
30. DES (1978b), op. cit., par. 6.12.
31. DES (1975), op. cit.
32. Ibid.
33. Ibid.
34. Ibid.
35. DES (1978a), par. 1.2.
36. See, for example, Tempest, N. R. (1974), *Teaching Clever Children 7–11*, London: Routledge & Kegan Paul.
37. DES (1978b), pars 6.13–6.17.
38. CACE (1967), op. cit., par. 872.
39. Tempest, N. R. (1974), op. cit.
40. DES (1978a), op. cit., par. 4.51.
41. CACE (1967), op. cit., par. 198.
42. DES (1985), *Education for All*, London: HMSO, p. xviii.
43. Parekh, B. (1985), 'Backdrop to the West Indian Tragedy', *The Times Educational Supplement*, 22 March 1985, p. 4.
44. DES (1985), op. cit., pars 5.14–5.15.
45. Ibid.
46. Described by Woodroffe, B. (1980), 'Primary Education: The Multi-Cultural Context', in Richards, C. (1980), *Primary Education: Issues for the Eighties*, London: A. & C. Black, p. 79.
47. DES (1985), op. cit., par. 5.5.
48. Woodroffe, B. (1980), op. cit., pp. 77–8.
49. Hill, J. *et al.* (1977) *Books for Children: The Homelands of Immigrants in Britain*, London: Institute of Race Relations.
50. Wilby, P. (1984), *1 plus 1 Equals an Anti Racialist Sum*, The Sunday Times 25 November 1984, p. 2.
51. Reported by Lodge, B. (1985), 'Honeyford Launches Attack on Left in Education', *The Times Educational Supplement*, 8 February 1985, p. 1.
52. *The Times Educational Supplement*, 28 December 1984, p. 13.
53. Winter, S. (1985), 'The Enemy Within', *The Times Educational Supplement*, 9 April 1985, p. 13.
54. DES (1978a), op. cit., par. 8.1.

21 No difference

1. Board of Education (1931), *Report of the Consultative Committee on the Primary School*, London: HMSO, p. 53.
2. Ibid., p. 32.
3. Quoted by Hannon, V. (1981), *Ending Sex Stereotyping in Schools*, Manchester: Equal Opportunities Commission, p. 1.
4. Hutt, C. (1972), *Males and Females* Harmondsworth/London: Penguin, pp. 88, 132.
5. Belotti, E. (1975), *Little Girls*, London: Writers & Readers.

6. Eysenck, A. J. and Eysenck, S. (1975), *Eysenck Personality Questionnaire (Junior and Adult)*, London: Hodder & Stoughton.
7. Galton, M. and Simon, B. (1980), *Progress and Performance in the Primary Classroom*, London: Routledge & Kegan Paul, pp. 159–61.
8. Ibid., p. 169.
9. Douglas, J. W. B. (1964), *The Home and the School*, London: MacGibbon & Kee, pp. 69–76.
10. 'The National Child Development Study', in CACE (1967), *Children and their Primary Schools*, Vol. 2, appendix 10.
11. King, J. S. (1974), *Women and Work – Sex Differences in Society*, London: HMSO, p. 1.
12. Hannon, V. (1981), op. cit., p. 1.
13. Good, T. L. *et al.* (1973), 'Effects of Teacher Sex and Student on Classroom Interaction', *Journal of Educational Psychology*, Vol. 65, No. 1, p. 83.
14. Galton, M. *et al.* (1980), *Inside the Primary Classroom*, London: Routledge & Kegan Paul, p. 66.
15. Douglas, J. W. B. (1964), op. cit., p. 71.
16. Galton, M. and Simon B. (1980), op. cit., p. 169.
17. DES (1976), *Joint Circular 2/76 Sex Discrimination Act*, London: HMSO.
18. DES (1975), *Curricular Differences for Boys and Girls: Educational Survey 21*, London: HMSO, p. 7.
19. Whyte, J. (1983), *Beyond the Wendy House: Sex Role Stereotyping in Primary Schools*, London: Longman for the Schools Council, p. 66.
20. Ibid., p. 66.
21. In 1982 Devon Education Committee, for example, accepted a recommendation of a paper suggesting single-sex classes for mathematics, and Holland Park School is at present trying one all-girl physics set in the fourth year. (Reported in *The Times Educational Supplement*, 24 September and 22 October 1982, letters.)
22. Tann, S. (1981), 'Grouping and Group Work', in Simon, R. and Willcocks, N. (1981), *Research and Practice in the Primary Classroom*, London: Routledge & Kegan Paul, p. 53.
23. Lobban, G. (1974), *Presentation of Sex Roles in British Reading Schemes*, Forum for the Discussion of New Trends in Education, 16, Spring, pp. 57–60.
24. Frazier, N. and Sadker, M. (1973), *Sexism in School and Society*, London: Harper & Row.
25. Dahl, R. (1984), *Revolting Rhymes*, Harmondsworth/London: Penguin.
26. Walden, R. and Walkerdine, V. (1982), *Girls and Mathematics: The Early Years*, Bedford Way Papers, 8, London: University of London Institute of Education.
27. Coote, A. (1976), *Child's Guide to Male Chauvinism*, The Sunday Times 11 April, 1976, p. 16–17.
28. From 'What Is Sexist Language?', in Hannon, V. (1981), op. cit., p. 20.
29. Weiner, G. (1978), 'Education and the Sex Discrimination Act', *Educational Research*, Vol. 20, No. 3, p. 172.
30. Turner, B. (1974), *Equality for Some*, London: Ward Lock, p. 217.
31. See McKeith, L. and Reid, S. (1975), 'Free Schools', *Women in Education Newsletter*, October 1975.

23 Even the kitchen sink: conflict over resources

1. Education Department (1895), London: HMSO, pp. 58–9.
2. Broudy, H. and Palmer, J. (1965), *Exemplars of Teaching Method*, Chicago: Rand McNally, p. 115.
3. Board of Education (1895), *Circular 369*, London: HMSO.

4. Dodd, C. I. (1901), *Introduction to the Herbartian Principles of Teaching*, London: Swan Sonnenschein, pp. 2–3.
5. Miall, L. C. (1897), *Thirty Years of Teaching*, London: Macmillan.
6. In Bainbridge, J. W. (1978), 'Origins of the Nature Study Movement', Natural Science in Schools, Vol. 16, 1.
7. Ibid.
8. DES (1905), *Handbook of Suggestions for Teachers*, London: HMSO, p. 59.
9. Stewart, J. (1981), *The Potential of Microcomputers in Aiding the Teaching of Primary Science*, unpublished M. Phil. thesis, University of Nottingham, p. 157.
10. DES (1978), *Primary Education in England*, London: HMSO.
11. Ibid., par. 5.87.
12. Ibid.
13. Parker, S. (1972), *Working with Wood: A SC5/13 Unit*, London: Macmillan for the Schools Council, p. 32.
14. See Association for Science Education (ASE) (1966), *Science for Primary Schools: Children Learning through Science*, London: Murray, p. 5.
15. Ministry of Education (1961), *Science in Primary Schools*, London: HMSO, p. 29.
16. ASE (1966), op. cit., p. 5.
17. Bainbridge, J. W. *et al.* (1967), *Nuffield Junior Science Guide 1*, London: Collins.
18. DES (1967), *Children and their Primary Schools*, London: HMSO, par. 97.
19. DES (1975), *A Language for Life*, London: HMSO, par. 21.19.
20. Ibid., par. 21.20.
21. Ibid., par. 21.27.
22. DES (1978), op. cit., par. 2.16.
23. Pollard, M. (1976), *A Handbook of Resources for Primary Schools*, London: Ward Lock, p. 25.
24. DES (1978), op. cit., par. 7.30.
25. Pollard, M. (1976), op. cit.
26. Whittaker, M. (1974), 'Realities of Primary Science', Natural Science in Schools, Vol. 12, 3.
27. Pollard, M. (1976), op. cit., p. 27.
28. Bainbridge, J. W. (1980), 'Tchirrip . . . Tchichirrip, Tseep: An Alarm Call for Primary School Science', Schools Science Review, Vol. 61, No. 217 pp. 623–638.
29. Pollard, M. (1976), op. cit., p. 27.
30. Ibid., p. 25.
31. Grundin, H. N. and E. H. (1978), *Reading: Curriculum Demands* in Grundin, H. N. and E. H. (eds) (1978), *Reading: Implementing the Bullock Report: Proceedings of the Fourteenth United Kingdom Annual Course and Conference*.
32. Body, W. (1982), 'Tell Another Story', *The Times Educational Supplement*, United Kingdom Association London: Ward Lock.
33. Warburton, F. W. and Southgate, V. (1969), *ita: An Independent Evaluation*, London: Murray & Chambers.
34. Ashton Warner, S. (1966), *Teacher*, Harmondsworth/London: Penguin, p. 48.
35. DES (1975), op. cit., par. 7.14.
36. Fletcher, H. (1975), *Mathematics for School: an Integrated Series (Levels I & II)*, London: Addison Wesley.
37. Blenkin, G. M. and Kelly, A. V. (1981), *The Primary Curriculum*, London: Harper & Row.
38. Pollard, M. (1976), op. cit., pp. 62–3.
39. Fawdry, K. (1974), *Everything but Alf Garnett: A Personal view of BBC Broadcasting*, London: BBC Publications, p. 21.
40. Hayter, C. G. (1974), *Using Broadcasts in Schools*, London: BBC Publications.
41. DES (1978), op. cit., par. 5.73.
42. Ibid., par. 5.98.

43. Ibid.
44. Clarke, J. (1966), 'The Development and Use of Linear Programmed Instruction in a Rural Primary School', in Unwin, D. and Leedham, J. (1966), *Aspects of Educational Technology*, London: Methuen, p. 43.

25 The micro: another white elephant?

1. Jones, R. (1978), *Microcomputers: Their Uses in Primary Schools*, London: CET, p. 35.
2. Reported in *Guardian*, 2 June 1980.
3. Quoted in 'Microcomputers in the Primary School: An "Education Digest"', *Education*, 18 February 1983, p. 1.
4. Obrist, A. J. (1983), *Microcomputer and the Primary School*, London: Hodder & Stoughton, p. 1.
5. Quoted by Burkhardt, H. (1984), *How Can Micros Help in Schools? The Research Evidence*, Shell Centre for Mathematical Education: University of Nottingham, p. 2.
6. 'Passing your Test on the Micro', *Primary Teaching and Micros*, March 1985, p. 20.
7. 'Passing your Test on the Micro', *Primary Teaching and Micros*, January 1985, p. 14.
8. *The Micro at Work* first appeared on the schools' television service of Granada Television, spring term 1985, 12 January to 28 March.
9. See Evans, C. (1980), *The Mighty Micro*, London: Gollancz.
10. Chandler, D. (1984), *Young Learners and the Microcomputer*, Milton Keynes: Open University Press, p. 1.
11. Quoted in Burkhardt, H. (1984), op. cit., p. 4.
12. Ibid., p. 4.
13. Papert, S. (1981), *Mindstorms*, London: Harvester.
14. Fraser, R. (1984), 'Microworlds', in Stewart, J. (ed.) (1984), *Micros and Project Work*, Winchester: MEP, pp. 92–107.
15. Fraser, R. (1984), 'A Beautiful Genius or An Ugly Moron', in Hughes, J. (ed.) (1984), *Computers and Education: Dreams and Reality*, Computer Education Group of New South Wales, pp. 8–17.
16. Papert, S. (1981), op. cit., p. 9.
17. Shiengold, K. *et al.* (1982), *Micros in School; Impact on the Social Life of Elementary Classrooms*, New York: Centre for Children and Technology, Bank Street College of Education.
18. Stewart, J. (1981), *The Potential of Microcomputers in Aiding the Teaching of Primary Science*, unpublished M. Phil. thesis, University of Nottingham, p. 176.
19. Ball, D. (1983), 'What Do You Really Think of Logo?', *Maths Teacher*, 105, December, p. 38.
20. Field, G. (1985), *Logo on the Sinclair Spectrum*, Basingstoke: Papermac/Macmillan, back cover.
21. Suppes, P. (1966), 'The Uses of Computers in Education', *Scientific American*, September 1966, p. 207.
22. Weizenbaum, J. (1976), *Computer Power and Human Reason: From Judgment to Calculation*, San Fransisco: W. H. Freeman, p. 8, footnote.
23. Howe, J. A. M. and du Boulay, B. (1981), 'Microprocessor-Assisted Learning: Turning the Clock Back?', in Rushby, N. (1981), *Selected Readings in Computer-Based Learning*, London: Kogan Page, p. 121.
24. Chandler, D. (1984), op. cit., p. 1.
25. See, for example Makins, V. (1981), 'Getting Brains Buzzing', *The Times Educational Supplement*, 24 April 1984.
26. Chandler, D. (1984), op. cit., pp. 1–7.

27. Smith, F. (1981), 'Demonstrations, Engagement and Sensitivity: The Choice between People and Programs', *Language Arts*, 28, No. 6, September 1981, p. 638.
28. Hughes, B. *et al.* (1984), 'Microprimer Software', *Mathematics in School*, September 1984, pp. 9–10.
29. Chandler, D. (1984), op. cit., p. 4.
30. Grand, D. (1984), 'Recording and the Slow Learner: Where a Micro Might Help', in Stewart, J. (ed.) (1984), op. cit., pp. 77–8.
31. See, for example, Hall, G. (1985), 'Learning Machine', *The Times Educational Supplement*, 7 July 1985, p. 9.
32. Grand, D. (1984), op. cit., p. 78.
33. Ross, A. (1984), 'Local Studies Projects and Information Retrieval', in Stewart, J. (1984), op. cit., pp. 30–1.
34. Ibid., p. 47.
35. Fraser, R. (1984), op. cit., p. 8.
36. Whalley, D. and Stewart J. (1985), 'Evaluating Software for Primary Science', in Stewart, J. (ed.) (1985), *Exploring Primary Science and Technology with Microcomputers*, London: CET, p. 25.
37. Fraser, R. (1984), op. cit., p. 12.
38. Cockcroft, W. H. (1982), *Mathematics Counts*, London: HMSO, par. 243.
39. Phillips, R. (1984), *Micro Primer Maths – There's More than Meets the Eye*, Shell Centre for Mathematical Education: University of Nottingham, p. 4.
40. Ibid., p. 5.
41. Fraser, R. (1984), op. cit., p. 13.
42. Ibid., p. 13.

Software details

LOGO. Versions are available from Acornsoft, Logotron Logo Systems, and the open University.

EUREKA, PIRATES SEEK and SLYFOX are part of the ITMA 'Micros in the Primary Classroom' course materials and are available from Longman.

ELIZA. Various versions of the original are available. See, for example, *Language Development in the Primary School: The Role of the Microcomputer*, Winchester: MEP.

WORDAMATICS. Available from ILECC.

WRITERIGHT. Available from Interface Software, 42 Radstock Road, Midsomer Norton, Bath.

DATAPROBE. Addison Wesley.

QUEST. Available from AUCBE, Hatfield Polytechnic.

Hardware details

The 'concept keyboard' is a touch-sensitive pad linked to the microcomputer by a cable. It removes the complexity of the QWERTY keyboard and is particularly useful for young or physically handicapped pupils. It is available from Star Microterminals in different sizes.

27 Deals on meals

1. Board of Education (1907), *Circular 552*, London: HMSO.
2. See the *Education (Provision of Meals) Act 1914*; and Board of Education (1940), *Circular 1520*, London: HMSO.
3. Dickens, C., *Nicholas Nickleby*, London: Dent, 1907 edn, p. 88.
4. Ibid., p. 89.
5. Brontë, C. (1847), *Jane Eyre*, Edinburgh: Nelson, 1955 edn, pp. 48, 76–7.

6. Dickens, C., *The Adventures of Oliver Twist*, Oxford: OUP, 1964 edn, p. 12.
7. Brontë, C. (1847), op. cit., p. 66.
8. Ibid., p. 66.
9. Leff, S. and Leff, V. (1959), *The School Health Service*, London: Lewis, p. 60.
10. Chief Medical Officer (1910), *Board of Educational Annual Report*, London: HMSO.
11. Chief Medical Officer (1923), *Board of Education Annual Report*, London: HMSO.
12. Robson, P. A. (1911), *School Planning*, London: HMSO, pp. 35–6.
13. Quoted by Leff, S. and Leff, V. (1959), op. cit., p. 71.
14. Corry Mann, H. C. (1926), *Medical Research Council: Special Report*, Ser. No. 105, London: HMSO.
15. Leff, S. and Leff, V. (1959), op. cit., p. 84.
16. NUT (1955), *The School Meals Service*, London: NUT Publications.
17. Reported in *The Times Educational Supplement*, 9 November, 1984.
18. Corry Mann, H. C. (1926), op. cit.
19. Orr, J. B. (1928), *Lancet*, 1, 202.
20. Leff, S. and Leff, V. (1959), op. cit., p. 99.
21. Ibid., p. 99.
22. Parker, S. and Doe, B. (1985), 'The Lunchtime Bomb', *The Times Educational Supplement*, March 1985, p. 20.
23. The continental school day begins and ends much earlier than ours so that lunch-time feeding is not necessarily required.

29 And what did you do at school today, Teacher?

1. Quoted by Broudy, H. and Palmer, J. (1965), *Exemplars of Teaching*, Chicago: Rand McNally, p. 106.
2. Berliner, W. (1984), 'Pay Arithmetic Makes the Teachers Wince', *The Times Educational Supplement*, 8 May 1984, p. 2.
3. Broudy, H. and Palmer, J. (1965), op. cit., p. 106.
4. Wilby, P. (1985), *The Sunday Times Magazine Good Careers Guide*, London: Times Newspapers, 25 November 1984, p. 60; in July 1985 published in book form, London: Granada.
5. Hilsum, S. and Cane, B. S. (1971), *The Teacher's Day*, Windsor: NFER.
6. Garner, G. (1985), 'Why Teachers Don't Stop Work when the Bell Goes', *The Times Educational Supplement*, 25 January 1985, p. 10.
7. Wilby, P. (1985), op. cit., pp. 51–67.
8. NUT (1985), *Today's Teacher*, London: NUT Publications.
9. Quoted by Wilby, P. (1985), op. cit., p. 60.
10. Pigache, P. (1984), 'When the Only Way Up Is Out', *The Times Educational Supplement*, 19 June 1984, p. 7.
11. Hochschild, A. R. (1983), *The Managed Heart: Commercialization of Human Feeling*, Berkeley: University of California Press.
12. Wilby, P. (1985), op. cit., p. 60.
13. The findings may be found in *Report*, the AMMA journal, September 1984.
14. Metropolitan Borough of Rochdale (1978), *Record Keeping in Primary Schools*, Rochdale: Borough Education Department.
15. NAS/UWT (1981), 'Three Statements of Teacher Union Policy on INSET', in Donaughue, C. et al. (eds), *In-service, the Teacher and the School*, London: Kogan Page for the Open University.
16. Amongst the pioneers of this approach to training is Pat Ashton of the University of Leicester, who directs the Centre for Evaluation and Development in Teacher Education. The emphasis on the centres work is on the development of the most effective processes for tackling classroom-based issues and helping individual

schools evaluate and develop their own curricula. They feel that teacher education at all levels should be school-focused, school-based, centred on classroom practice and routed in activity through thoughtful participation in what happens within classrooms. Ashton's work has naturally inspired others, so that schools will become increasingly involved in professional training.

17. The 1981 *DES Statutory Instruments (630)* gives detailed specifications of contents for school or LEA brochures.

18. See report of policy statement by the NAS/UWT in 'Parents Fill Teaching Jobs', *The Times Educational Supplement*, 11 January 1985.

19. Ireland, T. (1984), 'United We Stand', *The Times Educational Supplement*, 21 September 1984, p. 29.

20. CACE (1967), *Children and their Primary Schools*, London: HMSO, par. 111.

21. Interested readers can write directly to the school for a copy of its booklet on this reading approach.

22. Reported by Kirkman, S. (1984), in ' "No" to Extra Homework', *The Times Educational Supplement*, 21 September 1984, p. 1.

23. Reported by Durham, M. (1984), in 'PTAs Reject, "Majority"', *The Times Educational Supplement*, 21 September 1984, p. 5.

Index

Acland, H 243
acoustics (noise) 38, 41, 53, 55–6, 58, 60
ACSET 144
AEC 171
aesthetics 89, 109, 111–12, 156
aims of education 83, 110, 112
Aitken, M 92, 93, 242
Alexander, R 123, 244
AMMA 227, 251
ancilliary staff 40, 41, 171, 213, 216, 221, 231
Anderson, R. C. 87, 241
apparatus and equipment 70, 73, 78, 94, 141–55, 160, 165–6, 167–71, 173, 177–9
architects (*see also* DES Architects and Buildings Branch) 33, 34, 38, 53, 55, 56, 58, 61
architectural constraints 45–61
arithmetic (*see* mathematics)
Arnold, M 8, 235, 236
art and craft (*see also* 'practical education') 22, 50, 55, 65, 70, 71, 73, 94, 108, 125, 169–70, 180
ASE 170, 248
Ashton, P 126, 244, 251
Ashton-Warner, S 148, 174, 248
assemblies 38, 55
assessment: all round 90, 99, 114; and the curriculum 110, 112–13, 233; APU 110, 111, 112; criteria 25; by children 121; for secondary education 10, 13, 20, 24, 111; for streaming 25; informal 112–3, 228; materials, bias in 157; objectives and 112; of aesthetics 111–12; of basic skills 19, 89–90, 108, 110, 157; of creativity 146; of curriculum match 113, 126; of ethnic minority needs 146–7; of giftedness 146; of logic 111; of national standards 110, 111; of personal development 112; of practical skills 13; of progress 90, 110, 126; of project work 126–7; of short-term memory 156; of spatial ability 156; of special need 140–2, 150; of teachers 100, 226–7, 233; of teaching style 87–98; of verbal reasoning 13, 111; with computers 192–4, 206
audio visual aids 177–8, 180
Auld Report 86, 107, 241
Ausubel, D. B. 74, 84, 240, 241, 244

Bainbridge, J. W. 75, 84, 172, 240, 241, 248
basic skills 69, 72, 82, 84, 85, 86, 89, 96, 106–14, 118, 157, 192, 193, 194, 195, 199
Ball, D 190, 249
Bantock, G. H. 241
Barker-Lunn, 88, 93, 114, 244
Barnes, R. 121, 244

Bassey, M. 93, 109, 123, 125, 243, 244, 245
Bell, A. 34, 35
Bellotti, E. 246
Bennett, N. 41, 50, 51, 53, 54, 55, 56, 77, 86, 87, 88, 89, 90, 91, 92, 93, 97, 98, 99, 107, 109, 113, 123, 124, 125, 237, 238, 240, 241, 242, 244, 245
Blackie, J. 75, 240
Black Papers 85, 98, 106, 107, 109, 113
Blenkin, G. 112, 122, 125, 176, 244, 245, 248
Boards of Education, School Boards 9, 10, 33, 36, 235 also:
  and meal provision 215;
  and progressive teaching 73
  and the curriculum 111
  Architects and Buildings Bulletins 9, 36, 38, 58
  Birmingham 36
  Circulars 11, 35, 168, 239, 247, 250
  London 9, 36, 57, 142, 235
  Newcastle Upon Tyne 57
  Reports (also see Hadow Reports) 237, 239, 241
books:
  appearance of 171; content of 108–9, 171–3, 176–7; for ethnic minorities 148, 149, 152; home made 170; of tests 111; provision in school of 171–3, 180, 228; readability of 172; reading 134, 148, 174, 172–3, 180; reference 126, 171–2, 180; sex-bias in illustrations of 161; sexual equality and 161; text 24, 175–6, 180
Boulay, B du 192, 249
Boultwood, M. E. A. 70, 237, 239
Boyson, R. 85, 86, 243
Breakthrough to Literacy 161, 174
Brennan, W. 138, 139, 142, 245, 246
Broudy, H. 247, 251
Brown, M. 76, 83, 240
Brown, R. 111, 244
Bruner, J. S. 74, 84, 239, 241
Brunetti, F. A. 55, 238
Bryce, J. S. 111, 243
building(s) 31–61
  adaption of 47, 56–7, 58, 60; bulletins 34; cost limits on 40; flexibility in 41; influence of 47–61, 77, 96, 215–8, 218; maintenance of 47, 56–7, 58, 60; prototypes 34, 41; regulations for 36, 38, 40, 58, 211; replacement of 47

Bullock Report 86, 98, 109, 126, 138, 145, 171, 245, 246, 248

Cane, B. S. 226, 251
cassette recorders 166, 177, 178, 180
centres of interest (*see also* 'projects', 'topics', 'themes') 122
Chandler, D. 113, 186, 192, 194, 244, 249, 250
Clark, E. 20, 236
class(es):
  alternatives 76; mixed ability 19, 23, 24, 25, 27, 72; organisation of 54, 94–7; origin of 19, 36, 37; reception 21, 231; teaching of (see teaching methods)
classrooms 34, 35, 36, 37, 38, 39, 40, 41, 43, 44, 46, 50, 52, 53, 54, 56, 59, 60
class size:
  effects of 21, 96; in central hall schools 36; large 21, 23, 36, 68, 76, 168; small 21, 76
cloakrooms 39, 40, 46, 47, 48, 53, 54, 59, 115
Cockcroft Report 201, 250
Committee of Council for Education 9, 36
comprehensivisation 13, 15, 16, 24, 26, 79, 107
Concept keyboard 194, 250
cookery 22, 71, 221
Coote, A 161, 247
corridors 33, 39, 40, 44, 51, 53, 74
Corry Mann, H. C. 219, 251
Cox, C. B. 241, 243
creativity 106, 111
cross ventilation 38, 44
curriculum: 106–128; *also* balanced 88, 125; bidden 107–8; core 107, 108, 110; consistency 108, 125; evaluation of 77, 126–7, 252; integrated (see also 'projects') 83, 89, 91, 92, 118–28; individualised 127; match 96, 126, 145, 146; models 108; objectives 110, 112, 113; of the primary school 72, 78, 106–128; organisation 124, 89; parental understanding of 232; planning the 77; separation for sexes 158–9; teaching 77; the Inspectorate and 108–9; unified 109
Curtis, S. J. 70, 237, 239

Dalton Plan 71, 78, 118, 239
Daniel, M. V. 73, 239

Daniels, J. C. 25, 236
Dean, J. 53, 238
Dearden, R. F. 83, 122, 240, 244
Department of Industry 183, 194
DES (*see also* DES publications)
  Architects and Buildings Branch 34,
    43, 47, 53, 56; conflict with
    Inspectorate 106; on open plan
    schools 41, 54, 237, 238; support
    for science workcards 175, 177;
    1978 Survey (see HMI
    reports/Surveys)
design of schools 23–47
DES publications:
  A Framework for the School
    Curriculum 108, 110, 243;
    Curriculum Differences for Boys
    and Girls 246; Education in Schools
    (Green Paper) 107, 243; Education
    in Schools (Yellow Paper) 107, 243;
    Education Survey 16; Open Plan
    Primary Schools 237, 238;
    Organisation and Content of the
    5–16; Curriculum 108, 243; Report
    on LEA Arrangements for the
    Curriculum 108, 243; Special
    Needs in Education (White Paper)
    139; The School Curriculum 108,
    243; The Story of Post War School
    Building 237
de-streaming 24, 79
Dewey, J. 70, 71, 78, 118, 119
diarrhoea 45–6, 218
dining rooms 40, 44, 54, 215
discipline 12, 24, 25, 31–2, 37, 38, 69,
    76, 78, 84, 86, 95, 227, 229, 233
discussion 68, 90, 92, 94, 95, 110, 120,
    121, 169, 178, 187, 202, 231
Douglas, J. W. B. 157, 158, 247
Dow, G. 121, 244
drama 41, 120, 125, 157, 216
Durham, M. 238, 252
dyslexia 138, 146
Dyson, R. E. 241, 243

Education Acts/Codes: *1862* 20, 111;
    1870 9, 10, 21, 235; *1872* 9; *1876* 10;
    1880 10; *1902* 10; *1906* 213; *1918* 10,
    235; *1921* 136, 245; *1944* 13, 23,
    108, 136, 245; *1981* 139, 142–4,
    146, 150, 151
economic aspects of schooling 33, 34,
    39, 40, 43, 44, 52, 56, 57, 58, 59,
    60, 61, 142, 150–1, 171, 180, 213–5
educational psychologists 140

EFL/ESL 147
eleven plus, the 10, 20, 24, 111
Elzey, F. F. 88, 241
English (*see also* 'language', 'literacy'
    and sub skills) 92, 108, 114, 149
entry ages for school 8, 9, 235
Entwistle, N. 86
environmental studies 125
Equal Opportunity Commission 158
equal opportunity 20, 135, 153–166
ethnic minorities 135, 146–50, 151, 152
Eysenck, A. J. & S. 157, 247

family grouping 21
Flanders, N. A. 87, 93, 241
Fletcher Maths 175, 176–7, 248
Ford Teaching Project 88
Forster, W. E. 9, 168
Fraser, R. 187, 190, 201, 205, 237, 249,
    250
Frazier, N. 161, 247
free place system 10, 20
Froebel, F. 70, 78, 94

Gage, N. L. 87, 241
Gagne, R. M. 83, 84, 241
Galton, M. 24, 88, 89, 90, 91, 92, 94,
    95, 96, 97, 98, 99, 156, 157, 158,
    180, 192, 202, 236, 241, 242, 243,
    245, 247
games 35, 158–9, 201
gardens 40, 73
Gardner, D. E. M. 89, 90, 242
Gardner, K. 85, 241
Garner, G. 251
Geddes Commission 213
geography 108, 120, 121, 123, 125, 175
gifted pupils (*see also* 'high ability
    pupils') 146, 151
Gittins Report 122
Good, T. L. 158, 247
Grand, D. 195, 250
Gray, J 92, 93, 99, 242
group work (*see* teaching methods)
Grouws, D. A. 91, 242
Grundin, H. U. and E. H. 172, 248
Goodman, K. S. 113, 244

Hadow Reports:
  The Education of The Adolescent 11,
    192, 235
  The Primary School 11, 235, 236,
    237, 238, 239, 242, 244;
    (co-education) 20; (curriculum) 72,
    78; (membership of committee for)

Hadow Reports – *cont.*
　23; (project work) 118, 125; (school
　design) 38; (separate
　infants/juniors) 11, 12; (sex
　differences) 155, 156; (streaming)
　23, 25, 78; (teaching methods)
　72–3, 78; (value of infant
　atmosphere) 14
　The Infant and Nursery School 235,
　236, 239; (buildings) 38, 58;
　(teaching methods) 72–3, 78;
　(vertical grouping) 21
halls (*see also* central hall schools) 31–2,
　36, 37, 38, 39, 40, 43, 51, 54, 222
Handbooks of Suggestions for Teachers
　72, 168, 190
handicapped pupils 135–45, 150
Hannon, V. 246, 247
Hargreaves, D. 226
headteachers 3, 4, 5, 18, 37, 47, 48, 59,
　77, 140, 229
heating 47, 52, 56, 58, 59
Hendrix, G. 74, 239
Hesketh, J. 92, 93
high ability pupils (*see also* 'gifted
　pupils') 23
　acceleration through 'standards' for
　20
　advantages of group work for 75
　allocation of teachers to 25
　and special needs 146
　separate classes for 23, 229
　special provision for in elementary
　schools 11
　streaming and 25
　vertical grouping and 22
Hill, J. 49, 246
Hilsum, S. 226, 251
history 121, 123, 125, 175
HMI
　and design of buildings 34, 42
　and de-streaming 24
　and object lessons 118
　and progressive teaching 73, 75, 79
　and teacher development 110
　and the condition of schools 56, 57
　and the curriculum 108–9, 113
　conflict with teachers and Colleges
　106
　conflict with the DES 106, 109
HMI Surveys/Reports:
　1978 Survey 236, 242, 244, 245, 246,
　248, 249; (able pupils) 146;
　(assessment) 126; (criticisms of
　findings) 124, 126; (curriculum

areas tested) 89; (curriculum
　consistency) 125; (group teaching)
　24; (integrated curriculum) 119,
　126; (less able pupils) 145; (match)
　96, 126, 145, 146; (observation)
　168–9; (posts of responsibility) 171;
　(reading schemes) 172; (resources)
　177, 178; (teaching styles) 87;
　(topics) 119, 122; (vertical
　grouping) 22
A View of the Curriculum 109, 243
Report on the Effects of Local
　Authority Expenditure Policies on
　Educational Provision 239
The Curriculum from 5 to 16 109,
　243
The Curriculum from 11–16 123,
　243
The School Building Survey (1985)
　238
　1982 Survey 125, 245
Hochschild, A. R. 227, 251
Hoggart, R. 3, 235
home bases 41, 54, 96
home economics 55, 221
Honeyford, R. 149
HORSA 58
horizontal grouping 20–3, 26
Howe, J. A. M. 192, 249
humanities 228, 229
huts (see temporary school buildings)
Hutt, C. 156, 246

Infant School Society 35
information handling 74, 83, 121, 126,
　195–9
inservice courses (*see* teacher training)
integrated day 75–6, 77, 79, 83, 95
interests 83, 119, 124, 126
Invalid Children's Aid Association 137,
　245
Ireland, T. 179, 252
Isaacs, S. 23, 236
ITA 6, 173
ITMA 202

Jackson, B. 25, 236, 237
JEPI 157, 247
Jones, R. 249
Joseph, K. 233
Junior Training Centres 138

Kelly, A. V. 110, 112, 122, 125, 176,
　243, 244, 245, 248
Keisler, R. 74, 240

keyboard skills 184, 205
Kersh, B. Y. 74, 240
Kilpatrick, W. H. 71, 78, 118, 119, 127,
    128, 244
King, J. S. 157, 247
Kinnock, N. 142
Kirkman, S. 238, 252
kitchens 40, 218
Kruchten, P. M. 55, 238

labelling in school 22, 24, 26, 27,
    135–162
Lancaster, J. 34, 35, 69
Language (*see also* 'English', 'Literacy'
    and sub skills): 109, 110, 121, 125,
    187, 151, 229
  disorders 137
  Language Experience Approaches
    174–5
  Language Master 177
  of immigrant children 148
  sexist, in books 161
  swearing 124, 227
lavatories 45–6, 47, 48, 57, 59
Lawrence, D. H. 68, 239
Learning 74, 75, 79, 83, 91, 121, 126,
    168, 178, 179, 187, 191
Learning Processes 108, 110, 111, 112,
    122, 190
Leff, S. & V. 219, 251
less able pupils (see also remedial
    children) 145:
  and word processors 195
  assessment of 'needs' of 150
  'standards' system of organisation
    and 20, 21
  streaming and 25
  vertical grouping and 22
Leicestershire Plan 16
Leith, S. 122, 124, 126, 127, 244, 245
libraries 56, 171, 229
literacy (see also 'Language', 'English'
    and sub-skills eg. reading) 26, 107,
    109, 173, 180
Lobban, G. 161, 247
Local Education Authorities:
  administrative officers 34
  advisers 75, 79, 88, 110
  and PTA's 232
  assessment procedures 113
  book provision 171
  Bradford 149
  checklists for giftedness 146
  DES Buildings Branch, consultancy
    with 34

duties and handicapped pupils 136,
    137, 139, 140, 141, 142, 150
  establishment of 10
  ILEA 73, 113, 148, 149, 244
  Leicestershire 16, 73, 76
  maintenance of buildings 56
  medical officers 136
  'named person' (for handicapped
    pupil) 141, 143
  Northumberland 239
  Oxford 73
  policy for the starting age of
    schooling 7
  provision for gifted pupils 146
  provision for remedial pupils 144, 145
  provision of buildings 10
  provision of school meals 221
  provision of school meal supervisors
    221–2, 223
  records 110, 112, 113
  Rochdale 251
  secondary schooling and 15
  streaming and 24
  West Riding of Yorkshire 58
LOGO 186, 187, 190, 191, 201
Lowe, R. 39, 237, 239

Maclure, J. S. 239
maintenance (*see* buildings)
maladjustment 139, 142, 146
management 24, 88, 90, 94, 96
Mare, W de la 93, 242
match (*see* curriculum)
Mathematical Association 194, 199
mathematics 22, 25, 35, 72, 75, 89, 92,
    93, 106, 107, 108, 109, 110, 111,
    121, 125, 156, 161, 175, 192, 194,
    199, 201, 202, 205
McIntyre, D. 87, 237, 241
meals (*see* 'school meals')
medical officers (*see* school)
Miall, L. C. 168, 248
microcomputers 26, 150, 180, 181–206,
    228–9
milk (*see* school milk)
Milk Marketing Board 219
Ministry of Education 170, 245, 248
Montessori, M. 70, 78
moral development 112, 156
Moodie, A. G. 55, 238
Moran, P. E. 95, 240, 242
Morrison, A. 87, 237, 241
motivation 83, 90–1, 127
multicultural education 109, 148, 149,
    152

music 22, 38, 44, 55, 65, 108, 125, 216

Naish, M. 83, 240
NAS/UWT 230, 251, 252
National Child Development Study
    Group 157
National Education Union 235
NEDC 56
Neill, A. S. 71
NFER 15, 93, 108, 112, 114, 236, 241,
    244
Nuffield Junior Science 84, 170, 175
NUT:
    on building standards 56, 216, 238
    on courses for teachers 144, 246
    on open plan schools 41, 54, 237, 238
    on school meals 216, 218, 222, 251
    response to HMI 1978 Survey 124,
        245
    on teacher stress 226, 251, 266

object lessons 35, 118, 167, 179–80
Obrist, A. J. 184, 249
observation (teaching of) 168, 169, 179
ORACLE project 89, 90, 94–8, 99, 109,
    124, 158, 243
organisation 3–27, 76, 77, 88, 94, 99,
    113, 124:
    into age groups 20–3
    of separate teaching groups 18
    separation of ages/sexes/abilities
        19–20, 22, 23–6
    split day 124
Orr, J. B. 219, 251

Palmer, J. 247, 251
Papert, S. 186, 190, 249
Parekh, B. 147, 148, 246
parents:
    and different treatment of sexes 156
    and choice of primary schooling 16
    and gifted children 146
    and support for first/middle
        organisation 15
    home reading 232
    involvement in school of 41, 43,
        231–33, 234
    maintenance of buildings by 56, 57
    provision of books in home 171
    PTA's 60, 181, 231, 232, 233
    representation of in books 30
    rights and handicapped pupils 140,
        141, 143, 144
    working 8, 212
Parker, S. 248, 251

Parkhurst, H. 71, 78, 118
Parliamentary Select Committee on
    Immigration and Race Relations
    147
payment by results 9, 10, 20, 68, 71, 111
Pearson, E. 53, 238
Pestalozzi, J. H. 168, 225
Peters, R. S. 240
Phillips, R. 202, 205, 250
physical education 38, 44, 55, 70, 108,
    109, 158–9, 216
Pidgeon, D. 25, 236
Pilkington Report, The 54, 60, 238
play 12, 14, 37, 41, 51, 59, 73, 94, 107,
    156
Plowden Report 107, 178, 236, 237,
    238, 239, 240, 242, 244, 245, 246,
    248, 252
    analysis of sex bias in illustrations of
        156–7
    authors of 85
    criticism of 83, 96
    on aims 83
    on building standards 54
    on class teaching 73
    on combined primary schools 12
    on design of schools 41, 54
    on effective teaching 93
    on entry into schooling 15, 20
    on ethnic minorities 147
    on gifted pupils 146
    on group work 79, 93, 97
    on handicapped pupils 137
    on ideal ages for entry/transfer of
        schooling 15, 21
    on informal methods 73, 96
    on integrated day 75–6, 79
    on learning 73–5, 79, 83, 96, 122
    on project work 199, 122
    on PTA's 232
    on value of infant school 14
    on vertical grouping 22
    philosophy of 76
Pollard, M. 171, 172, 248
Poor Law 213
posts of responsibility 171, 228–9
practical areas 48
practical education:
    assessment of skills in 13
    facilities for 48, 54
    in central schools 10
Precious, N. 76, 83, 240
Pritchard, P. 55, 238
problem solving 26, 71, 78, 95, 114,
    119, 122, 190, 191, 202, 206

programmed learning 178–9
programming 186–90, 206
progress
    accelerated 20
    checklists of 120
    in learning 91, 95
    in infant school 21
    of pupils with special needs 20–1, 141
    retardation of 11
projectors 120, 126, 167, 177
project work (*see also* 'topic
    work'/'thematic work') 71, 78, 79,
    103–5, 115–128, 165–6, 172, 178,
    201

quiet areas 48, 55

Race Relations Act 147
radio 178, 184, 205
Rance, P. 122, 124, 244, 245
Rattenbury, P. 42, 237
reading: (*see also* 'Language', 'literacy',
    'books')
    attainment 25, 92
    books 148, 171–5
    Breakthrough to Literacy 161, 174
    commercial materials for 175, 176
    drill 72
    dyslexia 138, 146
    home 232
    individualised 174
    informal inventories 113
    ITA 173
    language experience approaches
        174–5
    Language Master 177
    listening to 96–7
    ORACLE findings on 157
    organisation of 35
    Plowden Report and 73
    remedial 133–4, 144–5
    schemes 172–3
    standards 84, 85, 93, 108
    teaching methods for 14, 174–5
    tests 26, 89, 93, 157
    with computers 192, 193, 195
    word games 36
record keeping 77, 110, 112, 113,
    193–4, 206, 228, 233
registers 6, 35, 77, 160
relationships in school:
    between groups with special needs
        133, 152
    between teachers/parents 230–3
    between teachers/parents/pupils 21

between schools 10, 17–18
between different ethnic groups 148,
    149
in team teaching 77
religious education 108, 109, 123, 125
remedial pupils/teaching (*see also* 'less
    able pupils') 6, 19, 23, 25, 26,
    144–5, 150, 151, 177
research 25, 82, 86, 87–98, 99, 109, 142,
    155, 156, 157, 161, 172, 212, 219
resources (see also separate items) 56,
    76, 113, 119, 125, 127, 140, 142,
    147, 150–1, 152, 167–206
revolution, the primary 65–7, 75, 79,
    85, 107
Richards, C. 108, 125, 243, 246
Ridgway, L. 24, 236
Rintoul, K. A. P. 77, 240
Root, B. 85, 241
Rosenshine, B. 93, 242
Ross, A. 196, 250
Rousseau, J. J. 69, 70, 78, 239

Sadker, M. 161, 247
Salmon, D. 69, 239
Satterly, D. 92, 93, 99, 242
scholarship, the 10, 11
school:
    accounts 229
    Attendance Committees 10
    Boards 9, 10, 33, 36, 57
    compulsory attendance at 11, 179
    entry age for 8, 9, 14
    environment 40, 41, 45–61, 73, 74,
        76, 78, 168, 184
    fees 8, 10, 11
    governors 143, 233
    grants 20
    homework 232
    involvement in community 228, 229,
        230–3, 234
    meals 37, 44, 54, 211–8, 221, 222
    medical officers 38, 39, 43, 136, 140,
        215, 251
    milk 209–10, 215, 219–20, 222
    reorganisation 13, 16
    roles 8
    Rules for Planning and Equipping 9,
        36
    School Library Association 171
    size 35, 41
    small 12, 19, 23, 72
    tuck 220, 222
    visits 75, 126, 168

school designs:
  central hall 31–2, 36–7, 40, 44, 51, 53,
    55, 59
  corridor 39–40, 44, 53
  finger plan 33, 39, 44
  one-room 34–6, 43, 52
  open-air 37–8, 44
  open-plan 33, 41–3, 44, 50, 53, 54–5,
    60, 77, 79, 96, 97, 124, 216
  pavilion/verandah 37–9, 44, 51, 59
  quadrangle 39, 59
  two-roomed 13, 36, 43
school (fittings):
  carpets 41
  benches 35
  desks 35, 54, 60
  chairs 54, 60
  doors 39, 51, 53, 54
  floors 41, 47, 53, 54, 56
  galleries 35, 36, 69
  lighting 47, 50–2
  roofs 40, 50, 56, 60
  walls 39, 40, 42, 51, 54
  water supply 47, 50, 56, 59
  windows 37, 39, 47, 50, 59
schools (named)
  Amersham 41, 216, 237
  Belfield 232
  Bishop Carpenter 47
  Borough Road 34
  Brewers Green 8
  Cheadle Grammar 239
  Church Hill Infants/Juniors 76
  Courfields 65–7
  Delf Hill Middle 216
  Drygate, Glasgow 8
  Eastlea 4–5, 7, 12, 19, 22, 24, 33, 40,
    48, 66, 67, 75, 77, 115–17, 119,
    121, 177, 232
  Eveline Lowe 41
  Finmere 41, 237
  Ford Farm 5–6, 7, 12, 19, 22, 33, 51,
    54, 153–4, 173
  High Rise 1–2, 7, 17–18, 19, 20, 23,
    31–2, 33, 37, 45–6, 47, 48, 50, 51,
    54, 216, 230
  Holland Park 247
  Jonson Street 35, 36
  New Lanark 8
  North Surrey District 58
  Summerhill 71
  Spitalfields 8
  Westminster Free and Day Asylum 8
  William Tyndale p. 85–5, 98, 107, 113
Schools Council Projects:

Aims in Primary Education 112
  criticisms of 124
  Learning through Science 176
  Progress in Learning Science 112
  Science 5/13 123, 170, 175
school types
  all age 12
  board 9, 10
  central 10, 11
  charity 7
  church 36
  combined primary 7, 11–13, 16, 19
  combined first/middle 15
  comprehensive 13, 15, 16
  council 10
  county 10
  dame 8
  elementary 10, 11, 12, 20, 26, 33, 37,
    68, 108, 136, 167, 213, 222
  first 7, 13–15, 16
  grammar 11, 13, 23
  higher 16
  higher grade 10
  infant 7–9, 10, 11, 12, 13, 14, 16, 20,
    21, 26, 37, 72, 123
  junior 7, 9, 10–11, 12, 13, 16, 19, 22,
    24, 73, 88, 123
  middle 7, 13–15, 16, 19, 149, 216
  monitorial 8, 35, 43
  national 35
  non-provided 10
  nursery 8, 9, 14, 21, 70, 147, 156, 231
  parochial 7
  preparatory schools 16
  private 19, 26, 222
  provided 10
  public 213
  rural 12, 36, 72
  secondary 10, 11, 13, 23
  secondary modern 11, 13, 216
  single sex 19–20, 26
  special 135, 136, 137, 139, 141, 142,
    143, 150, 151
  state 8, 19, 26, 214, 225
  sunday 7
  technical 13
  voluntary 10, 34, 36, 43
science 50, 69, 74, 75, 84, 92, 108, 109,
  111, 120, 121, 122, 125, 156–7,
  159, 161, 165–6, 168, 170, 175,
  178, 199, 221, 232
Seaborne, M. 39, 51, 58, 237, 238, 239
Secretaries of State 106, 109, 110, 113,
  143
SEF Survey 55, 238

Sex Discrimination Act 155, 158–62, 247
sex education 232–3
Sheingold, K. 187, 249
Simon, B. 89, 95, 96, 97, 98, 157, 242, 243, 247
smells in school 38, 48, 50
Smith, F. 193, 250
social development 8, 70, 71, 74, 78, 86, 88, 112, 121, 156
social studies 92, 109, 123, 169
Somerhill, H. J. 22, 236
Southgate, V. 96, 242, 248
space 38, 39, 40, 41, 42, 43, 44, 47, 52–5, 60
  circulation 53
  dual use of 40, 44, 54, 216, 22
  floor 40
  MTA 40, 53, 60
  storage 59
special needs, pupils with 133–162
specialist teaching 15, 76, 145
special units 141, 150–1
spelling 84, 85, 96, 106, 114, 193, 195
SRA 176
staff meetings 4, 31–2, 228
staff rooms 40, 54, 59, 162
standards (academic) 72, 82, 85, 86, 103–5, 106, 108, 110, 111, 113
standards (class groupings) 9, 20, 21, 26
Stewart, J. 187, 201, 248, 249, 250
Stow, David 8, 36
Strathclyde Regional Council 55, 124, 238, 240, 245
streaming: 13, 21, 23, 26, 27, 39, 44, 72, 73, 88, 175
subject specialisation 13, 15, 121, 127
Swann Report 147, 148, 149, 246

Taba, H. 88, 241
Tann, S. 159, 247
teacher:
  accidents 56
  accountability 109–12, 227–9
  attention to pupils 158
  attitudes to equal opportunity 162
  day 225–34
  initial training 9, 37, 44, 73, 78, 142, 144, 226, 230
  inservice training 144, 162, 178, 229–30, 233, 251–2
  meal supervision 216, 221–2, 223
  mid-day breaks 211, 216, 221–2
  parent relationships 230–3

pay 100, 223, 224, 225, 226
promotion 75, 100
pupil 34, 35, 37
stress 56, 60, 227, 233
treatment of different sexes 156
teaching machines 178–9
teaching: 68–105, 82–99
  activity 69, 73, 79
  class 41, 44, 68–9, 73, 76, 80–1, 94, 95, 96, 98, 9, 145
  didactic 15, 69, 78, 87, 93
  discovery 69, 73, 74, 76, 78, 79, 83, 84, 96, 100
  effective 82–99, 127, 202, 206
  formal 25, 68–9, 80–1, 86, 90, 92, 94, 98, 100, 176
  group 5, 24, 26, 70, 71, 72, 74, 76, 78, 79, 86, 91, 93, 94, 95, 96, 97, 99, 159, 201, 229
  individual 69, 70, 71, 72, 73, 74, 75, 76, 78, 79, 86, 91, 94, 95, 96, 99, 109, 113, 127, 174, 175, 180, 191–2, 193, 202, 206
  informal 85, 86, 90, 92, 94, 98, 100, 112
  mixed ability 96
  progressive 68, 69, 70, 78, 82, 83, 85, 86, 87, 88, 93, 94, 98, 100, 106, 108, 121
  prussian system of 36
  simultaneous instruction 35
  team 43, 76–7, 79, 83, 86
  traditional 39, 68, 78, 82, 88, 90, 93, 94, 100
television 167, 178, 184, 185, 186, 205
Tempest, N. R. 146, 246
temporary school buildings 5, 6, 48, 57–9, 60
tests (*see* assessment)
Thatcher, M. 184, 220
thematic work (*see also* 'project work'/'topic work') 118, 122, 123
Thorne, K. P. C. 77, 240
timetable 22, 76, 86, 108, 109
toilet paper 45–6, 48
topic work (*see also* 'project work'/'thematic work') 94, 98, 122, 123, 124, 125, 127, 172
transfer in schooling 11, 12, 13, 14–15
tri-partite system 23
'turtle' 186, 187

UNESCO 170

vertical grouping 20–23, 26, 41, 96, 97

Walden, R. 161, 247
Walker, D. 85, 86, 107, 243
Walkerdine, V. 161, 247
Warnock, M. 138
Warnock Report 138, 139–42, 143, 148,
    151, 245, 246 also:
  Advisory and Support Service 141
  assessment 140–2
  ethnic minorities 147
  gifted pupils 146, 151
  named person 141
  remedial pupils 144, 151
  special educational need 139, 140,
    150
  special educational provision 140,
    141, 142
Weiner, G. 161, 247
Weizenbaum, B. 191, 249
welfare 37, 77, 229

Whalley, D. 201, 250
Whittaker, M. 171, 248
Whyte, J. 123, 247
Wilby, P. 225, 227, 246, 251
Wilderspin, Samuel 8, 35, 36
Winter, S. 150–1, 246
Wisbey, A. 137, 245
Woodroffe, B. 148, 246
wordprocessors 195
workbooks 175–6, 180
workcards 24, 91, 175–6, 180
Wragg, E. C. 91, 242
Wright, N. 90, 241, 242
writing 22, 34, 72, 73, 106, 114, 121,
    126, 170, 175, 177, 195, 198, 202

Yates, A. 25, 236
Young, Baroness 184
youth clubs 229